A HISTORY OF BRIT
CRIMINOLOGY

A History
of
British Criminology

Edited by

PAUL ROCK

This Book First Appeared as a
Special Issue
of the
British Journal of Criminology

CLARENDON PRESS · OXFORD
1988

Oxford University Press, Walton Street, Oxford OX2 6DP

Oxford New York Toronto
Delhi Bombay Calcutta Madras Karachi
Petaling Jaya Singapore Hong Kong Tokyo
Nairobi Dar es Salaam Cape Town
Melbourne Auckland

and associated companies in
Beirut Berlin Ibadan Nicosia

Oxford is a trade mark of Oxford University Press

Published in the United States
by Oxford University Press, New York

British Library Cataloguing in Publication Data
Rock, Paul
History of British criminology.
1. Great Britain. Criminology, to 1987.
I. Title II. British Journal of Criminology
364.0941
ISBN 0–19–825635–3

Library of Congress Cataloging in Publication Data
History of British criminology/edited by Paul Rock
"First appeared as a special issue of the
British Journal of Criminology."
1. Crime and criminals—Great Britain—History.
I. Rock, Paul Elliott.
HV6021. H58 1988   88–1901
364'. 941—dc 19   CIP
ISBN 0–19–825635–3

Printed in Great Britain by Henry Ling Ltd.,
at the Dorset Press, Dorchester, Dorset

Contents

i	Foreword *Paul Rock*	vii
I	British Criminology Before 1935 *David Garland*	1
II	Hermann Mannheim *Sir Leon Radzinowicz*	18
III	British Criminology: 1935–1948 *Terence Morris*	20
IV	The Development of Criminology in Britain: 1948–1960 *J. P. Martin*	35
V	The Sociology of Crime and Social Control in Britain, 1960–1987 *David Downes*	45
VI	The Present State of Criminology in Britain *Paul Rock*	58
VII	Methodological Developments *Ken Pease*	70
VIII	Psychological Contributions to Criminology *D. J. West*	77
IX	Feminism and Criminology in Britain *Loraine Gelsthorpe and Allison Morris*	93
X	Criminal Justice and the Criminal Process *Andrew Ashworth*	111
XI	The History of Crime *J. A. Sharpe*	124
XII	British Criminology and the State *Robert Reiner*	138
XIII	Radical Criminology in Britain: The Emergence of a Competing Paradigm *Jock Young*	159

Foreword

The last major review of the history of criminology was Mannheim's *Pioneers in Criminology* but it was published long ago in 1960 and much has happened since. The criminology that was pioneered then has been transformed and the ambitions and ideas of our predecessors have changed. Administratively and practically, British criminology has acquired a new character which deserves description. It appears to have moved beyond its sometimes precarious childhood to become a recognized part of the life of universities, polytechnics and government departments. Financially, precariousness has returned and there is apprehension about the future funding of research and appointments. Intellectually, the discipline has achieved a great deal and it has grown in reflectiveness. There are new historians of ideas who are starting to interpret what has occurred. But, as yet, the story has not been told and newcomers do not seem to know their past. They construct a history out of fragments of polemic, gossip, myth and old analysis. British criminology needs a written record of its own development.

The editorial board of *The British Journal of Criminology* thought it timely to commission a special issue focusing on the past and present condition of their discipline. Tony Bottoms, Nigel Walker and I came together to identify the issue's broad themes and specific contributions. The subsequent work of editing was mine.

Papers were commissioned on the evolution of thinking about the police and prisons but they were not completed. The remaining articles are an otherwise useful reflection of the discipline. Some are essays in the history of criminological ideas. Others describe the formation of particular emphases, methods and problems. And others are, in effect, personal accounts of major phases in the growth of the discipline. Together, and perhaps for the first time in many years, they give British criminology a clear report about its own history and present standing.

Paul Rock
January 1988

THE BRITISH JOURNAL

OF

CRIMINOLOGY

Vol. 28	Spring 1988	No. 2

BRITISH CRIMINOLOGY BEFORE 1935

DAVID GARLAND (*Edinburgh*)*

I

"Criminology", as a professional academic discipline, did not exist in Britain before 1935, and was established only gradually and precariously thereafter. So whatever this essay is about, it cannot be about criminology in quite the sense we think of it today. Instead, it examines some of the lines of emergence of that discipline, and in particular, the theoretical and institutional processes which gave rise to a scientific criminology in Britain. Given the short space available to me here, this can be no more than a very selective account, highlighting a few important currents, while ignoring much that would be essential to a proper genealogy of the subject. My central concern will be to show that the development of British criminology can best be understood by concentrating less upon the spread of ideas from abroad and more upon the ways in which penal and social institutions acted as a practical surface of emergence for this kind of knowledge. What is presented is not an abstracted history of ideas, but instead an attempt to situate criminology within the institutional practices and power relations which have formed its immediate context and foundation. It should be possible, in turn, to situate this history of institutional pragmatics within a wider field of social forces—see Garland (1985)—but no such analysis is attempted here.

By convention, modern scientific criminology[1] is said to have begun with

* Lecturer in the Centre for Criminology, University of Edinburgh and currently Visiting Professor at the Center for Law and Society at Berkeley California. I am grateful to Peter Young, Beverley Brown, Phillipe Robert and Roger Hood for their comments on an earlier draft of this article.

[1] The term "scientific" is used in this essay to discuss those forms of talking about crime and criminals which were self-consciously undertaken within a framework derived from natural science. In using the term I intend to distinguish such criminologies from other ones which were phrased in moral, religious or common-sense vocabularies. This uncritical use of the term "science" is intended as an historical attribution, repeating actors' conceptions, not an epistemological evaluation. For a critical discussion of criminology's claims to be a science, see Garland 1985, Ch. 3.

Lombroso's criminal anthropology in the 1870s, and in one sense this is true enough, since it was the impact of Lombroso which sparked off the international congresses and debates of the 1880s and brought the idea of a criminological science to public prominence for the first time. But criminology in Britain did not develop out of the Lombrosian tradition. Nor did it derive from the European movement, despite the way in which Edwardian penal reforms appeared to follow its lead—even despite the fact that it would later be a group of European *émigrés* who did most to establish an academic profession of criminologists in this country. In fact the scientific approach to crime and punishment was not something which Britain reluctantly imported from abroad. On the contrary, there existed in Britain, from the 1860s onward, a distinctive, indigenous tradition of applied medico-legal science which was sponsored by the penal and psychiatric establishments, and it was this tradition which formed the theoretical and professional space within which "criminological science" was first developed in this country.[2] If we are to understand criminology and its social foundations it is important not to confuse these two traditions, or to collapse one onto the other. In particular, we should avoid assuming that any criminological work which is "positivist" in style is somehow derived from the "Scuola Positiva" of Lombroso. Much of the early British criminology which I will describe falls into the broad epistemological and methodological categories which we nowadays call "positivist"—but it had little to do with Lombroso's Positivism, nor indeed with that of Comte.

Lombrosian criminology grew, somewhat accidentally, out of an anthropological concern to study man and his natural varieties. The identification of human types led Lombroso and others to isolate such types as the genius, the insane, the epileptoid and the criminal, and to subject them to scientific scrutiny and categorisation. To some extent this was effectively the rediscription in scientific language of distinctions which were already established in cultural terms, and certainly the excitement which followed Lombroso's identification of "the born criminal" occurred because his work allowed a spectacular convergence between human science and the concerns of social policy. His differentiation of "the criminal type" chimed with deep-rooted cultural prejudice and also with the real processes of differentiation which were then being established by the expanding prison system, so that the apparent policy implications of Lombroso's work immediately became a focus for widespread attention. But although Lombroso was well aware of the social policy relevance of his anthropology, and took pains to promote it, he was not, at first, particularly well informed about the practical realities of crime and punishment. In consequence, his penology was not just radical and at odds with current practices: it was also naive and uninformed, demonstrating a

---

[2] There were of course other, indigenous traditions of criminological thought in nineteenth century Britain, most notably the ecological and social survey work of writers like Joseph Fletcher and Henry Mayhew. See on this, Lindesmith and Levin (1937), Morris (1957) and Carson and Wiles (1971). This particular genre was to be retrieved as an important strand in twentieth century British criminology, but it was not the central, continuous tradition through which the discipline initially developed in this country. For a comprehensive discussion of early criminology in Britain, see Radzinowicz and Hood (1986), Part I.

lack of familiarity with the normal range of offenders and with the institutions which dealt with them.[3] In fact it is clear that Lombroso had developed his conception of the criminal type more out of theoretical commitment than from practical experience or observation. And although exposure to criticism and his increasing involvement in penal affairs eventually led him to amend his initial framework, and to tone down his more outrageous propositions, it was the clear and unqualified claims of his early work which continued to define the Lombrosian tradition, particularly for those who viewed it from afar.

The psychiatric and medico-legal framework within which Britain developed its early criminological science was different from the Lombrosian tradition in a number of important respects.[4] Unlike anthropology, psychiatry was not concerned to isolate discrete types of human individuals and classify them by means of racial and constitutional differences.[5] Instead, it was a therapeutically oriented discipline based upon a classification system of psychiatric disorders which, like the disease model of nineteenth century medicine, discussed the condition separately from the individual in whom it might be manifested. Within the classification system of morbid psychology there were a variety of conditions which criminals were typically said to exhibit—insanity, moral insanity, degeneracy, feeble-mindedness, etc. But generally speaking, *the* criminal was not conceived as *a* psychological type. Instead the spectrum of psychiatric conditions might be usefully applied to a part of the criminal population: there was no separate criminal psychology or psychiatry, based upon ontological difference.

But more important than this *theoretical* difference was the way in which British psychiatry contrasted with Lombrosian anthropology in its *practical* commitments and its relationship to the institutions of criminal justice. Theorising about the condition of criminals was not done in the abstract, but instead was linked to professional tasks such as the giving of psychiatric evidence before a court of law, or the decisions as to classification, diagnosis and regimen which prison medical officers made on a daily basis. This practical experience was crucial in shaping the psychiatric approach to criminological issues because it ensured that psychiatrists and prison medics were well aquainted with the day to day realities of criminal justice and with the need to bring psychiatric propositions into line with the demands of courts and prison authorities.[6]

[3] For a critical discussion of Lombroso's penology, see the review by Arthur St. John (1912). St. John contrasts Lombroso, who has "never quite thought out the practical part of the subject", with the practical common sense of James Devon and his book *The Criminal and the Community* (1912).

[4] I do not intend to imply here or elsewhere that the criminology of other countries can be accounted for by reference to the Lombrosian tradition. My discussion here relates only to Britain and my intention is to show how the history of British criminology differs from its conventional description—not from that of other countries.

[5] These theoretical differences were not, however, absolute; there was a certain fluidity and overlap between all of the mid-century "sciences of man". Although psychiatry was primarily concerned with mental or psychic phenomena, it was at times intensely "physicalist" in its mode of explanation, and readers of the British psychiatric journals were kept well informed of developments in European anthropology, craniology and biology. The same overlap can be seen in Lombroso's own work, which draws indiscriminately upon all of these different "sciences".

[6] On this process of conflict and adjustment, see R. Smith (1981).

One can see the developing effects of this professional experience by reading through the psychiatric journals of this period and noting the changing terms in which criminals are discussed. In the 1860s Henry Maudsley and particularly J. Bruce Thomson could write, quite unguardedly, about "the genuine criminal" and "the criminal class", variously calling them "morally insane", "degenerate", "defective in physical organisation—from hereditary causes" and "incurable" in a way which is, for all the world, Lombrosian before Lombroso. Others though, like G. McKenzie Bacon, took care to distinguish between the "wilful" criminal on the one hand, and "the diseased" on the other,[7] and from the 1870s onward, prison doctors such as David Nicolson and later John Baker set about redefining "the morbid psychology of criminals", so as to differentiate a range of conditions rather than a single type. Nicolson emphasised that professional observation made it clear that only a minority of criminals were in any sense mentally abnormal, and he forcibly dispelled any suggestion that the general reformation of offenders was put in question by psychiatric science.[8] At the same time, the wider profession was learning—sometimes to its cost—that the criminal courts would not tolerate any psychiatric evidence which contradicted legal axioms about the general nature of action, or the importance of responsibility for conduct, and it gradually developed a practical *modus vivendi* which aimed to minimise conflict between psychiatry and the legal institutions. By the 1880s, leading figures of the new profession such as Needham, Hack Tuke, Nicolson and the mature Maudsley were able to distance themselves from the kind of embarassing or outrageous claims made by psychiatrists in earlier years—claims which were now being taken up again by the new criminal anthropologists.[9]

The British tradition of scientific thinking about criminals was thus, from an early age, situated within an institutional framework which had the support of the prison establishment and the prestige of medicine behind it. Partly in consequence, it was generally modest in its claims, and very respectful of the requirements of institutional regimes and legal principles. As far

[7] See G. McKenzie Bacon (1864); H. Maudsley (1863); J. Bruce Thomson (1867), (1869–70) and (1870–71).

[8] See D. Nicolson ("D.N.") (1872–73) where he stresses the importance of studying "the mental condition of the mass [of prisoners]"—not just the minority of insane or weak-minded inmates. In Nicolson (1873–74) (continued in subsequent volumes) he sets out a typology ranging from the "accidental criminal" to the "habitual and thorough criminal" and talks of the "psychical range" which the population of criminals displays. See also Nicolson (1878–79) where he criticises the claims of J. Bruce Thomson as "rash and misleading and fallacious" (p. 18) as well as Maudsley's tendency to generalise the link between insanity and crime. His concern is with the dangers such exaggerations present to the hope that "... there may be found a consentatious principle upon which the law and medical psychology may be able to harmonise in the matter of criminal responsibility" (p. 20). See also John Baker (1888), (1891) and (1896).

[9] See H. Maudsley (1889): "... first, there is no general criminal constitution, predisposing to and, as it were, excusing crime; second, ... there are no theories of criminal anthropology so well-grounded and exact as to justify their introduction into a revised criminal law" (p. 165) and the remarks made in discussion by Dr. Needham and Dr. Hack Tuke (ibid.). See also D. Nicolson (1895) and the discussion by Sir Edmund Du Cane, Dr. Clouston and Dr. Conolly Norman: "... any address which exposes the puerilities of criminal anthropology is distinctly an advantage" (pp. 589–590). Finally, see H. Maudsley (1895) where he criticises the "lamentable extravagances" of the latest school of criminology: "...although they make the vulgar stare, they make the judicious grieve" (p. 662).

as most prison doctors and experienced psychiatrists were concerned, the majority of criminals were more or less normal individuals; only a minority required psychiatric treatment, and this usually involved removing them from the penal system and into institutions for the mentally ill or defective. And although the diagnostic and therapeutic claims of psychiatry changed over time, from an early stage there was a recognition that, for the mainstream of offenders, the normal processes of law and punishment should apply. Compared to the sweeping claims of criminal anthropology, the psychiatric tradition was, by the 1880s, somewhat conservative in appearance.

But conservative or not (and here it depends on point of view) it was within this framework that most scientific-criminological work was done in Britain up until the middle of the twentieth century. It is, for example, almost exclusively within the Reports of the Medical Commissioner of Prisons and of the various Prison Medical Officers that one will find any official discussion of criminological science in the period before 1935. Similarly, most of the major scientific works on crime, written in Britain before 1935, were written by medics with psychiatric training and positions within the prison service, among them J. F. Sutherland (1908), R. F. Quinton (1910), J. Devon (1912), M. Hamblin Smith (1922), W. C. Sullivan (1924) and W. Norwood East (1927).

The first university lectures in "Criminology" delivered in this country—given at Birmingham by Maurice Hamblin Smith from the 1921/1922 session onwards—were directed to postgraduate medical students within a course entitled "Medical Aspects of Crime and Punishment", and long before Mannheim began teaching at the London School of Economics (LSE) in 1935 there were courses on "Crime and Insanity" offered at London University by senior prison medical officers such as Sullivan and East.

As for professional journals, although there was no specialist periodical devoted to criminology before 1950 (if one excludes the crime enthusiast's magazine *The Criminologist*, one issue of which appeared in 1927), a variety of medical and psychiatric journals devoted regular sections to issues of criminological science, above all the *Journal of Mental Science* (JMS), which had a criminological review section and regular articles, and the *Transactions* of the Medico-Legal Association, which from 1933, was renamed *The Medico-Legal and Criminological Review*. In contrast, journals such as *The Sociological Review*, which would later become an important outlet for criminological publications, carried nothing substantial on the subject from its inception in 1908 until the first British publications of Mannheim and Radzinowicz in the late 1930s.

Set against this background, the scepticism which greeted Havelock Ellis' campaign to introduce to Britain the teachings of criminal anthropology can be understood rather differently.[10] It was not, as historians have suggested, that the idea of a scientific approach to crime was culturally alien to the British. In fact Ellis' book was warmly welcomed by eminent representatives of the new scientific spirit such as Francis Galton, and many lay reviewers

[10] See H. Ellis (1890), (1890a) and his "retrospects" section in the *JMS* where he reviewed works on criminal anthropology from 1890 until 1919.

considered it to be of great interest[11]—as, apparently, did the literate public, which continued to buy it through three editions and several print runs. Rather, what the book encountered was a professional scepticism, based not upon anti-scientism but upon a rather different scientific tradition—one which was more modest, more acceptable to the institutional authorities, and was organised by engaged professionals rather than by maverick intellectuals. In his later years, the first Medical Commissioner of Prisons, Sir Horatio Bryan Donkin, gave clear expression to the distinction between the two traditions. Professing some discomfort at having to use the term at all, he contrasted what he understood as "criminology" properly so-called—namely the investigations undertaken by "persons concerned in some way with prison authorities who strive to discover just principles on which to base their work"—with the newer "doctrine and debate on the causation of crime" which he condemned as "theories based on preconceived assumptions regardless of fact".[12] A similar position was still being argued by Norwood East in the 1930s, when he occupied this same leading office.

In fact Havelock Ellis perfectly epitomised Donkin's view of the "theoretical" criminologist, whose knowledge was based entirely on book learning and second-hand doctrine.[13] Of the all criminological experts of this period, he was the only one with no practical involvement or experience, which was why he was able to approach the work of Lombroso, Benedict and Ferri with such unqualified enthusiasm. It was also why he continued to think of men like Maudsley and Nicolson as being forerunners of the Lombrosian tradition, even after they had done their vehement best to distance themselves from it.[14] In the end, Ellis' popularisation of criminal anthropology had little impact upon the thinking of practitioners, though it was important in other ways. His introduction into English of the term "criminology" in 1890 had the effect of firmly associating that name with the "criminal type" doctrines of Lombroso, thereby making it the subject of considerable scepticism, even where the Lombrosian heritage was actually negligible. In the same way, his much-referenced historical account of the subject has tended to link British criminology to criminal anthropology, and to assimilate all indigenous work to this single, European tradition. Less importantly, it was Ellis (followed by Bonger (1936)) who first made the now conventional attribution of the term "criminology" to remarks by Topinard in 1889. In fact the word—or rather its French and Italian equivalents—was certainly in use earlier than this. It was, for instance, the title of Garafalo's major work of 1885.

Interestingly, the only other person to take up the continental writers in the 1890s was the Revd W. Douglas Morrison, a Canadian who became a prison

[11] See the anonymous review of *The Criminal* in *The Atheneum*, 6 September 1890. Francis Galton's review appears in *Nature*, 22 May 1890 at pp. 75–76. See also the anonymous review in *The Saturday Review*, 30 August 1890 which doubts the scientific wisdom and practical use of criminal anthropology.

[12] H. B. Donkin (1917) p. 17.

[13] For Ellis' own account of his writing of *The Criminal*, see Ellis (1940).

[14] See Ellis' footnote in "The Study of the Criminal" cited above: "In recent utterances Dr. Maudsley seems to ignore, or to treat with indifference, the results of criminal anthropology. These results are, however, but the legitimate outcome of the ideas of which it is his chief distinction to have been the champion" (p. 6).

chaplain at Wandsworth and whose radical criticisms of the system helped provoke the appointment of the Gladstone Committee in 1894. Morrison was responsible for establishing and editing "The Criminology Series", a rather quirky, short-lived venture, which published translations of works by Lombroso (1895), Ferri (1895), and Proal (1898), as well as Morrison's own *Juvenile Offenders* (1896). Significantly though, Morrison's utilisation of these European theorists—as demonstrated in his "Introductions" to their texts and in his own work[15]—placed greatest emphasis upon the penal reform arguments which the new movement provided. Indeed his reduction of the new criminology to a scientific argument for penal reform which could strengthen the evangelical and humanitarian campaign, was perhaps the most characteristic way in which the European tradition was received in this country. When Major Arthur Griffiths, the retired Prison Inspector and one-time delegate to the Congress of Criminal Anthropology in Geneva, 1896, was commissioned to write the first ever entry on "Criminology" for the 11th (1910–11) edition of the *Encyclopaedia Britannica*, he showed the same broad scepticism for the theory of criminal types, together with a cautious interest in the penological ideas which were by now emerging from the movement.

II

The British tradition of institutionally-based, administratively-oriented criminology was, by its nature, a dynamic, evolving tradition. The "criminological" texts which it generated grew out of practical contexts which were forever changing, since institutions continually redefined their operations and took on new concerns, and also because new methods, theories and techniques became available to the professionals responsible for administering them.

Much of nineteenth century criminology, in this sphere, had grown out of the reclassification of selected offenders as being primarily psychiatric cases, rather than criminal ones, either because of moral insanity, or later, because of the less severe but more widespread diagnosis of feeble-mindedness. Underlying this process and the theoretical texts it produced was, of course, the institutional division between the asylum and the prison, or more broadly, between medicine and law. After about 1895 this simple division began to be reformulated to accommodate the much more complex world of penal-welfare institutions, with its more refined classifications and selection procedures, and the allocation of offenders to a greatly extended range of institutions and regimes. One result of this was an important extension of the specialist's role within the system, and a corresponding increase in the production of criminological literature which theorised those new diagnostic and classificatory tasks and the principles upon which they should be based. Such work as *Alcoholism* (1906) by W. C. Sullivan, *Recidivism* (1908) by J. F. Sutherland, *The Psychology of the Criminal* (1922) by M. Hamblin Smith and

---

[15] See W. D. Morrison (1889) and (1891).

"The Psychology of Crime" (1932) by H. E. Field are significant examples of criminological work derived from this developing context.

In 1919, the new penological emphasis upon individual character and specialised treatment—together with concerns about the large numbers of shell-shocked and mentally disturbed men returning from the War—led the Birmingham Justices to establish a permanent scheme for the clinical examination of adult offenders who came before the courts. Previously such work had been done on an occasional, *ad hoc* basis, and depended upon the skill and interest of the local prison doctor. By appointing M. Hamblin Smith and W. A. Potts, both psychiatrically-trained prison medics, and charging them with these new duties, the Justices (together with the Prison Commission) effectively created a new specialism for applied criminology. Before long, Potts, and particularly Hamblin Smith, were adapting the standard forms of mental tests for use in this specialist area, publishing the results of their clinical studies, and writing extensively about the need for this kind of investigation and its implications for the treatment and prevention of crime. In *The Psychology of the Criminal* (1922) and in a series of articles in the JMS, The Howard Journal and elsewhere, Smith emphasised the importance of criminological study, though for him this meant the kind of clinical examination of individuals which the Birmingham scheme employed.[16] As Britain's first authorised teacher of "criminology", and the first individual to go under the title of "criminologist", it is significant that Smith, too, rejected the search for "general theories" in favour of the "study of the individual".[17] Significantly too, the centres of criminological research and teaching, which he called to be set up in each university town, were envisaged as places where "young medical graduates" would be trained to become expert in the medical examination and assessment of offenders.

Hamblin Smith was also one of the first criminological workers in Britain to profess an interest in psycho-analysis, which he utilised as a means to assess the personality "make-up" of offenders, as well as proposing it as a technique for treating the mental conflicts and abnormalities which, he claimed, lay behind the criminal act. In this respect, Smith met with much official opposition, particularly from W. Norwood East,[18] but there were others, outside the establishment, who were more enthusiastic about the role of psycho-analysis. In the winter of 1922–23 Dr. Grace Pailthorpe voluntarily assisted Smith in the psycho-analytic investigation of female offenders at Birmingham, and went on to complete a 5-year study at Holloway, funded by a grant from the Medical Research Council (MRC). Her Report—completed by 1929, but delayed by the MRC until 1932—and its claim that crime was a symptom of mental conflict which might be psycho-analytically resolved, met with some consternation in official circles (see East 1936, 319) but it excited the interest

[16] See M. Hamblin Smith (1921), (1922) and (1925) and the reviews which Smith contributed to the JMS in this period. See also W. A. Potts (1921) and (1925).

[17] M. Hamblin Smith (1922) at p. 25.

[18] See, for example, East (1924–25). This kind of opposition seems to have restrained Smith somewhat, as East noted in his obituary: "Hamblin Smith was a convinced determinist and an omnivorous reader of philosophy and speculative psychology, but he retained a clear distinction between assumptions and facts, and his theoretical inclinations never obtruded in his daily duties" East (1936a) at p. 292.

8

of a number of analysts and medical psychologists who formed a group to promote the Report and its approach. Out of their meetings emerged the Association for the Scientific Treatment of Criminals (1931), which, in 1932, became the Institute for the Scientific Treatment of Delinquency (ISTD).[19]

In fact most of the founder members of this group were in some way or other involved in the new and expanding out-patient sector of psychiatric work, made possible by the opening of private clinics such as the Tavistock (1921), the Maudsley (1923), the new child guidance centres, and eventually, the ISTD's own Psychopathic Clinic (1933) (later moved and renamed the Portman Clinic (1937)). Once again this new field of practice gave rise to its own distinctive brand of criminological theory. The early publications of the ISTD emphasise the clinical exploration of individual personality, and in that sense are continuous with much previous work. But they also manifest a new preventative emphasis, which reflected the fact that the new clinics operated outside the formal penal system, and could deal with individuals before their disturbed conduct actually became criminal. Eventually the group's emphasis upon psycho-analysis, and its open hostility to much official penal policy, ensured that the ISTD remained essentially outsiders, usually operating at arms length from the Home office and the Prison Commission.[20] This outsider status forms an important background to the later decision of the Home Office to establish a criminological institute at Cambridge, rather than under ISTD auspices in London, for although "the formation of such a body was one of the original aims of the ISTD" (Glover 1960, 70) the Home Office appears not to have even considered such an option.

Despite its subsequent neglect, the work of W. Norwood East—particularly *Forensic Psychiatry* (1927) and *The Medical Aspects of Crime* (1936)—better represents the mainstream of British criminology in the 1920s and 1930s. East was a psychiatrically trained prison medical officer who became a leading figure in the 1930s as Medical Director on the Prison Commission, and President of the Medico-Legal Society, and his views dominated official policy-making for a lengthy period. East was himself a proponent of a psychological approach to crime, but he viewed its scope as being sharply delimited, and consistently warned against the dangers and absurdities of exaggerating its claims. In 1934, he established an extended experiment at Wormwood Scrubs, whereby those offenders deemed most likely to respond to psychological therapy—particularly sex offenders and arsonists—were subjected to a period of investigation and treatment by Dr. W. H. de B. Hubert. At the end of five years, East and Hubert's *Report on the Psychological Treatment of Crime* (1939)

---

[19] According to E. Glover's (1950–51) obituary of Dr. E. T. Jensen, this early group included the following individuals: Dr. E. T. Jensen, Mrs. Charles Tharp, Victor B. Neuberg, Dr. Jennings-White, Dr. A. C. Wilson, Dr. Worster Drought, Dr. David Eder, Dr. J. A. Hadfield, Dr. E. Miller and Dr. E. Glover himself. About the same time that Pailthorpe was completing her research at Holloway, Alice Raven published a number of articles setting out a psychoanalytical approach to crime. See Raven (1928) and (1929). See also Melanie Klein (1927) and (1934). The founding document of this psychoanalytical approach to crime was Freud's "Criminality from a Sense of Guilt" which was first published in 1915.

[20] Emanuel Miller recollects: ". . . . feeling like a conspiratorial group as the Establishment was hardly sympathetic; early criminological workers such as Norwood East, Hubert and prison administrator Lionel Fox were sympathetic but markedly orthodox" Miller (1970).

re-affirmed East's view that while 80 per cent of offenders were psychologically normal, and would respond to routine punishment, a minority might usefully be investigated and offered psychological treatment. The Report proposed a special institution to deal with such offenders—a proposal which was immediately accepted but not enacted until the opening of Grendon Underwood in 1962. East and Hubert also recommended that this proposed institution should function as a centre for criminological research, and it is significant that here, when a criminological centre is proposed for the first time in an official Report, it should be envisaged as a psychiatric institution, dealing only with a small minority of offenders.

An important departure from this series of clinically-based, psychiatric studies, was *The English Convict: A Statistical Study*, by Dr. Charles Goring.[21] This work also grew out of institutional routines, insofar as anthropometric measurement was used in prisons for the identification of habitual offenders during the 1890s, but it represented much more than the writing up of daily experience. In fact, in its final, expanded form, the study represents a major development because it signals the use of deliberately undertaken social science research to answer questions posed in institutional practice. The questions taken up here were numerous, and came from a variety of sources. Major Arthur Griffiths had previously suggested that data might be collected to test Lombroso's criminal type hypothesis against the evidence of English prisoners (Radzinowicz and Hood 1986, 20) and this may have been the original motivation of his name-sake, Dr. G. B. Griffiths, who began the work at Parkhurst Prison in 1901. It was probably a belief that other, useful information could be generated—for example, about the numbers of feeble-minded persons in prison, or the effect of prison diet and conditions upon the physical and mental health of inmates—which led Sir Bryan Donkin and Sir Herbert Smalley, the senior medical staff of the prison system, to take up the research and extend it considerably. The work was completed by Dr. Charles Goring, after a lengthy secondment at Karl Pearson's Biometrical laboratory, where he tabulated and analysed a vast quantity of data—motivated, no doubt, by a mixture of scientific curiosity and eugenist commitment.

As its sponsors intended, the study gave a definitive refutation of the old Lombrosian claim that the criminal corresponded to a particular physical type, thus confirming the position which the British authorities had held all along. However Goring's study went much further than this negative finding. In fact, in an important sense Goring's analysis *began* by assuming that there was no criminal type, as such, and although it was not much noticed at the time, his study is chiefly notable for demonstrating a quite new way of conceiving the criminal "difference". In the early part of the book, Goring set out extensive theoretical and methodological arguments which insisted that criminality should be viewed not as a qualitative difference of type, marked by anomaly and morbidity, but instead as a variant of normality, differentiated only by degree. Following the arguments of Manouvrier and Topinard, he pointed out that so-called criminal "anomalies" are only "more or less

---

[21] For a detailed discussion of this work, see Beirne (1987).

10

extreme degrees of character which in some degree are present in all men". Moreover, he made it clear that his use of statistical method necessarily presupposed this idea of a criminal characteristics which is a common feature of all individuals, and he went on to name this hypothesized entity "the criminal diathesis".

This conception of criminality as normal, rather than morbid or pathological, implied a new basis for criminological science, which Goring vigorously set forth. From now on, criminology could no longer depend upon the clinical gaze of a Lombroso and its impressionistic identification of anomalies. (Goring had, in any case, provided a devastating critique of such methods.) Instead it must be a matter of large populations, careful measurement and statistical analysis, demonstrating patterns of differentiation in the mass which would not be visible in the individual or to the naked eye. His own study, he concluded, had revealed a significant, but by no means universal, association between criminality and two heritable characteristics, namely low intelligence and poor physique.

Although *The English Convict* made a massive impact abroad, and especially in the U.S.A., in Britain it received a surprisingly muted response which dismayed both its author, and his mentor, Karl Pearson. On the one hand, Goring's attack had been centred upon theoretical positions which had little support in this country; and on the other, it appeared to have policy implications—eugenic and otherwise—which were not altogether welcome in official circles. The Prison Commission, while supporting the study's publication as a Blue Book, refused to endorse all of its conclusions. Sir Evelyn Ruggles-Brise provided a preface to the book which took care to render its finding compatible with the official brand of penal reform, while Sir Bryan Donkin distances himself from the study altogether, arguing that "even correct generalisations . . . . concerning convicted criminals in the mass are not likely to be of much positive value in the study or treatment of individuals . . . ".[22] In much the same way W. C. Sullivan, the medical superintendent of Broadmoor, argued in *Crime and Insanity* (1924) that clinical rather than statistical methods were the only reliable means to obtaining useful, policy relevant knowledge. Nevertheless, Goring's major argument—for the importance of statistical method in criminological research—was, in the long term, taken up by the British authorities. By the end of the 1930s, the Prison Commission and the Home Office had each embarked upon large-scale, statistically-based projects—eventually published as East (1942) and Carr-Saunders *et al.* (1942)—and this became the characteristics form of government sponsored research in the years after 1945.

The English Convict was a transitional work. Its conception of criminality as continuous with normal conduct, together with its statistical sophistication, opened up new research questions and methods for their solution, and gave British criminological work a scope and rigour which it had not possessed before. However its extensive engagement with older questions about

[22] Sir H. Bryan Donkin (1919). This article is part of an exchange with Goring, provoked by Donkin's (1917) paper. See Goring's response; Goring (1918).

"criminal types" and "physical anomalies" meant that for much of the book its language and concepts were those of a pre-modern idiom—an idiom which, even in 1913, was not much spoken in this country.[23] A mark of the book's success is that this idiom quickly became archaic, even in places such as the U.S.A. where it had once been strong.

III

When later criminologists such as Mannheim and Radzinowicz looked back upon their predecessors—and being the founders of a profession they were deeply concerned to establish a proper ancestry—they spent little time discussing the merits of *The English Convict*. Instead, they invariably picked out Cyril Burt's 1925 study of *The Young Delinquent* as the first work of modern criminology, and as an exemplar for the profession they were forming.[24] And indeed even now, more than sixty years after its publication, if one reads the 600 odd pages of *The Young Delinquent* it still seems strikingly modern in a way which even the best works of this period do not—not least because much of subsequent criminology was actually formed in its image. It seems appropriate then, to end this survey by asking what it was about Burt's work which gave it this major status and its aspect of "modernity".

Burt's book combined the statistical expertise of a Goring with the clinical experience and practical concerns of workers like Hamblin Smith, Sullivan and East, but was actually written for a wide popular audience, with a degree of verve and literary style rarely encountered in a scholarly text. Its analyses had all the marks of the scientist and disciplined researcher, but it also carried the transparent common sense of a practitioner who appeared to know his clients intimately (and compassionately) and who was concerned to specify viable modes of individual treatment as well as scientific claims about causation. As such, it could, and did, appeal to the widest range of readers—not just "criminological workers" but also parents, teachers, social workers, and social policy-makers—thereby linking scientific criminology into the other important traditions of writing and thinking about crime. It was a work which was able to open out criminological science, making it more relevant and comprehensible to a wider public than ever before.

Like most other British criminological texts, *The Young Delinquent* emerged from a specific field of practice, but in common with the subsequent work of the ISTD, and in marked contrast to most previous work in this genre, this field of practice was outside or on the margins of the penal system, rather than central to it. In his post as educational psychologist to the London County Council—the first post of its kind in Britain—Burt was responsible for the psychological assessment and advising of London's school-child population,

---

[23] In fact *The English Convict* was widely interpreted as presenting an alternative version of "the criminal type". See the review symposium in the American *Journal of Criminal Law, Criminology and Police Science*, Vol. 5 (1914–15) and also W. C. Sullivan (1924) pp. 9–10.

[24] See L. Radzinowicz (1961) pp. 173–176: " . . . it may be said that modern criminological research in England dates only from Sir Cyril Burt's study of *The Young Delinquent*, first published in 1925. Its excellence in method and interpretation was at once recognised and it has stood the test of rapidly advancing knowledge". See also H. Mannheim (1949) at p. 11.

which involved him in examining thousands of individual problem cases—
many of them behavioural as well as educational—and making recommendations for their treatment. His books from this period were thus a kind of
operational research, reflecting his practice, its problems, and the data he
derived therefrom.[25] It was thus an educational rather than a penal surface
of emergence which allowed Burt to develop his criminological study around
a wider than usual population—notably including pre-delinquents as well
as convicted offenders—and which also released his inquiries from the
narrowness of penal or prison-based issues. Rather than inquire about specific
classifications or distinctions, Burt was interested to specify all the possible
sources of individual psychological difference, and thereby to identify the
causal patterns which precipitate delinquency and non-delinquency.

The Young Delinquent was based upon the detailed clinical examination of
400 schoolchildren (a delinquent or quasi-delinquent group and a control
group), using a technical repertoire which included biometric measurement,
mental testing, psycho-analysis and social inquiries, together with the most
up-to-date statistical techniques of factor analysis and correlation. Its findings
were expansively eclectic, identifying some 170 causitive factors which were in
some way associated with delinquency, and showing, by way of narrative case
histories, how each factor might typically operate. From his analysis, Burt
concluded that certain factors, such as defective discipline, defective family
relationships and particular types of temperament were highly correlated
with delinquency, while the influence of other factors, such as poverty or low
intelligence, while not altogether negligible, had been seriously overstated in
the past. His major proposition was that delinquency was not the outcome of
special factors operating only upon delinquents, but was rather the result of a
combination of factors—typically as many as nine or ten—operating at once
upon a single individual. In consequence, the study of criminality must be,
above all, multi-causal in scope, while its treatment must be tailored to fit the
needs of the individual case.

Although Burt conceived his book as part of a larger study within individual
psychology, *The Young Delinquent,* more than any other work, set out the case
for an independent, self-constituting discipline of criminology. As glimpsed
through Burt's work, criminology was so broad in its eclectic coverage,
drawing upon a wide range of sciences and disciplines, and yet so focused in
its particular concerns, dealing with the peculiarities of offenders and the
institutional complex that surrounded them, that it cried out for specialised
expertise. The book suggested a vision of criminological research as an eclectic,
multi-disciplinary activity, based upon the clinical study of individuals,
and held together by statistical analysis. It also evoked an image of the professional criminologist, conversant with the quirks and characteristics of

---

[25] *The Young Delinquent* was completed about 20 years before the first occasion on which Burt is known to
have falsified data and findings. In his biography *Cyril Burt: Psychologist* (1979), L. S. Hearnshaw describes
how Burt's manipulation of data and manufacturing of results occurred at a time when he was out of
immediate touch with field research (having lost much of his original data as a result of the war) and was
responding defensively against challenges to his deeply held beliefs about the existence and hereditary
nature of general intelligence. He was probably also suffering from the psychosomatic condition known as
Menieres Disease.

deviant individuals, familiar with the vagaries of institutional practice, and able to translate scientific research into practical advice for the solution of important social problems.[26] Conceived in these terms, criminology could hardly be left as the passing trade of non-specialists from other disciplines, so it is hardly surprising that Burt's book would later hold such great appeal for those who favoured the idea of an independent criminology.

One might pause to reflect here that Burt's rationale for the discipline is based entirely upon the pragmatics of applied science and social necessity. It is a claim that criminological issues are important enough and complex enough to warrant specialised study, not that there is any distinctive object of study which can only be understood criminologically. In this respect it is very different from criminology's original Lombrosian claim that the criminal type is a naturally occurring entity which requires a scientific specialism of its own. And although this conception of criminology as rooted in the needs of social policy is perhaps more realistic and more enduring than one purportedly based upon a division of nature, it does raise questions about the nature of a knowledge which is linked so closely to forms of institutional power and policy. Or at least it should raise such questions: it would be some fifty years after Burt's work before criminologists began to take them seriously.[27]

Burt's work is thus important because it exhibits a framework which academic criminology would later latch onto and form itself around. But it would be historically short-sighted to concentrate too much upon texts which gave criminology its specific configuration at the moment of its professional inception—not least because that configuration has been changing ever since. This essay has concentrated instead upon some of the earlier work which helped prepare a social and institutional space for criminology in Britain. In particular it has discussed the institutionally-linked psychiatric tradition, which can be seen as the crucial route by which the idea of a scientific approach to criminals became implanted—however marginally[28]—in penal practice, in the courts, and in the policy thinking of governmental authorities. To some extent this might be seen as the "official criminology" of the period. It did not represent a general theory of crime, or even a full research programme which might produce one, and it would later be unpopular with academics for precisely that reason. But, as I have stressed, this tradition had no such ambition. Its goal was not general theory but instead particular understanding for specific, practical purposes, and it was bound to conflict with the intellectual ambitions of academic criminology in the 1950s, just as it had done with the continental work of the 1880s.

Criminologists in Britain, before the development of a university-based profession, were characteristically practitioners. Insofar as they had an expertise or a knowledge-base it was a detailed knowledge of the institutional terrain and its requirements, together with a general training in medicine or

---

[26] In his lecture "Should the Criminologist be Encouraged?" Paterson (1931–32), Alexander Paterson uses Cyril Burt as an exemplar of what "the criminologist" might amount to, given official support.

[27] Matza (1969) drew attention to the way in which criminologists had "separated the study of crime from the workings and theory of the state" (at p. 143). Much of the radical criminology of the 1970's and 1980's can be seen as an attempt to restructure the field so as to overcome this separation.

[28] Pat Carlen (1986) describes the contemporary operation of psychiatry in British prisons.

psychiatry, and later, psychology. It was this practical surface of emergence which largely accounts for the individualised, policy-based and theoretically limited criminology which was characteristic of Britain before 1935.

The history of British criminology has mostly been written by modern academic criminologists who searched in vain for "schools of criminology" and, finding none, have concluded that the subject was painfully slow to develop in this country. In doing so, they echo the complaints of Ellis or Morrison who also did not know, or did not like, the indigenous criminology of this early period. But if we cease to assume that "criminology" can take only an academic form, and instead ask about the ways in which scientific thinking about crime has previously been located in the social fabric, then the foundations of the criminological enterprise will be traced rather differently. By doing so, we can put ourselves in a position to judge the wider implications of these different traditions—their effects as forms of power as well as forms of knowledge.[29] At a time when a renewed vision of criminology as an engaged administrative knowledge has risen up to challenge the 1970s ideal of independent and critical theorising, there may be some value in pursuing this line of inquiry.

David Garland
University of Edinburgh
August 1987

REFERENCES

BACON, G. MCKENZIE (1864). "Prison Discipline". *The Social Science Review* (New Series) **II.**

BAKER, John (1888). "Some Remarks on the Relation of Epilepsy and Crime". *J.M.S.* **XXXIV,** 183–191.

BAKER, John (1891). "Some Points connected with Criminals". *J.M.S* **XXXVIII,** 364–369.

BAKER, John (1896). "Insanity in English Local Prisons 1894–95". *J.M.S.* **XLII,** 294–302.

BEIRNE, Piers (1987). "Carapace, Crab, Cranium Criminal: A Reconsideration of Charles Goring's *The English Convict*." Paper delivered at the British Criminology Conference, Sheffield, July 1987.

BONGER, William Adriaan (1936). *An Introduction to Criminology*. London.

BURT, Cyril (1925). *The Young Delinquent*. London.

CARLEN, Pat (1986). "Psychiatry in Prisons" In P. Miller and N. Rose (eds.), *The Power of Psychiatry*.

CARR-SAUNDERS, A., MANNHEIM, H. and RHODES, E. C. (1942). *Young Offenders*. London.

CARSON, W. G. and WILES, P. (eds.) (1971). *Crime and Delinquency in Britain, Vol. 1.* Oxford.

DEVON, James (1912). *The Criminal and the Community*. London.

DONKIN, H. Bryan (1917). "Notes on Mental Defect in Criminals". *J.M.S.* **LXIII.**

DONKIN, H. Bryan (1919). "The Factors of Criminal Action". *J.M.S.* **XLV,** 87–96.

---

[29] For a discussion of these issues, see Garland (1985a).

EAST, W. Norwood (1924–25). Report of the Medical Officer of Brixton Prison in *The Report of the Commissioners of Prisons for 1923–24*, pp. 1924–25, Cmnd. 2307 XV, at 44.

EAST, W. Norwood (1927). *An Introduction to Forensic Psychiatry in the Criminal Courts*. London.

EAST, W. Norwood (1936). *The Medical Aspects of Crime*. London.

EAST, W. Norwood (1936a). Obituary of M. Hamblin Smith *J.M.S.* **LXXXII.**

EAST, W. Norwood and HUBERT, W. H. de B. (1939). *Report on the Psychological Treatment of Crime*. H.M.S.O. London.

EAST, W. Norwood (1942). *The Adolescent Criminal; A Medico-Sociological Study of 4,000 Male Adolescents*. London.

ELLIS, Havelock (1890). *The Criminal*. London.

ELLIS, Havelock (1890a). "The Study of the Criminal" *J.M.S.* **XXXVI.**

ELLIS, Havelock (1940). *My Life*. London.

FERRI, Enrico (1895). *Criminal Sociology*. (Vol. 2 in "The Criminology Series"). London.

FIELD, H. E. (1932). "The Psychology of Crime: The Place of Psychology in the Treatment of Delinquents". *British Journal of Medical Psychology*. **12,** 241–256.

FREUD, Sigmund (1915). "Criminality from a Sense of Guilt" in "Some Character-Types Met with in Psycho-analytic Work" in S. Freud: *Collected Papers* Vol 4 (ed. J. Riviere) (1959) New York. (First published in *Imago*. IV (1915–16).

GALTON, Francis (1890). "Criminal Anthropology". *Nature,* 22 May 1890.

GARLAND, David (1985). *Punishment and Welfare*. Aldershot.

GARLAND, David (1985a). "Politics and Policy in Criminological Discourse". *The International Journal of the Sociology of Law*. **13,** 1–33.

GLOVER, Edward (1950–51). Obituary of Dr. E. T. Jensen *The British Journal of Delinquency*. **1.**

GORING, Charles (1913). *The English Convict: A Statistical Study*. London.

GORING, Charles (1918). "The Aetiology of Crime". *J.M.S.* **LXIV,** 129–146.

GRIFFITHS, Major Arthur (1910–11). Entry on "Criminology" in *The Encyclopaedia Britannica*. 11th edition.

HEARNSHAW, L. S. (1979). *Cyril Burt, Psychologist*.

KLEIN, Melanie (1927). "Criminal Tendencies in Normal Children". *The British Journal of Medical Psychology*. **VII.**

KLEIN, Melanie (1934). "On Criminality". *The British Journal of Medical Psychology*. **XIV.**

LOMBROSO, Cesare (1895). *The Female Offender*. (Vol. 1 in "The Criminology Series"). London.

LINDESMITH, A. and LEVIN, Y. (1937). "The Lombrosian Myth in Criminology". *American Journal of Sociology*. **XLII,** 653–671.

MANNHEIM, Hermann (1949). Contribution to *Why Delinquency?* published by the National Association for Mental Health.

MATZA, David (1969). *Becoming Deviant*. New Jersey.

MAUDSLEY, Henry (1863). Review of "Female Life in Prison". *J.M.S.* **IX.**

MAUDSLEY, Henry (1889). "Remarks on Crime and Criminals". *J.M.S.* **XXXIV.**

MAUDSLEY, Henry (1895). "Criminal Responsibility in Relation to Insanity". *J.M.S.* **XLI.**

MILLER, Emanuel (1970). "Retrospects and Reflections, 1950–1970". *The British Journal of Criminology*. **10,** No. 4.

MORRIS, Terrence (1957). *The Criminal Area: A Study in Social Ecology*. London.

MORRISON, W. Douglas (1889). "Reflections on the Theories of Criminality" *J.M.S.* **XXXV.**

MORRISON, W. Douglas (1891). *Crime and Its Causes*. London.

MORRISON, W. Douglas (1896). *Juvenile Offenders*. (Vol. 3 in "The Criminology Series"). London.

NICOLSON, David (1872–73). "Criminal Psychology". *J.M.S.* **XVIII**.

NICOLSON, David (1873–74). "The Morbid Psychology of Criminals". *J.M.S.* **XIX**.

NICOLSON, David (1878–79). "The Measure of Individual and Social Responsibility in Criminal Cases". *J.M.S.* **XXIV**.

NICOLSON, David (1895). "Crime, Criminals and Criminal Lunatics". *J.M.S.* **XLI**.

PAILTHORPE, Grace W. (1932). *Studies in the Psychology of Delinquency*. London.

PAILTHORPE, Grace W. (1932). *What We Put in Prison, and in Preventive and Rescue Homes*. London.

PATERSON, Alexander (1933). "Should the Criminologist Be Encouraged?" *Trans. of the Medico-Legal Society*. **XXVI**.

POTTS, W. A. (1921). "Justice for the Defective Offender". *The Howard Journal*. **1,** No. 1.

POTTS, W. A. (1925). "Delinquency". *J.M.S.* **LXXI**.

PROAL, Louis (1898). *Political Crime*. (Vol. 4 in "The Criminology Series"). London.

QUINTON, Richard Frith (1910). *Crime and Criminals 1876–1910*. London.

RADZINOWICZ, Leon (1961). *In Search of Criminology*. London.

RADZINOWICZ, Leon and HOOD, Roger (1986). *History of the English Criminal Law*. Vol. 5.

RAVEN, Alice (1928). "A Contribution towards a Psychological Conception of Insanity and its Relation to Crime". *The Sociological Review*. **XX.**

RAVEN, Alice (1929). "Murder and Suicide as Marks of an Abnormal Mind." *The Sociological Review*. **XXI.**

ST. JOHN, Arthur (1912). "Criminal Anthropology and Common Sense". *The Sociological Review*. **5,** 65–67.

SMITH, M. Hamblin (1921). "The Birmingham Scheme: A Review". *The Howard Journal*. **1,** No. 1.

SMITH, M. Hamblin (1922). *The Psychology of the Criminal*. London.

SMITH, M. Hamblin (1922). "The Medical Examination of Delinquents". *J.M.S.* **LXVIII.**

SMITH, M. Hamblin (1925). "The Psychopathic Personality". *J.M.S.* **LXXI.**

SMITH, Roger (1981). *Trial by Medicine*.

SULLIVAN, W. C. (1906). *Alcoholism*. London.

SULLIVAN, W. C. (1924). *Crime and Insanity*. London.

SUTHERLAND, J. F. (1908). *Recidivism: Habitual Criminality and Habitual Petty Delinquency*. Edinburgh.

THOMSON, J. Bruce (1869). "The Effects of the Present System of Prison Discipline on the Body and the Mind". *J.M.S.* **XII.**

THOMSON, J. Bruce (1869–70). "The Hereditary Nature of Crime". *J.M.S.* **XV.**

THOMSON, J. Bruce (1870–71). "The Psychology of Criminals". *J.M.S.* **XVI.**

HERMANN MANNHEIM (1889–1974)

Leon Radzinowicz*

Hermann Mannheim (1889–1974), criminologist, was born in Berlin 26 October 1889, the only child of Wilhelm Mannheim and his wife, Clara Marcuse. He came from a well-to-do background: his father represented a German firm in the Baltic seaport of Libau, where he was also vice-president of the chamber of commerce. After tuition at home and at a classical *Gymnasium,* Mannheim took up, at the age of eighteen, the study of law and political science at the universities of Munich, Freiburg, Strasburg, and Königsberg. By 1913 he had obtained the degree of Doctor of Laws. In World War I he served in the German artillery in Russia and in France; towards the end he was appointed judge of a court martial. By 1932 he had become a judge of the Kammergericht in Berlin (the highest court for the whole of Prussia) as well as Professor extraordinarius of the prestigious law faculty of the University of Berlin. He had to his credit many publications and was held in high esteem in governmental, judicial, and academic circles. He was barely forty-five years old.

The advent of the Nazi regime shattered this honourable and substantial achievement. He was forced to relinquish his professorship. Aware where all this would end he also retired from the bench, and in January 1934 this proud man moved to London to start life afresh. He became a naturalized British subject in 1940. Inevitably, the process of readjustment could not but be painful and tortuous. Yet, his capacity to face this new challenge was truly impressive. In this his wife, Mona Mark, whom he married in 1919, proved a gallant companion: they had no children. He switched the focus of his interest from criminal law and procedure to criminology and penal policy, and considerably improved his command of English. The London School of Economics, with its rich and adventurous tradition in social sciences, was the natural intellectual home for him. In 1935 he was appointed an honorary part-time lecturer in criminology. A year later he received the award of the Leon fellowship. In 1944 he became a permanent full-time lecturer and two years later the reader in criminology—the first post of its kind in Great Britain. He retired in 1955. He was a dedicated and enthusiastic teacher.

Between 1939 and 1965 he produced eight publications either as the sole author, co-author, or editor. In addition he wrote many articles, notes, and reviews: in the *British Journal of Criminology* alone there were seventy pieces. His most thought-provoking, original, and enduring books are: *The Dilemma of Penal Reform* (1939), in which he traced the implications of Bentham's famous principle of 'lesser eligibility' throughout the penological spectrum; *Criminal Justice and Social Reconstruction* (1946; 2nd impr. 1949), which is rightly recognized as his most influential and widely read work; and *Prediction Methods in Relation to Borstal Training* (with Leslie T. Wilkins, 1955), the first authoritative study of this kind in England. *Social Aspects of Crime in England Between the*

*This article was originally published in *The Dictionary of National Biography 1971–80*, edited by Lord Blake and C. S. Nicholls (Oxford University Press 1986, © Oxford University Press).

Wars (1940) was too ambitious and turned out to be rather uneven but it contained many useful hints for future researches into the environmental contents of crime. *Group Problems in Crime and Punishment* (1955) was largely a collection of his major articles, which in spite of the passage of time still repay rereading. But his three other books (*War and Crime*, 1941; *Young Offenders*, with A. M. Carr-Saunders and E. C. Rhodes, 1942; and *Juvenile Delinquency in an English Middletown*, 1948), though informative at the time of their appearance, were rather mechanical and pedestrian. *Pioneers in Criminology*, which he edited (1st edn. 1960; 2nd and enlarged edn. 1972), was a splendid pedagogical tool. *Comparative Criminology* 2 vols., 1965) failed to become the *magnum opus*, although it was well received, especially on the continent of Europe. An Italian translation appeared in 1972, a German in 1974. The treatise was confined to the strictly criminological aspect of the subject. It appeared at a time when criminological theory was changing direction and seemed in England and the United States already old-fashioned.

Mannheim's intellectual vitality was remarkable: as late as 1975 there appeared (posthumously) his massive comparative study of recidivism "Rückfall and Prognose" in the new edition of the *Handwörterbuch der Kriminologie*, Berlin, 1975, pp. 38–93). He helped greatly the Institute for the Study and Treatment of Delinquency; he was the founding editor of the *British Journal of Delinquency* (later *British Journal of Criminology*); he helped launch the International Library of Criminology and the British Society of Criminology. For twenty-five years he was closely associated with the Howard League for Penal Reform. He played a fruitful part in the work of the International Society of Criminology.

It is to the credit of the Federal Republic of Germany that he was appointed in 1952 to the rank of retired president of the division of Court of Appeal and in 1962 he received the Grosses Verdienstkreuz der Bundesrepublik Deutschland. In the same year he was awarded the Golden Beccaria medal of the German Society of Criminology. A volume of the German Encyclopaedia of Criminology (2nd edn. 1975) was dedicated to his memory. He was awarded the Coronation medal in 1953 and appointed OBE in 1959. He received honorary doctorates from the universities of Utrecht (1957) and Wales (1970) and was made an honorary fellow of the London School of Economics (1965). In 1965 he was presented with a Festschrift edited by three of his former students (*Criminology in Transition*).

There were many up and down the country as well as abroad who were taught by him and in their turn taught others. He was short in stature but robust, mild mannered but determined, sensitive but with a bite of his own. He maintained a formality characteristic of a German professor. He was disappointed that after so rich a contribution he was not made a professor by London University. It also grieved him that the first chair and Institute of Criminology found a home not in London but in Cambridge. Yet his reputation as a scholar–criminologist stands high and will remain high. Compelled to leave his country of birth he became a pioneer in the country which received him.

He died in London 20 January 1974.

19

BRIT. J. CRIMINOL.   Vol. 28   No. 2   SPRING 1988

BRITISH CRIMINOLOGY: 1935–48

TERENCE MORRIS (*London*)*

The starting date for this paper is arbitrary and will therefore be treated loosely; the concluding date is crucial since it is the year of the Criminal Justice Act which, as far as the treatment of offenders was concerned, marked the passage from the pre-war to the post-war world. That suggestion in itself may be objectionable to those who are repelled by an approach to history that seems to be characterized by a catalogue of events punctuated by dates. The criticism is not without substance, not least since all social and political life is suspended between a perpetual 'now' and an immediately recent past which was but an hour or a day away. Yet, notwithstanding the philosophical implications of Euclidian geometry, lines must be drawn, albeit that they have only length and points identified, even though they have but position and no magnitude. The position is further complicated by the fact that those who recount a history, of which they have not merely recollection but in which they played some part, have difficulties, when recalling their personal experience of events, in distinguishing between that which for others consists of a series of ossified events and those which for them are part of a continuity of personal experience. And that is not all; there are fashions in historiography, not least in what may, in substance, be largely oral as distinct from documentary history. Thus those who take down—generally with the aid of a recording machine—the recollections of elderly people who would readily identify themselves as 'working class' pursue a craft which is both as popular as it is useful. The middle and professional classes are supposed to be literate and keep diaries and papers with the result that when they too indulge in oral recollection, their accounts may be held as less desirable.[1]

Just as it has been said, and with some truth, that all history is the history of class struggles it is also true that in the history of an intellectual discipline its history is that of the prejudices and predilections of powerful and persuasive men. It tends to be their energies, constantly working upon the materials of their time, that shape its concerns and priorities. Nowhere has this been more true than in the field of criminology. If Beccaria and John Howard had not been the products of the eighteenth century Enlightenment *On Crimes and Punishments* and *The State of Prisons* would never have been written. Likewise Bentham's idea of the Panopticon prison—'a mill for grinding rogues honest and idle men industrious'—would never have seen the light of day, but for the fact that he was prepared to embrace both a newly fashionable Utilitarianism and an economics whose *fons et origo* was Adam Smith. So too with Lombroso,

---

*Professor of Social Institutions in the University of London (LSE), formerly Professor of Sociology with Special Reference to Criminology.

[1] When this paper was given in a somewhat shorter form at the British Criminology Conference at Sheffield in July, 1987, it was criticised, *inter alia*, for being a kind of 'history of the kings and queens of England sort of account' and at least one critic seemed to doubt its veracity altogether.

'father' of modern criminology (as some would have it); but for the positivism of Comte and the evolutionary theories of Darwin *L'Uomo Delinquente*
would have been stillborn.[2] It is therefore the substance of the argument of
this paper that the shape of British criminology during the period immediately
before and immediately after the Second World War owes almost everything
to the important figures who dominated the scene.

British society in 1935 was just emerging from the effects of the Great
Depression that had followed the Wall Street crash of 1929 and which had
touched bottom in 1931 when unemployment had reached 3 million.
Although it showed the marks of the changes that were the irreversible consequence of the war of 1914–18, it had more in common with the Britain of 1925
than the Britain of 1945. It was a relatively stable society, its character dominated by considerations of class and rigid social convention. Although fewer
than before 1914, large numbers of young women were still employed in
domestic service; illegitimacy was as heavily stigmatised as it was to have
had a criminal conviction. Social security was provided by a Poor Law that
had its origins in the Amendment Act of 1834—and which provided some 50
per cent of all the hospital beds in the country—and other health care was
provided by an inefficient combination of private means, private insurance
and a rudimentary state system that had been devised in 1911. It was a society
not only relatively stable but relatively tranquil. Demographically, the proportion of young people in the most crime prone age groups was lower than at
any period in this century; indeed, it was the era, *par excellence,* of the one
child family and of couples who preferred the baby Austin to the one in the
perambulator. Crime was rising but not alarmingly and it did not provide a
major theme for either political or general public debate. Such interest as
there was tended to centre around the notorious and the bizarre especially
where homicide was concerned. The Rattenbury trial, at which the older
married woman was acquitted and her younger, working-class chauffeur
lover was convicted, was a typical focus for the press. The public prints,
concentrating upon every detail of the most depressingly unoriginal domestic
crimes, were given over, as they had been since Dickens' day, to the prurient
voyeurism that anticipated the gallows.

In spite of the fact that prison conditions were in many respects every bit as
harsh as they had been in Victorian times,[3] inmate numbers were falling,
largely as a consequence of the growth of Probation orders, and some prisons,
like Shepton Mallet, were actually de-commissioned.[4] Innovations in prison
reform were also under way; the first 'open' borstal had opened at Lowdham
Grange in Nottinghamshire in 1931 and New Hall Camp, drawing prisoners
from Wakefield Gaol in 1934.[5] The kinds of crimes that were being committed
were essentially 'normal' in that although they might be presented as

[2] The influence of Lombroso on criminology has been at least as profound as that of Marx on political science.

[3] Penal servitude and hard labour, although they had fallen into desuetude by the early 1930s, remained on the statute book until 1948.

[4] After 1939 Shepton Mallet was put back into use as a military prison and was the scene of a number of executions following upon courts martial.

[5] See L. W. Fox *The English Prison and Borstal Systems.* London, Routledge. 1952.

'horrific'—like a brutal, sexually related homicide—they did not, by and large, represent the kind of departure from the familiar world of experience. Gratuitous violence was not part of the repertoire of even those offenders who might be termed habitual: they did their thieving and receiving and their burglary as they had for decades. There were, of course innovations, like the use of motor vehicles by criminals, notably in so-called 'smash and grab' robberies from jewellers' shops.[6] Most violence was localised to the areas around public houses on Saturday nights and such large-scale public dis-orders as there were tended to be both rare and specific, generally related to industrial disputes. 1936 was something of an exception in that the activities of Sir Oswald Moseley's British Union of Fascists, in emulating their National Socialist mentors in Germany by smashing up Jewish shops in London's East End and intimidating their proprietors, precipitated the Public Order Act, 1936.[7]

Poverty was widespread, although not high on the agenda of public debate, and was revealed in its magnitude during attempts to evacuate children from large centres of population, when it was found that among the children of the poor there were many without even rudimentary footwear. The unemployed were largely sullenly compliant of their lot and the Labour Party had still to recover from its crushing defeat in 1931—made worse by the defection of Ramsay MacDonald—and a further defeat in 1935. In that year George V and Queen Mary celebrated their Silver Jubilee; 25 years, as Claud Cockburn's banner had briefly proclaimed above Fleet Street to the passing cavalcade, of hunger and war. Hitler, now four years in power, had invaded the Rhineland in open defiance of the Versailles Treaty and had his eye on Austria for the following year. The Prince of Wales was taking his pleasures with Mrs. Simpson in the society of the super-rich and was but a year away from abdication. At Alexandra Palace John Logie Baird and the BBC were preparing for the first flickering TV transmissions to London. While the heavy industries of the North remained in decline, the fate of their people encapsu-lated in the monochrome photography of Bill Brandt, the south became more prosperous. Mars bars began to be made in Slough, Shredded Wheat in Welwyn Garden City and bakelite wirelesses in Southend. Unrestricted by any planning legislation the speculative builders raped the countryside of the Home Counties along every arterial road, building 'semi's' for a newly mobile and recently affluent white collar population. Ford knocked down the price of the 'Y' saloon built at Dagenham to £99 to undercut Sir Herbert Austin's famous 'Seven' and Morris's equally renowned 'Minor'. In such vehicles on summer Sundays the new lower middle classes headed in their droves for the coast or rural beauty spots. It was hardly a society in travail and those who suffered did so with little by way of articulate complaint. Social mobility was a function of changes in the labour market for new goods and

---

[6] See Ruby Sparks *Burglar to the Nobility*. London. 1961. The present writer possesses an autographed copy of this rare work.

[7] This Act was replaced by the Act of 1986. What is impressive about its fifty year history is the comparative infrequency of its use after about 1939 when many of the fascist trouble-makers were interned for the duration of the war under Regulation 18B.

services rather than of the educational system; grammar schools were few and hardly anyone save the children of the affluent and a minuscule number of scholarship winners went to University.

There was relatively little public debate about crime and punishment outside a narrow circle of people who in turn formed part of a small intellectual élite. Almost all of them in the pre-war period, with the exception of Margery Fry who had been Principal of Somerville,[8] were outside the universities, as indeed were so many of the important figures in British intellectual life at the time. Writers and poets, painters and social thinkers were then, as now, somewhat suspect.[9] This was in contrast to the traditions of mainland Europe where in the great university centres café society had flourished in their midst. The principal issues were the reform of prison conditions, such that they could be the source of the offender's rehabilitation and regeneration as a citizen; the development of forensic psychiatry so that the mentally disordered offender would not only get treatment within the penal system but would benefit from changes in the criminal law that could properly accommodate his handicap; and, not least, the abolition of capital punishment. Of the three issues, that of capital punishment probably excited the most general interest. Abolition had been a *cause célèbre* among penal reformers since the 1860s and the abolition of public executions in 1868 had been so far the campaigners' only, and very modest, achievement. The exotic figure of Mrs. Van der Elst stepping from her Rolls Royce to distribute abolitionist literature was to be seen outside prisons on the morning of executions, but apart from publicity she seems to have had little more effect than the one man demonstrations of the late Commander William Boaks.[10] The more effective campaigner was almost certainly Roy Calvert who, at the age of 28, had been persuaded to give up his Civil Service career to devote himself entirely to the cause of the abolition of the death penalty. He died in 1933 only 35 years old; had he lived to 78 he would have seen his efforts crowned with success.[11] Margery Fry was nevertheless the dominant figure on the penal reform scene for the whole period covered by this paper. As early as 1921 she and the Secretary of the organisation formed by the amalgamation of the John Howard Association and the Penal Reform League—nowadays known as the Howard League—had lobbied for the setting up of a Royal Commission on capital punishment. In the event they had to be content with a Select Committee whose report in 1930 recommended suspension for a trial period of five years—a suggestion that went unheeded. Margery Fry had been brought up a Quaker and as such not only followed in the footsteps of her illustrious kinswoman Elizabeth, who had brought Christian compassion to the gaols of Regency England, but

[8] For an account of the life of Margery Fry *see* Enid Huws Jones *Margery Fry*. London. 1966.

[9] A certain mental sluggishness seems to have been endemic in British academic life, even among those privileged to have the comparative leisure in which to think and write.

[10] For many years after the Second World War Commander Boaks ran a one man road safety campaign in London and was also active with regard to the immigration issue, often attempting to stand as a candidate in a multiplicity of constituencies at general elections. He was frequently involved with the law and was once remanded in custody for a psychiatric report, for which indignity he (unsuccessfully) sued the Chief Metropolitan Magistrate.

[11] *See* Huws Jones *op. cit.* pp. 123–4 and p. 158.

rejected the notion that there must be 'a life for a life' as being, like war, a negation of Christian pacifism.[12]

The Howard League was an articulate and essentially middle class pressure group. Its members were well connected socially and commanded the kinds of respect that prevented them from being sloughed off as either cranks or people of no account. Fry herself had managed, without too much difficulty, to gain access to the death cell to visit Edith Thompson before her execution in 1922 and several other condemned women afterwards. It was therefore natural that she and other leading members of the League, should be able to make ready connection with members of the Prison Commission.[13] The dominant Commissioner during the late 1920s and early 1930s was Sir Alexander Paterson. Although not Chairman of the Commission he was the engine of change within it. He was committed not merely to a humane prison policy but to a constructive criminal justice policy. He coined such aphorisms as 'You cannot train men for freedom in conditions of captivity' and was thus the driving force behind the open prison policy. He believed imprisonment to be so unnatural as to be damaging, arguing that 'prisoners are the unwilling monks of the twentieth century' and that after ten years of imprisonment the onset of mental and physical deterioration was irreversible.[14] The high public profile pursued by Paterson lent itself readily to his policy of recruiting young Oxbridge graduates with a social conscience to become housemasters in the borstal system whose ethos was increasingly modelled on that of the ideal-typical British Public School. These young men who had often gained some voluntary social work experience in the university Settlements—institutions redolent of the 'missions' whereby both Christian doctrine and charity were mediated to the poor and disadvantaged—became towards the end of their careers the backbone of the governor grades of the post-war prison service. By this the post-war Prison Commission was able to command the loyalty of a significant number of senior prison staff during a period of stressful change. Similarly, Paterson and, after the war, other Commissioners like Cape (who had a profound effect upon the shape of prison education)[15] and Fairn (who used to allay the fears of villagers threatened with the prospect of an open prison in the neighbourhood) often

[12] In 1954 she confided to the present writer that she approached death with an agnostic uncertainty. But even if she had lost some essential part of her Quaker faith, her commitment to the civilised decencies of penal reform remained wholly undiminished.

[13] The Prison Commission was established in 1877 after the local gaols (until then administered by the magistrates) were merged into a single prison system with the convict prisons hitherto run by central government. The Commissioners retained a public and individual identity until the Commission was abolished in the 1960s.

[14] This proposition has been frequently and successfully challenged, not least by the number of long term prisoners who have emerged from prison rather better, in a variety of senses, than when they went in. See Stanley Cohen and Laurie Taylor. *Psychological Survival*. London, Penguin. 1972. Paterson also travelled widely visiting prisons and penal establishments throughout the Empire. In 1966 the present writer found his signature and comments in the Visitors Book at the Salvation Army Reformatory for Boys at Baking Pot, Belize (formerly British Honduras) dated 1934.

[15] It was Cape who, as a housemaster, had led the first group of boys from Feltham Borstal in Middlesex on the long march to Lowdham Grange in Nottinghamshire, camping along the way until at their destination they began to erect the new buildings with their own hands. It was training 'in depth' of both character and building skill.

used Howard League meetings as public platforms for setting out their policies.

The subtle interaction between those in public office, and here one must include senior civil servants as well as the Prison Commissioners, and the penal reformers in this period is difficult to capture. The world of inter-acting pressure groups and power elites in British society was throughout the period comparatively small and remained so probably until as late as the end of the 1960s. It was, by and large, a leisured world in which the realities of the need to be earning a living did not always obtrude so uncom-fortably as they do today; private means had not yet been supplanted by the elusive grant.

That those who participated in public debate about crime and the penal system were limited in number, was almost certainly also affected by the fact that the mass media of communication—press, radio and television—were nothing like as extensive as they are today. They lacked both the omni-presence of the contemporary media and the raw immediacy of its current style. Programmes like *Any Questions* on which quite senior government ministers may debate with political opponents and the kind of terrier–like interviewing which has become the accepted mode for programmes like *The World at One* were quite unknown. It is possible, too, that a broad acceptance of a core of moral values effectively ensured that penal reform never emerged as a partisan political issue. Indeed, the bi-partisan nature of the politics of penal reform persisted until the rise of Thatcherism in the late 1970s. A further factor which might explain the limitation of debate was the fact that higher education was still, to all intents and purposes, so exclusive of all but the affluent middle and upper classes that many more people than today would have felt ineligible to participate.

What was to prove critical to the development of criminology in Britain was one of the very few positive outcomes of the growth of totalitarianism in mainland Europe. In 1935 Mussolini had been established as dictator of Italy for a decade and Hitler had just embarked on the first phase of his persecution of the Jews. This initially took the form of hounding them with thuggish violence, prohibiting them from holding public office, sequestrating their property and in some cases allowing them to leave Germany only on payment of a cash premium. Among the Jews who fled from this tyrannous regime were many distinguished scholars: one of the first to arrive was Hermann Mannheim. The biographical details of this distinguished scholar may be found elsewhere;[16] suffice it to say that his arrival at the LSE in 1936, where he was to spend the rest of his working life until his retirement in 1955, was to result in the introduction of criminology into university teaching in Britain for the very first time. He has been called 'The Father of modern British criminology' and with good reason. Indeed there is scarcely a professional criminologist in Britain today who was not either taught by him or taught by someone else who was. *Si monumentum requiris circumspice*. Mannheim at LSE

---

[16] *See* Terence Morris 'Hermann Mannheim'. *Encyclopaedia of the Social Sciences*. Vol. 18 *Biographical Supplement*. London, Collier MacMillan. 1972.

was followed by Max Grünhut who found refuge in All Souls.[17] The third member of what was to become a trio of distinguished émigrés did not finally settle in Britain until 1939. Leon Radzinowicz, much the youngest, was unlike either Mannheim or Grünhut in almost every way. He was not a direct victim of Nazi persecution but wisely (and fortunately for British criminology) had decided not to return to his native Poland. He had been one of the last students of the great Enrico Ferri in Rome and had already done important criminological research in both Poland and Europe generally. While the elder two remained essentially German while becoming superficially Anglicised, Radzinowicz—a brilliant linguist—retained a flamboyant cosmopolitan style which was much later to be such an essential element in integrating British criminology with a broader European scene. Thus London, Oxford and Cambridge within a decade became established centres of academic criminology. Of the three, the LSE was the most important both in terms of the numbers of students taught and the extent of research carried out, and remained so until the Institute of Criminology opened in Cambridge in 1959. In 1939 the LSE buildings were taken over by the Air Ministry and the School was evacuated to Cambridge. Little is directly known of the interaction between Mannheim and Radzinowicz in this period, the former being closely involved in research with Carr–Saunders and E. C. Rhodes, but it was clear by the early 1950s that there was some hostility between them. Mannheim, with the passage of time, came to regard Radzinowicz with feelings not so much of dislike as of detestation; Radzinowicz, to his credit, never reciprocated on that scale and has subsequently been most generous in print to the memory of his old adversary.[18]

Until the arrival of the émigrés, criminology in Britain was something little known, not studied in universities and associated in most people's minds with the work of Cesare Lombroso who was, of course, a foreigner. It formed no part of the legal education of those who would practice in the courts and magistrates, being appointed by the crudest forms of political patronage, would probably have associated it all with Sherlock Holmes. Yet, in all that bleak ignorance, there were glimmers of what was to come.

Lombroso had published *L'Uomo Delinquente* in 1876 and its influence had been profound, not least in eclipsing virtually all interest in the sociological study of crime. Charles Goring, far from rejecting Lombroso's positivism, merely substituted an alternative and infinitely more sophisticated set of propositions. Positivism was to early twentieth century criminology what the agrichemical industry has been to late twentieth century farming—something so vitally fundamental that to eschew it would be considered unthinkable. Thus those who did not follow directly in the steps of Lombroso nevertheless

---

[17] Both Mannheim and Grünhut persisted in wearing highly polished Edwardian style laced leather boots years after they had gone out of fashion.

[18] *See* Leon Radzinowicz 'Hermann Mannheim' in this volume. It is interesting to speculate upon what a powerful team they could have been but for Mannheim's paranoid hostility which, towards the end of his life had sadly reached pathological proportions.

explored similarly predicated hypotheses assuming, above all, *that the criminal was different*. Thus Goddard and Esterbrook plunged into the study of imbeciles and hereditary mental defect. Kretschmer explored physique and delinquency, a theme taken up by Earnest Hooton who wrote in his *American Criminal* in 1939 that

> Criminals are organically inferior. Crime is the resultant impact of environment on low grade human organisms. It follows that the elimination of crime can be effected only by the extirpation of the physically, mentally and morally unfit, or by their complete segregation in a socially asceptic environment.[19]

Hooton's work was soon to be followed by that of William H. Sheldon and that of Sheldon and Eleanor Glueck. (They dedicated one of their works to Hermann Mannheim. What they had in common was an interest in prediction studies). It was not until the 1960s, notably with the work of Becker and the development of labelling theory, that the intellectual tradition of this neo-positivism was eventually superseded although it rumbled on in the work of Hans Eysenck, whom some would regard as Lombroso's true heir.

By the turn of the century criminology had been successfully medicalised in the sense that since the criminal was seen to be a pathological specimen in both a social as well as often in a physiological sense, then the proper investigation would need to be undertaken by a skilled practitioner in physical or psychological medicine. Moreover, the unquestioned assumption that physical and mental abnormality were inextricably conjoined meant that the only people with legitimate access to the subject matter were either doctors or those within the newly expanding group of clinical and educational psychologists, who were interested in such things as education and delinquency and intelligence testing, and among whom the name of Cyril Burt springs immediately to mind.

The Young Delinquent, the first volume of Burt's two part study *The Sub-Normal Schoolchild,* appeared in 1925 and by 1945 it had gone through four editions as well as being reprinted no fewer than three times. Volume II, *The Backward Child,* is much less well known. The memorable figure of 'B.I.', capped and collarless, cigarette welded to lower lip and aged '$15\frac{7}{12}$' looking significantly from the frontispiece, seems to summarise so much about the delinquent youth of the early twentieth century. Yet in those days there were so many wretched and coarsely mis-shapen people about, suffering from poor nutrition and inadequate health care that the neo-Lombrosian vision had a tangible reality. Burt's work has now been largely discredited and is derisively dismissed as the psychological counterpart to the Piltdown fraud, but, in a sense, whether or not he did falsify some of his research findings is neither here nor there when estimating his position in the criminology of the period

---

[19] For a fuller account of this neo-positivist tradition of research *see* Terence Morris *Deviance and Control: The Secular Heresy.* London, Hutchinson. 1976.

1935–48. Then he would have been readily identified as a giant, head and shoulders above most others. And, it should be noted, he was certainly on the right track in a number of instances. He was opposed to corporal punishment for the deprived child.

> . . . to the child inured to wretchedness and benumbed by suffering, added hurt is only added injury. Hence if whipping is to be preserved as a official punishment the proper subject of it is not the street urchin from a struggling home hardened already by a succession of thrashings far more drastic than a humane legislature would allow, but rather, the over-indulged youth whose home is comfortable and easy going, who has been brought up under a lax and lenient discipline and who needs the smart tonic of a little pain to pull him sharply up after one or two weak lapses.[20]

Burt had also recommended to the London County Council that there be established under the aegis of its education service 'a psychological clinic for young delinquents'. The first child guidance clinic was probably set up in Glasgow (somewhat improbably given the enthusiasm of Catholic teachers for corporal punishment) in connection with a teacher training college run by an order of nuns. The idea spread but slowly, since 'psychology', especially where it seemed to 'excuse' crime, was held in great suspicion. By the middle of the period, however, (1935–48) two London clinics were well established; the Portman, run by the I.S.T.D., then the Institute for the *Scientific Treatment* of Delinquency and the Tavistock, where John Bowlby was to do his seminal work on *Forty Four Juvenile Thieves*.

It can be argued that those who saw the 'clinic' as a device for transforming delinquents into non-delinquents, had advanced significantly from the narrow positivism that saw the task of criminology as primarily one of identification of criminals in order that they might be contained or controlled. They fitted readily into the growing enthusiasm for 'therapy' that was to inform a great deal of work with difficult children[21] and with the 'rehabilitative ideal' that was to become the central focus of work in prisons and especially borstals. Even in the prison medical service there were small stirrings. Grace Pailthorpe, the medical officer at Holloway had published a monograph in 1932 that is of some historical significance, but it was in the field of forensic psychiatry that some of the most important steps were taken. Dr John Mackwood had experimented with psycho-therapy at Wormwood Scrubs prison as early as 1935 and shortly afterwards the distinguished forensic psychiatrist Sir Norwood East was asked by the Home Office to report on the possibilities of the psychological treatment of crime. The report appeared in

---

[20] Cyril Burt. *The Young Delinquent*. 4th ed. London, University of London Press. 1945. p. 123.

[21] The work of A. S. Neill at Summerhill and to a lesser extent schools like those at Dartington Hall and Frensham Heights were an integral part of this ethos. The tradition continued after the war in the work of the Dockar Drysdales at the Mulberry Bush School; The Dockar Drysdales were published in the early issues of the *British Journal of Delinquency*.

1939[22] and recommended, *inter alia*, the building of a psychiatric prison to be used for the treatment of inmates who would return to the community; this notion was quite distinct from that of the institutions for the criminally insane as they were then known, like Broadmoor which had opened in 1863,[23] and which were geared to keeping their inmates until they were released only by the agency of death itself. The war intervened and it was more than twenty years before the 'East-Hubert' institution, as it had come to be known, was finally opened as the maximum security prison at Grendon Underwood in Buckinghamshire. Psychological medicine was held in a wholly different regard by the Prison Commissioners and many senior civil servants in the Home Office than by judges and magistrates and most of the legal profession. While the latter were often stridently derisory in their scepticism, the former identified its role as being consistent with the promotion of the rehabilitative ideal.

The source of the psycho-therapeutic thrust came in part from the humanised expression of the interests of psychologists about their subjects; although his language seems archaic, Burt cared deeply about disadvantaged children and delinquents in particular. But the major thrust undoubtedly came from psycho-analysis. J. C. Flugel had become a lecturer in psychology at University College, London, in the early 1920s and his teaching and writing made much of Freud's work meaningful in a wider social focus, and other disciples had already spread the word of the Master before his arrival as an émigré in 1938. Edward Glover became after the war the doyen of forensic psycho-analysis and in later years came to regard criticisms of his sometimes implausibly bizarre theories as being somewhere between *lèse-majesté* and rank heresy; his friend Emmanuel Miller—who together with Glover and Mannheim founded the *British Journal of Delinquency* (as this journal was then known) in 1950—worked closely with him at the Portman Clinic and in the ISTD.

The Howard League, apart from its 'flagship' enterprise— the abolition of the death penalty—was especially concerned to advance the idea of rational, constructive sentencing that was aimed at rehabilitation rather than the sterile objective of the retributive punishment of crime in the manner that had been so eloquently expressed by Fitzjames Stephen some half a century before:

> I think it highly desirable that criminals should be hated, that the punishments inflicted upon them should be so contrived as to give expression to that hatred. . .[24]

Its Quaker element was strong and influential and in some ways reflected a continuity in that same Quaker spirituality which had a century before

[22] Sir W. Norwood East, MD, FRCP, late Medical Commissioner of Prisons and W. H. de B. Hubert, BA, MRCS, LRCP, late Psychotherapist, HM Prison Wormwood Scrubs. *Report on the Psychological Treatment of Crime.* London, HMSO. 1939. Price 2s. 6d. nett. The Report, which was of profound importance, arose from the original recommendation of the Departmental Committee on Persistent Offenders of 1932.

[23] One of its first inmates was the ageing Daniel M'Naghten, the would-be assassin of Sir Robert Peel and the misinformed killer of his secretary William Drummond, in 1843. His name is commemorated in the 'Rules' formulated to cover the insanity defence which arose from these events.

[24] Sir James Fitzjames Stephen, J. *A History of the Common Law.* London, 1883.

founded the Retreat at York, where the mentally ill had found compassion and treatment rather than oppression and incarceration. Perhaps one reason why the League and the Prison Commission were possessed of a shared empathy was on account of the fact that the Commissioners regarded religious commitment in their staff as a virtue. Among those recruited to the Housemaster grades for the borstals were not only saintly Quakers like Duncan Fairn but wonderful Anglican eccentrics like Almeric Rich.[25] But the urging along of legislation was another matter.

As far as what we would now term 'deviance' was concerned, the period of inertia that had followed upon the great cataract of Liberal legislation in the first decade of the century was coming to an end. In 1930 the Mental Treatment Act dealt, among other things, with 'certification' by magistrates. In 1932 the Salmon Committee had reported on the subject of persistent offenders and had recommended both reform of the Preventive Detention Act of 1908 and a new sentence of 'corrective training' which was not to see the light of day until the Criminal Justice Act of 1948. In 1933 a new Children's Act had been passed but prison matters were coming to a head and were expressed in a Criminal Justice Bill in 1938. The time could have scarcely been more inopportune. By 1938 the evil genius of Hitler, having re-taken the Rhineland and invaded Austria had engineered the Sudeten Crisis to make Czechoslovakia his next victim. Britain prepared for war; every man, woman and child acquired both an identity card and a gas mask. Meanwhile Neville Chamberlain (who had succeeded Baldwin as Prime Minister after the Abdication crisis) flew to see Hitler and concluded the Munich Agreement. To all intents and purposes, the period from its signing in 1938 and the outbreak of war following upon the invasion of Poland a year later, had the effect of neutralising all legislative activity save that which was directed towards the conduct of the war, which was by now quite inevitable. As the Anderson shelters[26] were set into suburban gardens, the Criminal Justice Bill with its proposals for Detention Centres and Attendance Centres—to be known as Howard Houses—was consigned together with the plans for the psychiatric prison, to a future when 'hostilities would be over'. Pentonville, which had up until 1939 been somewhat under-used, was soon full of both recently arrived Jewish refugees—'aliens'—as well as the jew-baiters of the British Union of Fascists and other detainees under Defence Regulation 18B, who were somewhat insensitively housed with them until the latter could be transferred to quarters more comfortable and befitting their social station on the Isle of Man. The borstal system was terminated almost overnight and the staff permitted to enlist.

With the progress of the war, prisons began to fill with all manner of

[25] Sir Almeric Rich, Bart. when Governor of Huntercombe Borstal was known to have sentenced a boy to scrub out the gymnasium for some misdemeanour and then get down beside him in dungarees to share the penitential task.
[26] These flimsy corrugated iron structures of Romanesque appearance, bearing the name of the Home Office Minister, Sir John Anderson, were designed to be erected in semi-excavated sites in private gardens. Later in the war a type of indoor shelter that also served as a table bore the name of the Labour Home Secretary in the coalition government (Herbert Morrison). Prison inmates had to take their chance during the air raids but only one prison, Pentonville, suffered other than superficial damage.

offenders including the flotsam of war such as aliens who had been convicted of offences and members of allied and Commonwealth armed forces.[27] The British prison system acquired a cosmopolitan character that it has never subsequently lost. By the time the war ended it had also acquired a problem of overcrowding which it has also never lost. The response of the Prison Commission in this immediate post-war period was to remain consistent with the rehabilitative ideal and to seek to acquire new properties for use as open prisons; at this time there were numerous camps with adequate if somewhat spartan accommodation recently vacated by the armed services. It was in this way that the ex-American Army hospital at Leyhill became an open prison. One of the effects of the war had been to develop a sense of bi-partisanship in political affairs and although the Labour landslide of the 1945 election re-opened the old political divisions there remained a common approach to both foreign and home affairs. If there were differences they tended to be about means rather than ends.

Thus the Attlee government, in spite of its steamroller majority, did not go about the business of penal reform with much that could be considered as either originality or greater enthusiasm. It was considered sufficient to dust down the aborted Criminal Justice Bill of 1938 and make amendments to it rather than embark upon some wholly new appraisal of the situation. Chuter Ede, the Home Secretary, could hardly be described as a memorable incumbent of the office. Attlee was above all, cautious in matters he considered to be socially tendentious.[28] Just as most of the important social welfare legislation, Beveridge notwithstanding, was in essence a continuation of the unfinished business of the Liberal government of 1906, so it was logical to base post-war legislation on the skeletal structure of a bill some ten years—and a world war— away. Indeed, the provisions for preventive detention and corrective training dating from the Salmon Committee were almost twenty years old. The Howard League mounted a vigorous Parliamentary campaign suggesting amendments to the bill early in 1948; amongst other things it wanted not only the abolition of judicial corporal punishment but that of the death penalty at which prospect the government baulked. It was left to Sydney Silverman as a back-bencher to introduce an amendment to that effect. It was opposed by the government and its law officers who included the Attorney General Sir Hartley Shawcross, who felt that to do so would be to run ahead of public opinion. The result was that the government bought off its back-benchers by the setting up of a Royal Commission[29] and suspending the execution of condemned persons during its sitting. Attlee employed the same

[27] In 1942 a Canadian Indian soldier, August Sangret, was executed at Wandsworth for the murder of Joan Pearl Wolfe. He waited longer to be hanged than any offender in English legal history. United States service personnel were dealt with by their own military who carried out executions from time to time.

[28] Attlee's conception of Parliamentary government was such that he did not take the view that his majority entitled him to discount a broader public opinion and the idea of an 'elective dictatorship' would have been wholly alien to him. Churchill, with a characteristic contempt, once dismissed him as 'a modest man, who has much to be modest about'.

[29]The Royal Commission on Capital Punishment finally reported in 1953 CMND·8932. Capital punishment was suspended during the parliamentary debates of 1947–48 and in consequence a number of murderers, who would certainly have otherwise hanged, escaped the gallows and have been subsequently released during the last thirty years.

ruse to turn away Irene White's attempt to reform the law of divorce in the
following year by setting up the Morton Commission. The terms of reference
of the Gowers Commission were also cunningly drafted so as to exclude any
direct consideration of abolition; it was to inquire into methods of execution
and ways in which the penalty might be limited. It was notable, not only in
having Sir Ernest Gowers as its Chairman and Francis Graham-Harrison, a
permanent civil servant of Victorian stature, as its Secretary, but in being the
first Royal Commission on a criminological topic to include a criminologist
among its members. That this was Leon Radzinowicz furnished nothing
by way of satisfaction to Hermann Mannheim, who was a member of the
Howard League executive.[30]

The Criminal Justice Act of 1948 can be seen in historical perspective then,
less as a post-war innovation than the closing of an agenda of unfinished
business. Persistent offenders, a topic that had been awaiting resolution since
1932, was dealt with in a 1932 fashion. The recommendations of the Cadogan
Committee on Judicial Corporal Punishment had only been awaiting enact-
ment since 1938. Abolition of the death penalty was still to come. It was not to
be until the Criminal Justice Act of 1967, enacted by perhaps the only Labour
administration to have had both the sensitivity and capacity to enact original
legal and penal reform that the struggle was finally won.

To contemporary eyes, the sum of criminological research during these
years may not seem to account to much. But given that this was an era in
which the Copeland-Chatterton Index Card (manipulated by knitting
needles through the holes punched around its edges) was high technology—
the Hollerith eighty column machine read card was not widely available
until well after the war—the achievements are not wholly to be despised. This
is not the place in which to evaluate such work, rather to place it in its
intellectual and political context. Effectively those between 1935 and 1948
were foundation years in which the subject was establishing its legitimacy in
the universities and in government circles; the political world was also becoming aware of there being something akin to a criminal science that extended
beyond such things as forensic pathology. The topics for research were predicted by a neo-positivism which had become enmeshed in a welfare model of
crime control that had in turn become the received wisdom of government. In
this sense the Children's Act of 1948 was as significant as the Criminal Justice
Act of the same year.[31]

What did not perceptually advance during the period was the course of
legal education which remained virtually unchanged by the passage of time
such that both practitioners and judges retained many of the beliefs and

[30] When visited in the early 1960s by the present writer and Louis Blom-Cooper, Gowers confided that
throughout the entire period of the Commission's work Radzinowicz had been alone amongst its members
in never giving the least hint of where he stood on the issue of abolition. It was not until 1969, at the time of
the final Parliamentary debate on abolition, that he 'went public' heading the list of signatories of a letter to
The Times advocating abolition, which included the name of every academic criminologist in Britain, save
one.
[31] The Act followed hard on the heels of the recommendations of the committee chaired by Dame Myra
Curtis set up after the death of Dennis O'Neill, a boy in foster care, in 1944. Forty years later, children are
still dying and solutions to the problem seem more remote than ever.

attitudes that were characteristic of figures like Fitzjames Stephen. Throughout the period the higher judiciary was distinguished by a complete unconcern for criminology in general or a critical attitude towards sentencing in particular. Not only would a law student know more about such things as reasonable estovers and the crimes of champerty and maintenance than about the role of schizophrenia or post-natal depression in homicide; legal education was, and still is, predicated upon a model of rationality in human action that bears scant resemblance to what goes on in the real world for most of the time. In the post-war period the office of Lord Chief Justice of England was held by one Rayner Goddard, arguably among the most Rhadamanthine figures ever to dispense justice from the Bench. He openly ridiculed much of what behavioural science had to say about human behaviour, not least the notion that if children were beaten and mercilessly abused they might not grow into adults who repeated the pattern. Many magistrates, including Stipendiaries, were given to purveying justice in similar vein. It was in sentencing that their effects were most inhumane.[32] On the other hand, there were exceptions. Recorders like Sir Leo Page[33] and Walter Raeburn took a different view. At the Howard League Conference in 1953 Raeburn maintained that he would, ideally, never allow lawyers to sentence by themselves

> ... because by their very training they have had the humanity dessicated out of them.

In the juvenile courts, and especially those in London, there was also a distinctly different atmosphere. But because the majority of lay justices were appointed by a system that had remained largely unchanged since Tudor times and underwent no training of any kind,[34] sentencing decisions were almost certainly at their worst at the level of petty sessions. The Magistrates' Association, which Margery Fry had helped to found in 1921, was still a somewhat radical organisation to which by no means all magistrates belonged; the contrast with today is acute, since now almost all justices belong and the Association is both conventional and cautiously conservative in its outlook.

   In sum, then, this was a period of primitive growth stimulated by a variety of individual figures; reformist academics, moral entrepreneurs, visionary civil servants and public administrators and some members of the medical and legal professions. Since many, indeed most of them, were financially comfortable and socially privileged they had access to the various élites whose influence could restrain or accelerate change in British society. Conversation across the dinner table, too, is often more productive than that which is conducted in the official office. The judiciary, often hard of hearing, was at

---

[32] The present writer recalls, *circa* 1948, an offender being sentenced by the Stipendiary at Tower Bridge Magistrates' Court to three months imprisonment for stealing a bar of soap, the property of his employers, the British Railways Board.

[33] *See* Sir Leo Page *The Young Lag*. London, Faber and Faber. 1950.

[34] The Royal Commission on Justices of the Peace (1948, CMND·7463) catalogued much of what was wrong. It was not until 1965 that a reforming Labour administration in the person of its Lord Chancellor, Gerald Gardiner, sought to put matters right.

best sceptical and at worst hostile to what it managed to discern, but forensic medicine provided a much needed source of legitimacy for many of the psycho-therapeutic endeavours that formed part of the practical expression of the rehabilitative ideal. The Diaspora engendered by Nazism had the beneficent effect of laying the foundations of academic criminology. It was a period in which genuinely charismatic figures carved great shapes upon the cliff face of the criminal justice system and set agendas for debate well outside the normal progenitory channels of politics. In the last three years from 1945 to 1948 there was, in spite of the many difficulties that had been exacerbated by the war, great optimism that the practical application of the knowledge derived from criminology could produce a more just and more effective criminal justice system. The irony was that crime was to continue to increase, regardless of what was done either by the courts or by the agents of the penal system. But if there was little by way of satisfaction on that score the contribution by way of humanising the treatment of offenders and establishing new canons of acceptable decency was considerable. It is perhaps one of the great mercies that flows from human mortality that almost none of the great figures of the period has survived to witness the degeneration and decay in our own time of so much of what they had built in confidence and hope.

BRIT. J. CRIMINOL.   Vol. 28   No. 2   SPRING 1988

THE DEVELOPMENT OF CRIMINOLOGY IN BRITAIN 1948–60

J. P. MARTIN (*Southampton*)

Introduction

The period which I am going to cover is conveniently marked by two significant events. 1948 saw the passing of the *Criminal Justice Act* while in January
1960 The Institute of Criminology began its existence in its temporary abode at
4 Scroope Terrace in Cambridge. Although these events provide a convenient
frame for this article I shall not treat them as rigid boundaries and shall say
something about the early days of the Institute in order to add a little to the
historical record. It may also be helpful to give an indication of why the
Institute began to work in the way it did, as this has not always been clear from
accounts published so far.

In a short paper such as this it is not appropriate to attempt highly
detailed documentation of relatively uncontroversial matters. The acts of
government—legislation, reports of advisory committees, ministerial statements and so on—are on record. What is not nearly so well recorded is what
people were reading and thinking—did they do what they did for the reasons
we now attribute to them, or for reasons all too clear to them, but not at all
obvious a quarter of a century later?

Needless to say there is no simple way of re-creating the intellectual life
of the era, but something can be gleaned from looking through the books
reviewed in the *British Journal of Delinquency* and in the *Howard Journal* but,
while that is helpful, one does not know how much to allow for the vagaries of
publishers, the prejudices of editors or the inefficiency of reviewers. I was also
able to consult the catalogue of the John Howard Library of Criminology and
Penology *c.*1963 which, no doubt, suffered from all these limitations and
probably more but provided a rough check on the more important books
published and being read during the period. Some of the gaps may be filled,
and interpretation based on, personal recollection. Terence Morris and I
began our criminological studies, and indeed first met, in Mannheim's lectures
and seminars at the London School of Economics (LSE) in the Autumn of
1951. Parts of this article therefore amount to self-recorded oral history and
its validity should be judged accordingly. They are included deliberately
because, when a preliminary version of this article was delivered as a paper to
the national Criminology Conference at Sheffield in July 1987, it became
clear that the nature of the intellectual climate of the period was simply not
understood by many people whose interest in crime and deviance began in the
1970s and 1980s.

Criminology 1948–50

By comparison with the situation of the 1980s the available literature was
scanty. *The Sociological Review* was published intermittently but had little

interest in criminology. Neither the *British Journal of Delinquency* nor the *British Journal of Sociology* were in existence in 1948, both being founded in July 1950. The list of books reviewed in the *Howard Journal* in 1948 contained, as it happened, four books of criminological significance: *Penal Reform: A Comparative Study* by Max Grünhut (1948): *Concentration Camps* by Eugen Kogon (2nd Ed., 1947): *Juvenile Delinquency in an English Middletown* by Hermann Mannheim (1948) and *A History of English Criminal Law and its Administration from 1750* (Vol 1) by Leon Radzinowicz (1948). In addition there were three books on children in need and child delinquency (two of a psychological/psychoanalytical character), the autobiography of a celebrated stipendiary magistrate and the 3rd edition of Charles Duff's *A Handbook on Hanging*, published by the Freedom Press. Significantly enough, at a time when there was a single public executioner and the average number of executions in England and Wales was about 13 a year (Royal Commission on Capital Punishment 1953, Table 6), Duff's publishers were prepared to publish *A Revised Handbook on Hanging* only six years later in 1954.

In 1948 only three people held jobs in British universities which potentially involved the teaching of criminology—Mannheim, Grünhut and Radzinowicz. Pre-eminent among them as a teacher was undoubtedly Hermann Mannheim, Reader in the subject at LSE. Not only did he lecture to undergraduates, but his postgraduate students already included Norval Morris, Tadeuz Grygier and John Spencer. A little later they were joined by John Croft, later to become Head of the Home Office Research Unit. Mannheim had a weekly two-hour lecture period held on Thursday afternoons in a very unattractive and unsuitable room on the ground floor of the LSE. It opened off the main corridor from which it was separated by double doors which swung to and fro rather noisily so there was continuous background noise interrupted by louder noises whenever the doors opened for latecomers. Mannheim's voice retained a German accent, and in any case was not strong, so he was difficult to hear; it was not surprising he found lecturing an ordeal until the end of his career. Much more congenial was his Seminar which was addressed by a variety of students and outside visitors. Altogether his teaching achievement was remarkable, not merely for its success in producing the first post-war generation of researchers, but for the personal courage and determination it entailed.

By contrast Max Grünhut at Oxford played a less prominent teaching role. Although he became a Reader before he retired, in 1948 he held a lectureship: he did some teaching at Barnett House and held a seminar at Nuffield College. He was in the slightly invidious position of being a member, but not a Fellow, of All Souls' College. In view of the importance attached to Fellowships at Oxford this was an unenviable status, but it should be said that the position was specifically created by the College in order that Grünhut could come to England. He was another charming, rather gentle, continental scholar. Radzinowicz, although technically a university teacher, did little if any teaching. He became a Life Fellow of Trinity College on the strength of Volume 1 of his History, and he enjoyed the support of G. M. Trevelyan,

Master of Trinity. This gave him a secure base on which to build the development of criminology in Cambridge.

All the founding fathers were highly industrious as researchers. Mannheim and Grünhut both went on writing well into their retirement, while Radzinowicz, under rather different circumstances, published the final volume of his *magnum opus* when in his eighties, 38 years after the appearance of volume one. Grünhut was possibly the more empirical, completing studies of Juvenile Court Sentencing, and a follow-up of the first Detention Centre detainees during this period. Although Mannheim did some survey work, mostly in collaboration, his strength was undoubtedly in his wide-ranging scholarship, exemplified not only in his books but in his numerous notes and comments in the *British Journal of Delinquency* and the *British Journal of Criminology*. His knowledge was encyclopaedic, but he tended to suffer from the complementary weakness of being unable to see the wood for the trees. He was least at home with the grand sweep of history and the broader concerns of theory.

As researchers Mannheim and Radzinowicz demonstrated almost exactly opposite qualities, with Radzinowicz being most at ease with broad issues. He was, perhaps, more of an organizer of research than an originator, though he could be very quick to recognize the possibilities of topics when they arose. He never displayed the interest in research technique which makes it easy to talk to fellow research workers of almost any persuasion. On the other hand he was deeply interested in language and style, and he had an acute judgement of people and political possibilities. It may be that he would talk about research methods with historians but he tended not to do so with social scientists.

Virtually the only other independent research workers of the period were D. H. Stott, who had undertaken his psychological study of juvenile delinquents for the United Kingdom Carnegie Trust *Delinquency and Human Nature* (1950), and John Mack of Glasgow University from whom the Carnegie Trust was shortly to commission a general appraisal of the juvenile crime situation.

All these early research workers, it should be stressed, were working with the barest minimum of support. Only Carnegie among the Foundations had shown much interest, and government support was non-existent.

This parlous situation, however, was about to change. Thanks to the advocacy of one persistent and far-sighted MP, Major Wilfrid Vernon, the Criminal Justice Act was to contain a power which would alter the face of research. Section 77(1) said:

> Any expenses . . . incurred by the Secretary of State. . . in the conduct of research into the cause of delinquency and the treatment of offenders, and matters connected therewith, shall, to such amount as may be sanctioned by the Treasury, be defrayed out of moneys provided by Parliament.

sub-section (3) similarly authorised payment

> towards the expenditure of any body or person approved by the Secretary of State in the conduct of research into the causes of delinquency and the treatment of offenders, and matters connected therewith. . .

At the time this last section, which had been suggested by an MP now unremembered, was included because, in the view of Home Office officials, "it might come in handy sooner or later and in any case could do no harm" (Lodge, 1974).

In recent years it has been asked why the criminologists of this period showed little interest in the sociology of deviance. The answer is simple. People were perfectly aware that there were problems about the boundary between criminality and deviance but these were not of immediate concern. The position of sociology itself was not strong. In 1948 the University of London had two Professors—Ginsberg and Marshall, and Marshall was not a member of the sociology department. David Glass was given a personal Chair in 1949. LSE, moreover, was virtually the only place in the country where sociology was taught on a large scale. Then, as later, the department was split between the theoreticians led by Ginsberg and the empiricists led by Glass. Most of the latter were involved in the classic studies of social mobility then under way. Only Mannheim kept an interest in empirical criminology alive.

That there was an interest in the boundaries of criminality was shown by the fact that the very first issue of the *British Journal of Delinquency* contained an article by N. Muller (1950) of Amsterdam entitled "The Group Factor in Crime and Punishment" which dealt with an episode in which, in some areas of that city, there was widespread use of "free" electricity obtained by the illegal by-passing of meters—"the offenders were for the greater part ordinary people with a mere sprinkling of real asocial types...only a tendency to belittle the criminal nature of the practices appeared to be characteristic of these otherwise perfectly ordinary people whose petty offences, by sheer weight of numbers, developed into a serious evil". This fascinating account of deviant behaviour was rounded off with a characteristically scholarly commentary by Mannheim linking such practices with pilfering in the London Docks, and with the question of White Collar Crime as developed by Sutherland. How he must have been irked by lacking the pupils to undertake such studies in Britain.

The intellectual concerns of criminology at the end of the 1940s were dominated by two major themes: capital punishment and psychoanalysis. Historians will recall that during the passage of the 1948 Criminal Justice Act an attempt had been made to include a clause abolishing capital punishment but this was sacrificed in order that the Act, which commanded a consensus of political support, should go through without undue controversy. As a result the Royal Commission on Capital Punishment, with Radzinowicz as one of its members, was set up and worked from 1949–53. In effect, therefore, Capital Punishment was *the* political issue for criminologists for almost a decade— attention died down somewhat after the passing of the Homicide Act 1957. Then, as now, a few MPs took a close interest in penal affairs, and one of them, George Benson was quite an expert and contributed several articles to the *British Journal of Delinquency*.

The other major intellectual interest was in juvenile delinquency and its treatment, particularly by psychoanalytic means. It is very hard today to comprehend how predominant this approach was. For at least a decade psychoanalytic principles were at the heart of the training of social workers and probation officers despite the fact that the method of treatment could only be applied to a handful of individuals, while in any case its efficacy was unproven. Not for the first time treatment was dominated by what powerful clinicians wanted to do. Criminologists who entered the field at this time had, therefore, to struggle to get some sort of balance to the subject so that it actually looked at the crimes committed by ordinary criminals.

The 1950s

During the 1950s criminology began to establish itself as a subject. Obviously there is room for argument as to what were the most significant events in the period but those that follow seemed then, and still seem, important turning points in the history of the subject.

The Founding of the British Journal of Delinquency

The *BJD* was first published in July 1950, within a month of the first appearance of the *British Journal of Sociology*. It had three joint Editors who retained their position unchallenged for a decade. Two were psychiatrists, Emmanuel Miller and Edward Glover (the High Priest of psychoanalysis at the time); Hermann Mannheim represented the Law and the rest of the social sciences, a role he was to discharge with unfailing conscientiousness for the rest of his life. Delinquency, especially Juvenile Delinquency, was seen as a subject in its own right and therefore required its own journal. Treatment required teamwork so the new journal would be multi-disciplinary but, as the first Editorial implied, there was a distinct pecking order of disciplines

> Under these circumstances it is perhaps unnecessary to add that the *British Journal of Delinquency* is not in the customary sense a clinical journal. Clinical contributions will of course receive special consideration, but it is hoped to publish articles, both theoretical and practical, from trained workers in the various departments of criminology; namely, medical psychology, psychiatry, psychoanalysis, organic medicine, educational psychology, sociology, economics, anthropology, psycho-biology and statistics; also from social workers, probation officers, prison and other institutional personnel, and from forensic specialists whose work brings them into intimate contact with the problem of delinquency.

The medical emphasis was clear.

From the beginning there was controversy over the title. Some argued for "Criminology" rather than "Delinquency" (a change in fact made ten years later), but the Editors argued for delinquency—interestingly enough on grounds very similar to those which were later to be used to stake the claims of the sociology of deviance, namely that "criminology" implied restricting interest to a category of individuals artificially delimited by the criminal law. Mannheim, of course, was very conscious of questions relating to the role and

39

the limits of law, as was shown by his treatment of the Dutch "electricity case" referred to above.

The *BJD* included sections on Events and on Current Research—there being no other record of such activities. Such lists, incidentally, quickly introduced names later to become well-known—Howard Jones, Gordon Rose, John Spencer, Peter Scott, Tadeuz Grygier, John Croft and others. Generally the overall plan seems to have been sound, the problem was its execution. At the beginning there was a shortage of articles and some rather unsophisticated efforts appeared: in later years Mannheim's pupils came along and standards became more professional. The imbalance of the subject placed a heavy burden on Mannheim as commentator—he covered most non-medical topics, and drew on several languages to do so—the breadth of his scholarship was very clear. The imbalance was shown by the predominance of articles on juvenile offenders and on psychoanalysis. These two areas *each* had more than three times as many articles as the next most widely discussed topic, the prediction of delinquency. Was this due to prejudice? At the time it seemed that there probably was some bias in favour of psychoanalysis, but the articles mainly reflected the volume and nature of activity in the subject.

The Mannheim-Wilkins Borstal Prediction Study

In 1951 the Home Office commissioned the Government Social Survey to assist Mannheim in carrying out a "pilot prediction study of borstal boys". The sum of £1000 was allocated from the £1500 which was the total amount the Home Office could include in its 1951/2 Estimates for criminological research. This was the first major use of the Home Office Power to support research (Lodge, 1974). Mannheim was expected to provide criminological expertise and Leslie Wilkins was assigned to look after the survey side. At that time Wilkins was probably the most celebrated member of the Social Survey, and his work was technically in a different class from all previous criminological research in this country. The results were published in 1955 in a book inelegant in format and title—*Prediction Methods in Relation to Borstal Training* which became No. 1 in the Home Office Research Series.

Both the book and its *de facto* leading author, Leslie Wilkins, played immensely significant roles at the time. The book was of fundamental importance because it began the process of evaluating the supposed effects/achievements of training/treatment. By showing that these could very largely be predicted by information about the inmates available *before* they entered the institution it raised the question whether the outcome was any more than a consequence of the selection procedure. This led directly to the cutting of the maximum period of Borstal Training from three to two years, and ultimately to the systematic undermining of the treatment ideology. Secondly, the technical innovations of the research laid the foundations for all evaluations involving the classification of people undergoing any form of "treatment". About a year after the publication of the book Leslie Wilkins was made Deputy Statistical Adviser to the Home Office and, in consequence, the Home Office Research Unit effectively began on 1st September 1956.

The importance of Leslie Wilkins in the development of criminology in Britain in this period has never been adequately recognised. From about 1953 onwards Wilkins advised unofficially almost everyone doing empirical research in criminology in the country. He was at the height of his fame in statistical circles for the brilliant studies which had done so much to establish the reputation of the Government Social Survey, but despite this he was unfailingly ready to help anyone, however junior and undistinguished, who approached him with a problem. Not only did he help with immediate problems but he was also successful in tempting people to work in criminology. This rather unorthodox influence continued until the early 1960s when he left the Home Office. He had not only the gift of great technical imagination and ability, which often found simple solutions to difficult problems, but also a warmth and enthusiasm which helped many a research student or young academic along the lonely and often depressing paths of quantitative research.

1955 was also marked by a personal milestone in that, having by dint of personal labour laid the foundations of the teaching of criminology in Britain, Hermann Mannheim retired. Terence Morris, one of his pupils, was appointed partly to replace him.

Signs of Change

The middle years of the 1950s were also marked by some significant publications. 1956 saw the production of the first home-grown textbook, written by Howard Jones, a pupil of Mannheim's, then teaching at Leicester. It probably reflected the type of course Mannheim himself gave at that time, with, perhaps, the difference that Howard Jones explicitly maintained that criminology should be avowedly reformist. Ultimately Mannheim produced his own two volume version *Comparative Criminology* published in 1966, well after his retirement. Both books rather rapidly became dated with the beginning of the sociology of deviance which, in England, might be said to have arrived with the publication of A. K. Cohen's *Delinquent Boys* in 1956. It was the precursor of much later work which, however, did not become widely known until the early 1960s. It was not surprising, therefore, that the sociology of deviance did not have much influence on criminology until the 1960s.

The same period also saw the publication of the first home-grown sociological study, T. P. Morris' *The Criminal Area* (1957). This was significant for three main reasons: first, it was the latest manifestation of a tradition of small area studied which had tended to flourish in England, and Morris traced the antecedents of his own work back to nineteenth century examples. Second, it not only made sociological observations but also pointed to various social policy implications, for example for the traditional policy of locating all "difficult" families in the same parts of council estates. Third, it set this empirical work in the context of a major review of ecological studies, and linked it to the established tradition of the Chicago school.

Although Morris' work was the first such study published in the period it was not the only work of its kind being undertaken. Professor W. J. H. Sprott of Nottingham with a team of colleagues did a study of crime in a

41

Nottinghamshire mining village which he called Radby. It contained fascinating sociological material but, unfortunately, never found a publisher and was only available in mimeographed form. Sprott, to his credit, published Morris' book in the Routledge series which he edited and, in fact, gave him considerable encouragement.

Foundation of the British Society of Criminology

Although in later years the society's reputation has fluctuated, its creation marked an important stage in the emancipation of the subject from the thrall of psychiatry and psychoanalysis. In the late 1950s the Institute for the Study and Treatment of Delinquency (ISTD) formed a "Scientific Group" to hold discussion meetings on matters relating to delinquency. Although it had non-medical speakers, such as the then Mr Justice Devlin, its meetings were held in the rooms of the Medical Society of London and the proceedings tended to be dominated by senior medical members, particularly Edward Glover who addressed the group at extreme length and tended to assume privileges of primacy rather like those of Privy Councillors pre-empting debating time in the House of Commons. The younger members decided this could not be allowed to go on and eventually achieved a successful breakaway by translating the Group into a Society in its own right.

Although Barbara Wootton was not a member of the Group or the society she exerted a powerful intellectual influence, particularly by the study she undertook with the support of the Nuffield Foundation, published in 1959 as *Social Science and Social Pathology*. This was a massive review of "the contributions which the social sciences have made towards the understanding, and thereby also towards the prevention and cure, of the social problems associated with unacceptable forms of deviant behaviour" (p. 9). It blew a fresh and cold wind through the scene which, among other things, demolished the pretensions of the psychoanalysts and exposed the dangers of the Glueck tradition of predicting delinquency. All this was done in a very pragmatic way drawing on both her own experience as a juvenile court magistrate and on the sceptical traditions of the English empirical philosophers. She did not attempt to erect a new system of beliefs but stated the need for better empirical work which paid more attention to social factors than the previous emphasis on individual qualities.

The use of the term Social Pathology, with its attempt both to use a medical term and, at the same time, appropriate it for adoption in a sociological context was perhaps symptomatic of the end of one era and the beginning of another. The term seemed to disappear from use as soon as the sociology of deviance became established, but at least it had the merit of trying to relate criminal behaviour to its social context.

The Establishment of the Cambridge Institute

The story of the establishment of the Institute has been told by two of the main protagonists from the Home Office side, R. A. Butler and T. S. Lodge (1974). At the time the decision seemed perverse to those of us at LSE who were well

42

aware of the School's primacy in teaching, but in fact the reasons were simple and compelling in terms of personalities and university politics. The University of London did not want to establish any more Institutes while Cambridge, inspired no doubt by the enthusiasm and drive of Radzinowicz, responded quickly and positively. In terms of potential for leadership Radzinowicz was the only one of the three "founding fathers" who held a strong position in a major university, being a Fellow of the College of which Butler's father had been Master, and of which Butler himself was to become Master within a few years. Thus it was that it fell to Radzinowicz, in the full vigour of his early fifties, to establish Criminology in a university where it had never been taught as an undergraduate course in the tripos and where research had only made a cautious beginning.

The tasks set for the Institute were ambitious. It was to conduct research, to establish a major specialist library as a national resource, and it was to be available to provide advice and expert guidance for government. It had also to undertake a substantial teaching programme. The corner-stone for this was to be a postgraduate instructional course leading to a Diploma, which was to provide a cadre of researchers and teachers both in Britain and worldwide. At undergraduate level Criminology was to be an optional subject in the Law Tripos with the aim of ultimately producing generations of Cambridge lawyers with some knowledge of the social and psychological contexts within which the criminal law operated. This introduction to the human face of the law became very popular and the course was taken by more than a hundred students each year. Additionally the Institute was to run, on a biennial basis, an Advanced or Senior course for a multi-professional group of high flyers in the professions in the criminal justice system.

A specification such as this was not unreasonable for a national centre, but it was probably too much for its few staff—initially three Assistant Directors of Research (research posts at Lecturer level) plus small research teams—to undertake successfully.

Perhaps it was not surprising that the Institute was not at all a typical university department. Only one of its founding staff had had an academic career in another English university, and the model of operations that developed was essentially of bilateral relationships with Radzinowicz. Staff meetings may have occurred, but if they did I cannot now remember them; certainly they were not regular events. Few staff seminars were held—no more than half a dozen in the first seven years. This was unfortunate because general discussion was in short supply and, indeed, only took place in the coffee room. What dominated our informal discussions was the sense of pressure the Institute and its staff were under. Fortunately the media did not see us as an important source of instant comment, so the pressure was not as bad as it might have been, but we were always aware that the fate of the Institute, and of course ourselves, depended on the success of our major activities. Thus it was that we talked much about the pressures and not as much about the subject as we should have done. It was mainly for these reasons that, as some of us said at the time, the Institute in its early days was a centre of criminological research but not of criminological thought.

What determined the Institute's research programme? Apart from Radzinowicz's own work on his History, all the projects were the responsibility of the Assistant Directors of Research, of whom there were three. McClintock had been working with Radzinowicz for a number of years and initially simply continued the project on robbery and violence against the person that was already under way. West had come without a definite project, and began by developing his interest in habitual offenders. My own and Douglas Webster's study of The Social Consequences of Conviction had already started in a small way from LSE and Radzinowicz had agreed that I would continue it before I accepted appointment to the Institute. His main concern in this connection was that I should undertake the study which became *Offenders as Employees* (1962) and which had been dropped from the Social Consequences proposal to reduce costs. However it could be completed quickly and so became one of the first products of the new Institute. No doubt it gained some credibility for the Institute to publish three books by its staff within the first three years of its existence.

Ironically it was the function of giving of advice to government which never developed as an Institute activity, although Radzinowicz himself was a member of the Home Secretary's Advisory Council. The rest of the staff was too heavily engaged to have the time to offer advice on an intermittent basis even if asked.

The Achievements and Limitations of the Period

The foremost intellectual achievement of the period was probably the cutting down to size of the psychoanalytical approach to criminology. The *coup de grâce* was delivered by Barbara Wootton in *Social Science and Social Pathology*.

Secondly, the beginnings of a home-grown sociological literature began to appear, while there was an increasing awareness of how the subject was being researched elsewhere, particularly in North America, Europe and Scandinavia.

Thirdly, there were the institutional developments—the increase in the numbers of people working in the subject, and in the number of places where it was taught. The Cambridge Institute was something of an exception, but most of this development was thanks to the work of Mannheim's and, to a lesser extent, Grünhut's students. It was a period of building on small, but good, foundations.

REFERENCES

BUTLER, R. (1974). 'The Foundation of the Institute of Criminology in Cambridge'. In R. Hood (ed.). *Criminology and Public Policy*. London, Heinemann.
LODGE, T. (1974). 'The Founding of the Home Office Research Unit'. In R. Hood (ed.). *Criminology and Public Policy*. London, Heinemann.

BRIT. J. CRIMINOL. Vol. 28 No. 2 SPRING 1988

THE SOCIOLOGY OF CRIME AND SOCIAL CONTROL IN BRITAIN, 1960–1987

DAVID DOWNES (*London*)*

The period under review saw the expansion of criminological studies from the scholarly cottage industry portrayed by Martin to the multi-institutional, academic enterprise documented by Rock. In 1960, perhaps a few dozen academics, including post-graduate students, and Home Office researchers, could be defined as criminologists. They were predominantly sited in London, Cambridge, Oxford and Liverpool. When the first National Deviancy Symposium took place at York University in Autumn 1968, its organisers were swamped by well over a hundred applications to attend. The first National Criminology Conference in 1987 had to limit attendance to 200 teachers and researchers in criminology. The Economic and Social Research Council Initiative on Crime and the Criminal Justice System in 1984 received applications for project-funding in designated fields from 147 individuals or teams, a large minority from departments other than those of criminology, sociology and psychology. All indicators point to a momentous enlargement of the field in terms of both the number of practitioners and the scope of the subject. Criminologists are now to be found at virtually every institution of higher education in the land. It is easy, nonetheless, to see signs of coming crisis in the subject. For several years now, the contraction in funding for post-graduate students, source of much that was best in the effluorescence of the subject in the 1960s and '70s, has implied a problem of succession when, in little over a decade from now, the members of the "fortunate generation" retire. Though the rate of expansion of the 1960–1980 period was unsustainable, the rate of contraction has been unwarrantedly sharp.

A recognisable first phase in the period lasted from the late 1950s until the first York Symposium of 1968. This phase saw relatively few published studies of real significance, but the ground work of training and recruitment was laid on the foundations described by Martin. As an entrant to the field in late 1959, it seemed to me to have been swept clean by Wootton's excoriating critique of that year. The only pointers in Britain to how useful work might in future be accomplished lay in the area study tradition developed so ably by Mays (1954), Sprott, Jephcott and Carter (1954) and Morris (1957). The work of John Mays, whose death in October 1987 overshadows the coming publication of a book of essays in his honour (Downes, ed., forthcoming), stimulated a small but penetrating number of area studies of delinquency in Liverpool (Parker, 1974; Gill, 1977) and Sheffield (Baldwin and Bottoms, 1976; Bottoms and Wiles, 1986; Bottoms *et al.*, 1987). Mays was at one with the British tradition of community studies born of Victorian social inquiry, which found its most formidable exponent in Henry Mayhew (1851–1861),

*Professor of Social Administration, London School of Economics.

and the poverty surveys of Booth, Rowntree and Bowley. In the 1950s, such studies as *Coal Is Our Life* (1956) and the stream of work from the Institute of Community Studies, beginning with Wilmott and Young (1957), employed a mixture of documentary research, interviews and a kind of mild ethnography to furnish data for more humanistic insights than the social survey and aggregated case-studies then in vogue allowed.

The later area studies in the crime and delinquency field were also influenced by American sociology. Terence Morris initiated the comparative awareness of American theory and research in his study of crime commission and delinquent residence in Croydon, (1957). Using the methods of the Chicago School to evaluate their theories in the distinctively British public housing estates of Croydon, Morris began what became successive plunderings of American sources: subcultural theory in Downes (1966) and Hargreaves (1967); labelling theory and interactionist perspectives in most work in the deviance and control field from 1968 on, but in particular that of Stanley Cohen (1971, 1972), Jock Young (1971a, 1971b) and Paul Rock (1973a, 1973b) who also went on to explore its intellectual origins (1979). Radical criminology in Britain owed much to Gouldner's critique of interactionism (1968), and control theory, as in Box (1971), to Hirschi (1969). For two decades, Britain became an off-shore laboratory for the distillation of ideas fermented in the U.S.A. The American influence reached its height in 1971, when Becker, Skolnick and others to the fore in the sociology of deviance there came, somewhat surprised by their celebrity, to the British Sociological Association conference on that theme. Two years later, at the same event in Edinburgh, Goffman, Lemert and Sacks engaged in debate on ethnomethodology. From the mid-1970s, however, that closeness of affinity receded, and the whirl of theoretical and methodological innovation that had resulted gave way to normal scientific pursuits. It was in part displaced by the renewed appeal of neo-Marxist European sources, well exemplified in Phil Cohen's "new" subcultural theory (1972) (see also Clarke *et al.*, 1976).

The attentiveness of sociologists of crime to American debates reflected the marginality of sociology to the criminological tradition in Britain. In the course of the expansion of higher education, and the rising popularity of sociology in the 1960s, a new generation of graduates found the medico-legal cast of much British criminology increasingly irksome. As posts were created and filled by a diaspora from such Departments, as well as from the centres of active research at the London School of Economics, Cambridge and Oxford, they found they lacked a forum. The biennial conferences held at the Institute of Criminology at Cambridge were felt to be too dominated by Establishment agendas, on which topics of interest to senior Home Office staff, police and members of the judiciary, such as the findings of the Cambridge longitudinal study, took precedence over debates of more concern to the rising generation, such as the impact of policing on drug use and the politics of vandalism. At the same time, deviance—which by the late 1960s was the preferred construction of the topic—was marginal as a subject in most Departments of Sociology. Doubly marginalised, the new generation of sociologists of deviance set up their own forum, at the University of York.

The political background was of some significance in these developments. The first phase of post-1960 work in the sociology of crime explored the limits of sociological orthodoxy, but did not break with them. The appeal of American theory was that it addressed a problem, and seemingly furnished a framework for its intellectual resolution, of the persistent rise in official crime rates despite the appearance of both greater affluence and diminishing inequality in the major industrial Western societies. Anomie theory and its subcultural variants seemed to supply the answer in terms of the frustration of rising expectations among socially disadvantaged youth. In the post-Wootton era, genetics and psychology were seen as offering little purchase on what were perceived as startling differences in crime rates both between societies and within societies over relatively short spans of time. Research in this tradition corresponded to the social-democratic reformism of the Labour Government in Britain and, until Johnson's presidency became ineluctably identified with the Vietnam war, with the reformism of the Democratic party in America. Criminology was seen as inescapably preoccupied with deterministic, individualistic and apolitical forms of intervention and correction. Sociology was seen as capable of furnishing a "vocabulary of motives" for delinquency which could be addressed by structural change and political action.

The second key phase in the field lasted for some ten years, from the late 1960s to the end of the 1970s. The National Deviancy Symposium (later Conference) (NDC) held at the University of York and, on occasions, Sheffield University was so-called and so-held to symbolise a deliberate break with what was seen as the stranglehold on the subject by the orthodox criminology of the South-East. The great appeal of the NDC was not only to sociologists of crime in search of a congenial forum, but also to younger sociologists who saw in deviance an escape route from the positivist methods and functionalist orthodoxy of much British sociology. The diversity of the topics discussed ranged from Max Atkinson's first forays into the phenomenology of suicide to Ian Taylor on soccer hooliganism, from Laurie Taylor and Paul Walton on industrial sabotage to Ken Plummer on 'men in love'. Representative collections of papers were published as *Images of Deviance* (edited by Stan Cohen, 1971) and *Politics and Deviance* (edited by Ian and Laurie Taylor, 1973, which appends a chronology of topics and speakers). The anchor-men of the NDC were Stan Cohen and Laurie Taylor, who also produced the best example of its approach in *Psychological Survival* (1972), their study of the experience of imprisonment under maximum security conditions in H Wing at Durham Prison. Its publication in defiance of the Official Secrets Act provisions governing research into penal and allied establishments was a stand against even liberal forms of censorship: interpretive sociology on behalf of the underdog was wedded to the refusal of co-optation by the State. Such work also bore the hallmark of what was known as the "politics of experience" (Laing, 1968). Many deviants seemed to be involved in projects similar to those of the sociologists, aiding identification and empathy, and making existential questions political.

The liberating effect of the NDC was exemplified by the flood of publications in the 1970s which reflect the diversity of theory and method and the catholicity of subject. Ethnography was to the fore in the search for appreciative authenticity, though signs of the tensions which were to fissure the NDC after 1973 occurred in such episodes as the criticism of Howard Parker (and, by extension, virtually all ethnographers) for "exploiting" their subjects. The politics of the NDC pivoted around the tensions between those who primarily sought intellectual as distinct from those who emphasised political radicalism. A number of sociologists, such as Jock Young, seem to have moved to the sociology of deviance because Marxism did not address their concerns. They then modified the sociology of deviance to incorporate Marxism. The context of the growing political schisms in the early 1970s, with a Conservative Government shaken from office by industrial unrest and devastatingly effective strike action by the National Union of Mineworkers, politicised NDC discussions to the point where the forum was ceded to the radicals in 1974. As a forum for the "new" criminology (Taylor, Walton and Young, 1973, 1975) it has provided some continuity into the present: but its salience for the sociology of deviance largely ended at that point.

If the NDC is to be judged by the calibre of the work produced by its adherents, it was a notable success. *Inter alia,* work by Brake (1980), Carson, (1970, 1981), Ditton (1976, 1979), Mungham and Pearson (1976) and Pearson (1975), Plummer (1975) and Wiles (1976) are representative achievements to add to those already cited. A climate of unfettered and free expression prevailed it its heyday, and an opening to new movements which gave many their first contact with criminologists from the continent, such as Nils Christie, and Thomas Mathiesen, whose work paralleled NDC concerns but added a novel comparative perspective. Radical if not feminist criminology was born at the NDC. Junior Home Office researchers and senior criminologists attended in sufficient numbers for the critical climate to be disseminated and given some durability. It is not impossible to discern its ethos in unexpected form in such radical Home Office studies as Clarke and Hough's *Crime and Police Effectiveness* (1984). Indeed, the momentous increase in the output of the Home Office Research Unit from the mid-1970s may have much to do with the breaking of the mould which stipulated that useful work could only flow from several years' laborious data-gathering by sample survey. At the NDC, good work could be born of play, casual conversations and the seizing of a novel research opportunity. It could even be trivial and ephemeral and lead onto better things.

It would be absurd to see all that was valuable in the sociology of deviance as bound up with the NDC, even in the short period of the 1970s. The creative, productive aspect of the NDC was accompanied by much factious and turbulent in-fighting. By 1974, several competing theoretical approaches were on offer, and much revisionist and synthesising activity under way. The appeal of ecological and subcultural theories had receded with the adoption of the labelling perspective, but labelling theory in the narrower sense had been swiftly challenged by radical neo-Marxist approaches. Control theory was combined with labelling by Steven Box (1971) but its potential remained undeveloped by British criminologists until several years later (Wilson and

Herbert, 1978; 1980; Clarke, 1980). Phenomenological critiques challenged the adequacy of most interpretive sociology at the methodological level. It was a dizzying scene, more a paradigmatic kaleidoscope than a clear-cut progression of superior paradigms delivering a knock-out blow to the inferior. And not all practitioners had the time, inclination or stomach for the fray. For example, King and Elliot (1976) and King and Morgan (1976, 1979, 1980) addressed the inefficiencies and injustices of the penal system largely outside its aegis.

The third phase of post-war work, from the late 1970s to the present day, has been conducted with a lower level of theoretical intensity but a greater attentiveness to method and project management, and to policy as well as political issues. As Bottoms (1978, p. 504) commented on an earlier attempt at stock-taking (Downes, 1978): ". . .in this new context, we can return to policy studies with a surer footing and a less restricted vision than before, and therefore (at least in principle) be able to understand and contextualise rather more meaningfully events such as Mrs. Thatcher's movement into the "law and order" debate. . . .Despite all the recent trauma and the continuing real intellectual disagreements, British criminology as a whole is in considerable better shape to tackle the issues than it was fifteen years ago." If one substitutes "because of" for "despite" in the passage above, it is possible to discern the makings of a "scientific revolution" in criminology in the sheer concatenation of competing theories and problem-shifts. In the period before the mid-1960s, a fairly narrow orthodoxy prevailed, in which the aetiology of juvenile delinquency and the relative efficacy of various penal measures dominated. In the period since the late 1970s, a relatively mature scientific community has emerged in which the levels of theoretical debate, empirical inquiry and critical response have been significantly raised. Themes and preoccupations were now as various as the emergence of victimisation studies (Maguire, 1982; Shapland *et al.*, 1986); the drift towards and nature of the "law and order" State (Hall, 1980); the transition from "Left idealism" to "Left realism" (Lea and Young, 1984); changes in urban policing and the accountability debate (see the Special Issue of this Journal, Winter 1987); the rise of control theory; the role of gender in deviance and control (see Gelsthorpe and Morris, this issue); and trends in "penality" and formal social control (Cohen, 1979, 1985; Garland, 1985; Garland and Young (eds), 1983). There are inevitably gaps, regressions and portents that may be read as ominous reflections of a political context hostile to a sociologically informed, critical criminology in its broadest sense. Thus, the ESRC Initiative attracted only three proposals for research into inner-city crime, out of 147 in total. This reflects the pervasive view that we already know all there is to know about the subject, whereas in fact we remain in considerable ignorance of its character and variety. Good ethnography is now in especially short supply, with some interesting exceptions, largely the work of female criminologists (Welsh, 1981; Foster, and Player, forthcoming). Work on public order can still proceed at a pre-Chicagoan level of sophistication (Coleman, 1985). And the overall level of funding for the social sciences in general has been cumulatively cut to the point where the continued employment, let alone productivity, of most of the subject's practitioners is now, with the cuts in research funds and the imminence of an Education Act to phase out academic tenure, at risk. Even now, key research centres, such as the Oxford Centre for Socio-Legal Studies, with a formidable list of successful projects to its credit in the realm of regulation and compliance strategies, has seen its staff reduced over the past decade from twenty-four to nine. There are limits to resilience in the face of such remorseless pruning.

If some sort of scientific revolution has occurred in criminology over the past twenty years, or at least since the pre-Wootton era, then this implies that a new and better game is being played, rather than the changes being accounted for by the vagaries of taste in topic and method, or the simple fact that the number of players has increased tenfold. What routine precepts are now being followed that were previously either absent, or anticipated by only the occasional insight or anomalous study? Three fundamental changes do seem to have taken place, in the nature of "taken for granted" criminological inquiry, though they are neither irreversible, nor do they account comprehensively for all that now commands attention as research topics.

First, it is now axiomatic that, whatever else may be brought to bear on the explanation of deviant behaviour, the motives and meanings that inform it should be addressed. The avoidance of the task of grounding explanation in the accounts given by the subjects themselves has, for much of the history of sociology and criminology alike, reduced human agency to drives or trauma accessible only to the clinician, or reified its causes to the macro-social level available only to the systems theorist, whether of functionalist, or Marxist persuasion. It is no simple matter, however, to bring men and women "back in" (Homans, 1964). If deviance implies deviousness, in Matza's terms, the eliciting of accounts is a problem-strewn business, and it is perhaps unlikely that the wealth of ethnography, particularly of youthful deviance, that was gathered in the 1970s in Britain will be easily revived (see, for outstandingly good examples, Parker, 1974; and Willis, 1977, 1978). Yet the very compounding of deviance by deviousness requires the use of unobtrusive measures, which occasionally become full-blown participant observation, to enable any appreciation of the phenomena to emerge (Matza, 1969). This need not imply miniaturisation, an endless unreeling of spools of abstracted ethnography. Meanings imply contexts, and contexts are formed in relation to encompassing cultural and social "structures". But it does imply profound difficulty in relating typical motives and meanings derived from accounts to questions of casual sequence (Wallis and Bruce, 1983). There are problems of mis-interpretation, over-interpretation (see S. Cohen, 1980, Introduction), and recurrent ethical pitfalls (Plummer, 1972), but on balance the gains of taking accounts seriously greatly outweigh the costs (though some control theorists would dispute this, e.g. Kornhauser, 1978).

Sociology "from below" preceded history from below: the Chicago "School" of the inter-war years went far to give primacy to accounts as relevant data. In Britain, John Mays in 1954 broke a century-long silence that had lasted since the work of Henry Mayhew in attempting a systematic trawl of young offenders' versions of their own delinquency. Subcultural studies in a prison (Morris and Morris, 1963), a high-delinquency area (Downes, 1966) and a school (Hargreaves, 1967) led onto a rich period of interactionist studies (Parker and Willis, *op. cit.* and Ditton, 1976; Corrigan, 1979; Pearson, 1976; Pryce, 1979; and Plummer, 1975, *inter alia*). The vein has thinned in the 1980s, in part because postgraduate students are far fewer in number, though the approach has become more prominent in the study of control and policy-making (Holdaway, 1983; Rock, 1986; Hobbs, forthcoming). It is important to rescue both deviants and controllers from what (to adapt Thompson's phrase) might be termed the enormous condescension of contemporaneity. Among the voids that remain, we lack any knowledge of "suite" crime as distinct from street crime (cf. Clarke, 1981); only one study of any substance exists on the "underworld" (Taylor, 1984); and the judiciary have—at least at senior levels—defied attempts to extend appreciation to their work (Ashworth, 1983). Clearly, some are still more equal than others in the process of transforming ourselves into objects of knowledge.

Secondly, the most fundamental reorientation of the field flowed from the impact made by the labelling perspective (as distinct from labelling theory) (Plummer, 1979). Lemert's (1967) view that "social control leads to deviance" may, as a proposition, prove more fruitful than its opposite, and Becker's banal-sounding axiom that "deviant behaviour is that which is so labelled" (1963), produced such reverberations not because they were utterly novel, but because they expressed, with exemplary elegance, the sterility of analysing deviance and control as two utterly distinct topics. For criminology had tended to proceed for most of its history as if social control was activated in a dispassionate, neutral and disinterested way by deviant behaviour when-ever and wherever it arose. There were acknowledged problems of the "dark figures" of unrecorded and unreported crime, and that the inhumanity of imprisonment might reinforce rather than reduce recidivism, but by and large the worlds of deviants and controllers were addressed as distinct social and moral universes. That social control was in itself a set of highly variable processes, both in terms of definitions of deviance and their selective use in relation to some groups rather than others, became the basis for an extensive research programme (Lakatos, 1970) from the mid-1960s in Britain. That programme gained in appeal in the context of two forms of youthful deviance neither predicted by existing theories nor adequately addressed by them, since they eluded the reach of "zero-sum" formulations: middle-class drug-taking and student dissidence. The irony that social control may amplify deviance, and generate more than would otherwise exist, lent continuity to much of the best British work on deviance and control from Wilkin's original modelling (1964) to Ditton's last-ditch attempt to re-define the field as "contrology" (1979).

In the Spring of 1964, in front of a huge montage of Mods leaping before the camera's eye on to Rockers from Clacton pier, a television presenter confided his puzzlement to me that "some people are even saying the media have got something to do with it". Days of innocence indeed, before Stanley Cohen's justly celebrated *Folk Devils and Moral Panics*, (1971) analysed the nuances of social control in that period as symbols of legitimation for a far harsher set of responses than the deviance in reality seemed to merit. The idea that "moral panics" emerged "from time to time" was radicalised in the more ambitious work of the Birmingham Centre for Contemporary Cultural Studies (Hall *et al.*, 1978) to synchronise with political crisis. In retrospect, under-stating the deviance and over-stating the reaction are criticisms which may justly be made of that work (Sumner, 1981; Waddington, 1986), but it brought into play an attentiveness to "the art of the State" which remains of central concern, particularly in an era of "law and order" politics (Bottoms, 1978; Taylor, 1981; Downes, 1983; Young, this issue). Whether or not the major shift from the separation of deviance and control as topics to their analytic inter-connectedness proves irreversible must, however, remain an open question: the work of James Q. Wilson (1975), some control theorists, and the contraction and centralisation of research funding could logically set the field back to a pre-Chicagoan moral economy of crime.

The third major shift in the era under review nevertheless remains an active and growing interest in the excavation of untilled deviant sites. The concept of the normalcy of crime takes on fresh meaning when the framework of analysis is extended to incorporate occupational deviance (Martin, 1962; Taylor and Walton, 1971; Ditton, 1977); domestic deviance (Dobash and Dobash, 1981; Edwards, forthcoming); the "hidden economy" (Henry, 1978; Mars, 1983) and corporate crime (Box, 1983). That the "fear of crime", in itself a growth area of research interest following the British Crime Surveys (Hough and Mayhew, 1983, 1985), remains most developed in relation to certain forms of street crime (Jones, Maclean and Young, 1986) is probably more to do with collective representations of unpredictable violence than that which more frequently occurs in the home, or that which is normalised as accidental, or where victimisation is indirect and dispersed, as with corporate crime. But lethal consequences flow more frequently from the offences which are defined as not "really" criminal. Their incorporation into analysis would do much to alter popular stereotypes of criminality, since their distribution is far less skewed than street crimes and often are limited to the in-work and higher status groups.

The focus on the sociology of crime and deviance has left much unsaid about the many forms of criminological work that fall outside its ambit, and some necessary caveats and qualifications should be entered to offset any risk that it is mistaken for a comprehensive guide. Such a guide would devote far more attention to several notable developments in the broader field. First, penal studies have, throughout this period, been something of a *forte* in British criminology. Radzinowicz completed the fourth and, with Roger Hood, the fifth in the masterly series on the history of English criminal law and criminal justice policy, bringing the story to 1914. Sean McConville (1981) produced an authoritative documentation of penal administration and policy until 1870. Nigel Walker's *Crime and Insanity* accomplished both historical and contemporary coverage of criminal psychiatry. Penal studies of a post-structuralist variety followed from the work of Foucault, and that of Stanley Cohen and David Garland in particular have set a distinctive form of research agenda for what might be termed the new penology. Distinctive again are the studies of courtroom processes by Carlen (1976) and Atkinson and Drew

(1979), and of legal process by John Baldwin and Michael McConville (1977). Secondly, the work of the Cambridge Institute set new standards of methodological rigour in the longitudinal cohort study (West and Farrington, 1969, 1973, and 1977). *Inter alia*, McClintock's pioneering studies of trends in particular offence groups, and Sparks's anticipations of penal crisis (1971) and victim studies (1977) are note-worthy. Thirdly, the Home Office Research Unit (now Research and Planning Unit) has not only housed seminal talents (Wilkins, 1964; Clarke, 1980) but has produced a spate of high calibre work which would, were one to be assembled, provide much of the basis for an integrated criminal justice policy (Bottomley, 1986).

These addenda fall far short of conveying the range and quality of sociological as well as criminological work conducted at the designated centres and other departments around the country as a whole. To give just one example, the University of Leicester has over this period produced such diverse work as Elias and Scotson's neglected study of divisions within a working-class community (1966); the media studies of Halloran and Murdoch (see especially their 1970 case-study); and the studies of deviance in sport by Dunning and his colleagues (see, e.g., Dunning and Williams, 1984; and Dunning and Elias, 1986). The period has been one of sustained activity and increasing sophistication. It has matched only fitfully, however, the trends in crime and its control. Much work has been stimulated by the worsening condition of the penal estate. A great deal has been inspired by the need to make up for lost theoretical and research time. But curious gaps persisted. The dynamics of crime and criminology have often been at odds. For example, until very recently, (Parker *et al.*, 1986; Pearson *et al.*, 1986), the anticipated stream of research into drug dependence has not materialised. With a few exceptions, such as Stimson (1973), Plant (1975) and Young (1971b), sociologists were not engaged by the drugs issue. Alcohol remains almost totally neglected as a topic. Despite high levels of productivity, much remains to be mapped, and the supply of cartographers is in foreseeably short supply.

REFERENCES

ASHWORTH, A. (1983). *Sentencing and Penal Policy*. London, Weidenfeld and Nicolson.

ATKINSON, M. and DREW, P. (1979). *Order in Court*. London, Macmillan.

BALDWIN, J. and BOTTOMS, A. E. (1976). *The Urban Criminal*. London, Tavistock.

BALDWIN, J. and McCONVILLE, M. (1977). *Negotiated Justice*. London, Martin Robertson.

BECKER, H. (1963). *Outsiders*. New York, Free Press.

BOTTOMLEY, A. K. (1986). "Blue-prints for criminal justice" Howard Journal, 25, 199–215.

BOTTOMS, A. E. (1978). *Comment* on Downes (1978). *Brit. J. Soc.* **29,** 503–505.

BOTTOMS, A. E. and WILES, P. (1986). "Housing tenure and residential community crime careers in Britain". In Reiss, A. J., Jr. and Tonry, M. (eds) *Communities and Crime*. Chicago: University of Chicago Press.

BOTTOMS, A. E., MAWBY, R. I. and WALKER, M. A. (1987). 'A localised crime survey in contrasting areas of a city". *Brit. J. Criminol.* **27,** 125–154.

Box, S. (1971). *Deviance, Reality and Society*. London, Holt, Rinehart and Winston.

Box, S. (1983). *Crime, Power and Mystification*. London, Tavistock.

Brake, M. (1980). *The Sociology of Youth Culture and Youth Subcultures*. London, Routledge and Kegan Paul.

Carlen, P. (1976). *Magistrates' Justice*. London, Martin Robertson.

Carson, W. G. (1970). "White collar crime and the enforcement of factory legislation". *Brit. J. Criminol.* **10,** 383–398.

Carson, W. G. (1981). *The Other Price of Britain's Oil*. Oxford, Martin Robertson.

Clarke, J., Hall, S., Jefferson, T. and Roberts, B. (eds.) (1976). *Resistance Through Rituals*. London, Hutchinson.

Clarke, M. (1981). *Fallen Idols: Elites and the Search for the Acceptable Face of Capitalism*. London, Junction Books.

Clarke, R. (1980). "Situational crime prevention". *Brit. J. Criminol.* **20,**

Clarke, R. and Hough, M. (1984). *Crime and Police Effectiveness*. Home Office Research Study No. 79. London, HMSO.

Cohen, P. (1972). "Subcultural conflict and working class community". *Working Papers in Cultural Studies*, **2,** 1–51.

Cohen, S. (ed.) (1971). *Images of Deviance*. Harmondsworth, Penguin.

Cohen, S. (1972). *Folk Devils and Moral Panics: The Creation of the Mods and Rockers*. London, MacGibbon & Kee.

Cohen, S. (1979). "The punitive city: notes on the dispersal of social control". *Contemporary Crises*. **3,** 339–363.

Cohen, S. (1980). *Introduction* to his (1972), 2nd. ed. Oxford, Martin Robertson.

Cohen, S. (1985). *Visions of Social Control*. Cambridge, Polity Press.

Cohen, S. and Taylor, L. (1972). *Psychological Survival*. Harmondsworth, Penguin.

Coleman, A. (1985). *Utopia on Trial*. London, Hilary Shipman.

Corrigan, P. (1979). *Schooling the Smash Street Kids*. London, Macmillan.

Dennis, N., Henriques, F. and Slaughter, C. (1956). *Coal Is Our Life*. London, Eyre & Spottiswood.

Ditton, J. (1977). *Part-time Crime*. London, Macmillan.

Ditton, J. (1979). *Controlology*. London, Macmillan.

Dobash, R. E. and Dobash, R. (1981). *Violence Against Wives*. London, Open Books.

Downes, D. M. (1966). *The Delinquent Solution: A Study in Subcultural Theory*. London, Routledge and Kegan Paul.

Downes, D. M. (1978). "Promise and performance in British criminology." *Brit. J. Soc.* **29,** 483–502.

Downes, D. M. (1983) *Law and Order: Theft of an Issue*. London, Fabian Society.

Dunning, E. and Williams, J. (1984). *Hooligans Abroad: The Behaviour and Control of English Fans in Continental Europe*. London, Routledge and Kegan Paul.

Dunning, E. and Elias, N. (1986). *The Quest for Excitement: Sport and Leisure in the Civilizing Process*. Oxford, Blackwell.

Edwards, S. S. M. (forthcoming) *Women and Policing*. London, Sage.

Elias, N. and Scotson, J. L. (1965). *The Established and the Outsiders*. London, Frank Cass.

Foster, J. (forthcoming) "Two stations". In Downes, D. M. (ed.) *Crime and the City: Essays in honour of John Mays*. London, Macmillan.

Foucault, M. (1977). *Discipline and Punish: The Birth of the Prison*. London, Allen Lane.

Garland, D. (1985). *Punishment and Welfare*. Aldershot, Gower.

Garland, D. and Young, P. (eds.) (1983). *The Power to Punish: Contemporary Penality and Social Analysis*. London, Heinemann.

Gill, O. (1977). *Luke Street: Housing Policy, Conflict and the Making of a Delinquency Area*. London, Macmillan.

Gouldner, A. (1968). "The sociologist as partisan". *American Sociologist*. May, 1968.

Hall, S. (1980). *Drifting into a Law and Order Society*. London, Cobden Trust.

Hall, S., Critcher, C., Jefferson, T., Clarke, J. and Roberts, B. (1978). *Policing the Crisis: Mugging, the State and Law and Order*. London, Macmillan.

Halloran, J. D., Elliot, P. and Murdock, G. *Demonstrations and Communications* Harmondsworth: Penguin.

Hargreaves, D. (1967). *Social Relations in a Secondary School*. London, Routledge and Kegan Paul.

Henry, S. (1978). *The Hidden Economy*. Oxford, Martin Robertson.

Hirschi, T. (1969). *Causes of Delinquency*. Berkeley, University of California Press.

Hobbs, R. (forthcoming) *Doing the Business: East London, the CID and Symbiotic Control*. Oxford, Clarendon Press.

Holdaway, S. (1983). *Inside the British Police*. Oxford, Blackwell.

Homans, G. (1964). "Bringing men back in". *Amer. Sociol Rev.* **29.**

Hough, M. and Mayhew, P. (1983). *The British Crime Survey*. Home Office Research Study No. 76. London, HMSO.

Hough, M. and Mayhew, P. (1985). *Taking Account of Crime*. Home Office Research Study No. 85. London, HMSO.

Jones, T., MacLean, B. and Young, J. (1986). *The Islington Crime Survey*. Aldershot, Gower.

King, R. D. and Elliott, K. W. (1978). *Albany: Birth of a Prison—End of an Era*. London, Routledge and Kegan Paul.

King, R. D. and Morgan, R. (1976). *A Taste of Prison: Custodial Conditions for Trial and Remand Prisoners*. London, Routledge and Kegan Paul.

King, R. D. and Morgan, R. (1979). *Crisis in the Prisons: the Way Out*. A Paper based on evidence submitted to the Inquiry into the United Kingdom Prison Service. Universities of Bath and Southampton.

King, R. D. and Morgan, R. (1980). *The Future of the Prison System*. Farnborough, Gower.

Kornhauser, R. (1978). *Social Sources of Delinquency*. Chicago, Chicago University Press.

Laing, R. D. (1967). *The Politics of Experience and the Bird of Paradise*. Harmondsworth, Penguin.

Lakatos, I. (1970). "Falsification and the methodology of scientific research programmes". In Lakatos, I. and Musgrave, A. (eds.). *Criticism and the Growth of Knowledge*. Cambridge, Cambridge University Press.

Lea, J. and Young, J. (1984). *What Is To Be Done About Law and Order?* Harmondsworth, Penguin.

Lemert, E. (1967). *Human Deviance, Social Problems and Social Control*. New Jersey, Prentice-Hall.

MARS, G. (1983). *Cheats at Work*. London, Allen & Unwin.

MAGUIRE, M. (1982). *Burglary in a Dwelling*. London & Heinemann.

MARTIN, J. P. (1962). *Offenders as Employees*. London, Macmillan.

MATZA, D. (1969). *Becoming Deviant*. New Jersey, Prentice-Hall.

MAYHEW, H. (1851–61). *London Labour and the London Poor*. 4 Vols. London, Griffin.

MAYS, J. B. (1954). *Growing Up in the City*. Liverpool, Liverpool University Press.

McCLINTOCK, F. H. (1963). *Crimes of Violence*. London, Macmillan.

McCLINTOCK, F. H. and GIBSON, E. (1961). *Robbery in London*. London, Macmillan.

McCLINTOCK, F. H. and AVISON, N. H. (1968). *Crime in England and Wales*. London, Heinemann.

McCONVILLE, S. (1981). *A History of English Prison Administration*. Vol. 1. London, Routledge and Kegan Paul.

MORRIS, T. P. (1957). *The Criminal Area*. London, Routledge and Kegan Paul.

MORRIS, T. P. and MORRIS, P. (1963). *Pentonville*. London, Routledge and Kegan Paul.

MUNGHAM, G. and PEARSON, G. (eds.) (1976). *Working Class Youth Cultures*. London, Routledge and Kegan Paul.

PARKER, H. (1974). *The View from the Boys*. Newton Abbott, David & Charles.

PARKER, H., NEWCOMBE, R. and BAKX, K. (1986). "Heroin and crime: the impact of heroin use on the rate of acquisitive crime and the offending behaviour of young drug users". Liverpool, Misuse of Drugs Research Project, University of Liverpool.

PEARSON, G. (1975). *The Deviant Imagination*. London, Macmillan.

PEARSON, G., GILMAND, M. and MILNER, S. (1986) *Young People and Heroin: An Examination of Heroin Use in the North of England*. Aldershot, Gower.

PLANT, M. (1975). *Drug-taking in an English Town*. London, Tavistock.

PLUMMER, K. (1975). *Sexual Stigma: An Interactionist Account*. London, Routledge and Kegan Paul.

PLUMMER, K. (1972). *Review* of Laud Humphreys's *Tearoom Trade*. *Brit. J. Criminol.*, **12,** 189–192.

PLUMMER, K. (1979). "Misunderstanding labelling theory". In Downes, D. M. and Rock, P. (eds.). *Deviant Interpretations*. Oxford, Martin Robertson.

PLAYER, E. (forthcoming). "Women and crime in the city". In Downes D. M. (ed.) *Crime and the City: Essays in Honour of John Mays*. London, Macmillan.

PRYCE, K. (1979). *Endless Pressure: A Study of West Indian Life-Styles in Bristol*. Harmondsworth, Penguin.

RADZINOWICZ, L. (1948–68). *A History of English Criminal Law and its Administration from 1750*. 4 Vols. London, Stevens.

RADZINOWICZ, L. and HOOD, R. G. (1986). *A History of English Criminal Law*, Vol. 5. *The Emergence of Penal Policy*. London, Stevens.

ROCK, P. (1973a). *Making People Pay*. London, Routledge and Kegan Paul.

ROCK, P. (1973b). *Deviant Behaviour*. London, Hutchinson.

ROCK, P. (1979). *The Making of Symbolic Interactionism*. London, Macmillan.

ROCK, P. (1986). *A View from the Shadows*. Oxford, Clarendon Press.

SHAPLAND, J., WILLMORE, J. and DUFF, P. (1985). *Victims in the Criminal Justice System*. Aldershot, Gower.

SPARKS, R. F. (1971). *Local Prisons: The Crisis in the English Penal System*. London, Heinemann.

STIMSON, G. V. (1973). *Heroin and Behaviour*. London, Irish University Press.

SPARKS, R. F., GENN, H. and DODD, D. J. (1977). *Surveying Victims*. London, Wiley.

SPROTT, W. J. H., JEPHCOTT, P. and CARTER, M. (1954). *The Social Background of Delinquency*. Nottingham University of Nottingham (unpubl.)

SUMNER, C. (1981). "Race, crime and hegemony: a review essay". *Contemporary Crises*, **5**,

TAYLOR, I. (1981). *Law and Order: Arguments for Socialism*. London, Macmillan.

TAYLOR, I. and TAYLOR, L. (eds.). (1973). *Politics and Deviance: Papers from the National Deviancy Conference*. Harmondsworth, Penguin.

TAYLOR, I., WALTON, P. and YOUNG, J. (1973). *The New Criminology*. London, Routledge and Kegan Paul.

TAYLOR, I., WALTON, P. and YOUNG, J. (eds.) (1975). *Critical Criminology*. London, Routledge and Kegan Paul.

TAYLOR, L. (1984). *In the Underworld*. Oxford, Blackwell.

TAYLOR, L. and WALTON, P. (1971). "Industrial sabotage: motives and meanings". In Cohen, S. (ed.) (1971), 219–245.

WADDINGTON, P. (1986). "Mugging as a moral panic". *Brit. J. Sociol.* **17**, 245–259.

WALKER, N. (1968, 1973). *Crime and Insanity in England*. 2 Vols. Edinburgh, Edinburgh University Press.

WALLIS, R. and BRUCE, S. (1983). "Accounting for action: defending the common sense heresy". *Sociology*, **17**, 97–110.

WELSH, S. (1981). "The manufacture of excitement in police-juvenile encounters". *Brit. J. Criminol.* **21**, 257–267.

WEST, D. J. (1969). *Present Conduct and Future Delinquency*. London, Heinemann.

WEST, D. J. and FARRINGTON, D. P. (1973). *Who Becomes Delinquent?* London, Heinemann.

WEST, D. J. and FARRINGTON, D. P. (1977). *The Delinquent Way of Life*. London, Heinemann.

WILES, P. (ed.) (1976). *The Sociology of Crime and Delinquency in Britain*. Vol. 2: *The New Criminologies*. London, Martin Robertson.

WILLIS, P. (1977). *Learning to Labour: How Working Class Kids Get Working Class Jobs*. Farnborough, Gower.

WILLIS, P. (1978). *Profane Culture*. London, Routledge and Kegan Paul.

WILMOTT, P. and YOUNG, M. (1957). *Family and Kinship in East London*. London, Routledge and Kegan Paul.

WILSON, H. (1980). "Parental supervision: a neglected aspect of delinquency". *Brit. J. Criminol.*, **20**, 203–235.

WILSON, H. and HERBERT, G. (1978). *Parents and Children in the Inner City*. London, Routledge and Kegan Paul.

WILSON, J. Q. (1975). *Thinking About Crime*. New York, Basic Books.

WILKINS, L. (1964). *Social Deviance*. London, Tavistock.

WOOTTON, B. (1959). *Social Science and Social Pathology*. London, Allen and Unwin.

YOUNG, J. (1971a). "The role of the police as amplifiers of deviancy, negotiators of reality and translators of fantasy". In Cohen, S. (ed.) (1971), *op. cit.*

YOUNG, J. (1971b). *The Drugtakers: The Social Meaning of Drug Use*. London, MacGibbon and Kee.

THE PRESENT STATE OF CRIMINOLOGY IN BRITAIN*

Paul Rock (*London School of Economics and Political Science*)

There has been no adequate survey of contemporary criminology in Britain. The discipline has evolved quickly and erratically, appearing sometimes to advance in opposing directions, and it has been more than a little difficult to make sense of its progress. There are only a few criminologists in post who might have wished to report its development, and they have at best reconstructed criminology in their own image. Indeed, any attempt to interpret current movements must refract the preoccupations of the observer. My own description will be just such a special organization of perspectives. It could not be otherwise. I shall focus on a small number of themes that I regard as important although I am aware that others might well have reviewed the field quite differently. In a short article, there cannot be a proper discussion of many things. For instance, I must neglect analysis of the important but vastly intricate exchanges that have occurred between British and foreign ideas about crime and control. British criminology has evolved in an intellectual environment constituted by others' thought, just as it has attained a modest presence elsewhere, but I shall not pay attention to that history. I shall concentrate instead upon the development of British criminology *in* Britain. In particular, I shall describe the negotiated order which has begun to emerge amongst the core members of a generation of criminologists who have worked together and known each other for some two decades.

In the autumn of 1986, for the purposes of this article, I conducted a census of all the 160 British university departments and institutes in which criminologists might be found. I also approached the Home Office Research and Planning Unit with questions about its staff and funding. I did, of course, appreciate that criminologists were to be found elsewhere, particularly in the polytechnics, but I could not undertake more than a sample survey of academic institutions in the United Kingdom. It is uncertain what effect the addition of polytechnics and colleges of further education might have had on my argument.

Excluding the Research and Planning Unit, 92 departments replied, and their replies produced some elementary demographic information about 118 specialist criminologists. Thirty-seven criminologists worked in law departments, eight in psychology departments, thirty-three in sociology

*I would like to thank A. Armstrong of the Association of University Teachers; David Downes and Margaret Savage of the London School of Economics; Don Harris of the Oxford Centre for Socio-Legal Studies; P. Oakley, General Secretary of the Universities Central Council on Admissions; the Law and the Social Sciences Committee of the ESRC; and Mary Tuck of the Home Office Research and Planning Unit for their help in the writing of this article. I am particularly grateful to David Garland and Peter Young of the University of Edinburgh, Pat Mayhew of the Home Office Research and Planning Unit and to Tony Bottoms of the Institute of Criminology, Cambridge, for their detailed comments on earlier drafts.

departments, twenty-seven in social administration departments, and thirteen in centres of criminology. It is not possible to establish how unusual those responding departments might be. My impression is that they contained the bulk of working criminologists and that the departments which did not reply refrained from doing so because they had no criminologists to report. I certainly knew of no criminologists in those departments. (There was also one "spoilt paper" from an ethnomethodologist representing a large department. I was accused of reifying the division of labour within sociology.)

The demography of British criminologists was moulded by a brief period of rapid university growth. Until 1950, there were only twenty-nine British universities. Thereafter came increase: eight universities were founded in the 1950s and fourteen in the 1960s, eight in 1966 and 1967 alone. 27 per cent of Britain's universities were chartered in that one decade of the 1960s. And the older universities were also enlarged. Student populations mushroomed: the total numbers of "home acceptance" undergraduates more than doubled between 1963 and 1969, and then increased by another two-fifths by 1980. As they became established, so in time the burgeoning universities began to acquire new staff, recruiting most energetically in the 1970s: there were 13 per cent more staff in universities in the second half of the decade than in the first. After that time, new universities ceased to be built. None was founded in the 1970s and only one, in Ulster, was established in the early 1980s.

Criminology and criminologists were part of that bounded phase of expansion. Bottoms observed that, twenty-five years ago, "at the beginning, despite the existence of several major theories and some significant empirical research, there was really very little that could properly be classed as established criminological knowledge" (Bottoms, 1987). He may have been a little too emphatic. After all, there was a rudimentary framework in place, the framework established by Radzinowicz and Mannheim and others, and it was against that framework that criminology reacted, but it was really in the 1970s that criminology took off. Few (2·5 per cent) of the staff in my sample had been hired in the 1950s, and only 19 per cent had been hired in the 1960s. 58 per cent had been recruited in the 1970s, 30 per cent in the years between 1973 and 1976 alone. Recruitment in the 1980s then declined: two people were reported to have been hired in 1981, none in 1982 and only a few each year thereafter. 20 per cent of practising criminologists were hired this decade.

In effect, the social organisation of criminology has been bifurcated. The bulk of contemporary teachers and researchers moved into place in the late 1960s and 1970s, and it was they who manufactured the intellectual framework that continued to be used into the 1980s. A second and smaller wave of younger criminologists then entered in their wake, inhabiting the environment which their predecessors had created. As I shall argue, appointments made in the 1980s were different in kind: the younger criminologists find it difficult to be paradigm changers: they are not *virtuosi* but professional scholars. Importantly, too, they do not appear to constitute a distinctive intellectual generation in their own eyes. They are not organised. They have not met collectively as their predecessors had done in the National Deviancy Symposium. For example, one significant member of the second wave, David

Garland of Edinburgh, confers principally with older criminologists: "one reason why my generation seems to lack cohesion or an invisible college is that there has been no central forum to bind it together" (Garland, 1987). It is with the earlier prime group that I shall remain for a while.

The recent history of criminology in Britain has been largely, if not wholly, the work of a fortunate generation appointed in and around the single decade of the 1970s. Although that generation never enjoyed a monopoly of teaching and research, it did represent a substantial force that was moved into position within a very short space of time. Its attempt to provide an intellectual habitat and identity for itself was accompanied by a corresponding proliferation of argument. Publishing also exploded during the 1970s. Firms recognised an expanding market and fed it with books. The catalogues of publications received for review by the journal *Sociology* between May 1973 and November 1986 reveal a great swelling of works in criminology and the sociology of deviance in the later 1970s. Of the 342 criminological books that were mentioned throughout that total period, 164 (or 48 per cent) were listed between 1976 and 1979. The 1970s were evidently turbulent and factious. There was a polemical time before the new criminologists began to settle down. In their search for intellectual definition and territory, they tended to bind themselves together and set themselves apart in an intricate dialectic of attraction and repulsion. They sought to discover what they *were* by proclaiming what they were *not*, working on what Gouldner once called a "conflictual validation of the self". Thus the York Deviancy Symposium was established in 1968 by embryo criminologists in their last months of graduate research or in the very first months of teaching. When they published their first anthology of papers in 1971, members of the Symposium allowed themselves to be described as entertaining:

> feelings towards official criminology [which] ranged from distrust at its orientation towards administrative needs and impatience with its highly empirical, anti-theoretical bias, to simply a mild lack of interest in the sort of studies that were being conducted. . . So, as our own theory might put it—we found ourselves with a common identity problem. . . (Cohen, 1971).

In a conference held in 1971 by the British Sociological Association, a conference which seemed to mark the "coming out" of the new sociology of deviance, Cohen was to talk of the neglect of meaning by orthodox criminologists (Cohen, 1974), and the phenomenologists, Phillipson and Roche, of reification (Phillipson and Roche, 1974). A year later, the Marxism of the Birmingham Centre for Contemporary Cultural Studies was turned on

> mainstream sociology [which] is dominated by official or authoritarian perspectives in the service of the present organisation of interest and privilege . . . many radical students of society and culture have themselves moved into a closer alliance with the deprived and stigmatised groups (Jones, 1972).

In 1973, the Marxist exegetists, Taylor, Walton and Young, pointed to the hidden politics of bourgeois criminology (Taylor, Walton and Young, 1973). In 1977, the feminist Carol Smart listed the patriarchal attitudes which buttressed criminology (Smart, 1977). And almost everybody professed to recoil from positivism (Platt, 1981). In effect, the new generation were refracting and amplifying wider debates, bringing into criminology the definitional quarrels and developments of sociology. Within that rather tumultuous jostling for space, encouraged and displayed in the books of the 1970s, there may well have been a purposeful exaggeration of conflict. In retrospect, many of the differences seem to have resided more in style and vocabulary than in substance (Cohen, 1980). (Bottoms has talked of how "political challenges to mainstream criminology... [were] a mixture of truth and exaggeration" (Bottoms, 1987).) Yet, at the time, they were thought to be substantial enough. They gave a useful order to an emerging field.

I have written elsewhere about the principal features of the sociology of crime as it appeared in the late 1970s (Rock, 1981). I described the administrative criminologists who had a practical bent; the systemic analysts who, seeking to develop global theories, turned to deviance from time to time as a source of material; and the phenomenalists who subordinated theory to a mapping of the substantive world. Some were indissolubly committed to the discipline. Administrative criminologists in centres of criminology and the Home Office had an occupational and organizational stake in the preservation of applied research. Interactionist, ethnographic and other phenomenalist sociologists typically did not work with an abstractness or scale of thought that threatened to remove them from the prolonged study of a single empirical area. But the systematic sociologists were ill-prepared to linger in one small portion of the social world: their interest lay in form and not in substance, in wholes and not in parts. It seemed as if the sociology of deviance was fated to become the intellectual property of administrative researchers, phenomenalists and renegades from systemic analysis.

Some of the systematic theorists who had marked the discipline in the 1970s did indeed veer off to pursue other concerns. Thus, Phillipson, Hirst, Hall and Douglas no longer write extensively about crime and deviation. In large measure, it has been the other members of the fortunate generation of the 1970s who have stayed to superintend the progress of the sociology of deviance into the 1980s. The loss of the more abstract thinkers has transformed the character of debate. The sociological criminology of the 1980s is no longer quite as metaphysical, abstract and argumentative. If it has retained any ambitions to advance a wider social theory, they are to be found in such areas as Garland and Young's sociology of control and punishment (Garland, 1985), a sociology which began with labelling theory, passed through an examination of social control and moved on to a discussion of state structures and their workings. But those areas are few.

The rump remain in universities that have suffered contraction. The numbers of graduate students in sociology departments rose from 2480 in 1974–5 to 2514 in 1979–80 and then declined to 2122 in 1983–4. The population of undergraduates decreased from 4355 in 1979–80 to 3533 in 1983–4.

The total teaching and research staff of British universities shrunk by 11 per cent from 1979–1980 to 1984–85 (Universities Statistical Record, 1986). Contraction has affected criminology itself. An older cohort of criminologists, including Eryl Hall Williams, Nigel Walker, Donald West and Leon Radzinowicz, has begun to enter retirement. A few critical members of the prime generation have emigrated: Stanley Cohen to Israel, Kit Carson to Australia, Ron Clarke and Stuart Henry to the United States, and Ian Taylor to Canada. Fifteen criminologists were reported in my census to have left teaching and research in the last five years but there was small prospect of replacing them. Forty-five of the departments had no plans to recruit new staff in the field. Only nine departments did have such intentions, and six of them were law departments. The stock of sociologists of deviance is not being fully replenished and it is ageing. In late 1986, the average age of a criminologist in a law department was 40, in a sociology department 42, and in a department of social administration 43.

Since that Golden Age of the 1970s, no comparable body of young criminologists has been allowed to rise up to make their own mark on the world of theory. Graduate research training has declined. The chief patron of graduate students, the ESRC, has been awarded a budget which contracted steadily from the *annus mirabilis* of 1978 until it became lower in real terms in 1986 than it had been in 1974. A smaller proportion of that smaller budget has been allocated to postgraduate training, shrinking from two-thirds in 1978 to two-fifths in 1986 (*Network*, 1987). Indeed, the Director of the London School of Economics wrote rather wistfully, "one gathers the impression that there is a tendency in some influential quarters to question the very usefulness of Ph.D. degrees as a vehicle for research in social sciences" (Patel, 1986).

The fortunate generation remains the major executor of the British tradition. And there appears to have been a consequent fall in the rate of intellectual innovation. Theoretical revolution no longer follows theoretical revolution in a dizzy procession. Instead, sociologists of deviance seem still to be investigating the ramifications of the ideas which were introduced in the 1960s: they have become the normal scientists of ethnography, interactionism, feminism (Heidensohn, 1985) and Marxism. To be sure, the bearers of each of those separate traditions might phrase that intellectual history differently, discovering a greater consistency of purpose and a more solid achievement. Garland has certainly written to me arguing that there "*is* a continuous legacy" of a "self-conscious movement towards both the theory and politics of Marxism", a movement which has been disrupted by recent political change. Others would probably point to other strains which have also been preserved and advanced. But revolution-making is in palpable decline.

It is the emergence of a routine competence which distinguishes criminological work from the first giddy phase of sociological criminology. The earlier books of the 1970s were usually bravura pieces, published versions of doctorates produced by graduates who had worked in some intellectual isolation. They were the bold creations of lone autodidacts who forged new, venturesome, eccentric and sometimes precarious syntheses between Marxism and interactionism, or interactionism and cybernetics (Young, 1971; Cohen,

1972). Many were influential but they were also too individual to permit simple replication.

The period of disputation set the character of the field and it has gone. Later publications have become professional studies produced in a matter of fact manner. The second generation of the 1980s consists chiefly of a smaller and younger group of professional scholars. It is a group that missed the period of major recruitment to teaching posts, having to turn instead to research contracts in applied criminology. Their work has necessarily been empirical and policy-oriented, and it has disclosed much. Thus the Oxford Centre for Socio-Legal Studies was founded in 1972 with four part-time staff and it began to flourish two years later. It set people to work on long-term, empirical and co-operative projects that would be beyond the scope of solitary crimin-ologists in teaching posts. It has emitted a steady flow of elegant ethnographic studies of law and law enforcement, attending above all to the compliance based strategies of such organisations as offices of fair trading, environmental health departments and water boards (Cranston 1979; Hawkins, 1984). The Centre has its own distinctive and communicable intellectual idiom. Similarly, the Oxford Centre for Criminological Research acquired a presence in 1976 and its staff, Shapland, Maguire, Corbett, Player, Vagg and others, write professionally as a matter of course. The Institute of Criminology at Cambridge has Trevor Bennett on research contract, and he has begun to reveal some of the situated rationality of criminal decision-making. Proficient scholarship is no longer an extraordinary or virtuoso accomplishment. It has become uneventful, transmitted routinely and competently in Cambridge, Edinburgh, Hull, Keele, London, Oxford and Sheffield. (Sadly too, it is now also somewhat insecure, threatened by precarious funding in a country which has begun to devalue scholarship and research (see Martin and Irvine, 1986).)

The era of manifestos passed largely because an ageing group of scholars in the prime generation had no need repeatedly to fight the battles of its youth. The generation has not been effectively challenged from behind. (Perhaps, as Garland has suggested to me, it is so heterodox that it does not *need* to be challenged from behind. Too many identities are on offer to warrant opposition.) It has attained a satisfactory respectability and influence. It has as much power as any to command resources. To be sure, there are always a few who lose none of their combativeness: Sumner and Brogden are instances. But the fortunate generation has come into its own and there is apparent agreement that many of the earlier problems of theoretical definition and identity have grown stale or have been resolved for most practical purposes. Differences remain but there is decreasing profit in stressing them. A law of the diminishing marginal utility of academic criticism would hold that less and less will be gained by continual, repetitious attacks on others. After a point, much that could be said without moving on will have been said. The central terrain of the sociology of deviance is no longer subject to bellicose dispute, most criminologists having become more conciliatory and catholic, engaging in a reasonably civil trade in one another's ideas. It is about the margins that skirmishes are now being fought. There are battles where criminologists explore regions abutting the preserves of others: the sociology of the police has

63

begun to encroach on analyses and polemic about the State, industrial disputes and civil order (Reiner, 1985); and the sociology of crime in the inner city has collided with the politics and study of race (Lea and Young, 1984).

Indeed, those politics have jolted almost all criminologists. The civil disorders of 1981 and 1985 and the Miners' Strike of 1984–85 stirred disparate and sometimes conflicting reflections about Saturnalia, collective bargaining by riot, criminal areas, the dangerous classes, the politicisation of policing and the oppressiveness of life in the inner city. Criminologists have had to think anew about crime as a collective process formed in the politics and geography of race and class. In the work of Alice Coleman, Anne Power, Frances Reynolds, the Priority Estates Projects, the Safe Neighbourhoods Unit, the Home Office Research and Planning Unit and the Middlesex Centre for Criminology, there has been a resurrection of interest in the difficulties of policing crime-ridden communities. Indeed, according to Bottoms, those communities may be something new, special and disturbing in the social and criminal ecology of Britain, a resurrection of the rookeries: there may be a "major qualitative difference between such areas—or some pockets of such areas—and the remainder of the country" (Bottoms, 1987).

An ageing, shrinking generation that has come into its own has tended also to find itself surrounded by a new, interesting and increasingly diverse environment of sponsorship. It has become, as it were, the established group, virtually the sole repository of expertise and authority. There is no other for outside funding agencies to support.

It is difficult to ascertain patterns of movement in research grants. One strategic sponsor has been the Education and Science Research Council (ESRC), the patron of the Oxford Centre for Socio-Legal Studies. The only records available to the ESRC about its own research funding touch on the awards made to criminology by its Social Sciences and the Law Committee between 1972 and 1984 (ESRC, 1984). Those records disclose rather modest numbers and sizes of awards until the mid–1970s: £334 was shared between two projects in 1972 for instance. One award was made annually between 1972 and 1976. Funding did become more substantial by 1978: £63,450 was given to three projects in that year. Thereafter, the ESRC made yearly awards totalling tens of thousands and, in two years, over a hundred thousand pounds. Most recently, its "Crime and Criminal Justice Initiative" has allocated £750,000 to research over several years.

Another strategic sponsor has been the Home Office, the patron of the Cambridge Institute of Criminology and the Oxford Centre for Criminological Research. In the era of collective contention, a different Home Office was much criticised by younger and rather more belligerent members of the fortunate generation (see Cohen and Taylor, 1976). But people and stances have changed. The Home Office's research history has been something of a mirror of wider academic work, moving from essays in abstracted empiricism to small, clever artisanal studies in applied theory. There was the need to formulate a policy response to the fragility of race relations and the unrest of the 1980s. There was a loss of faith in the "medico-psychological model" and the rehabilitative powers of the penal system. Together, they combined to bring about movement from abstracted empiricism and a seemingly obsessive penology to a much wider analysis of situational crime prevention, civil disorder, police-community relations and victimisation (Clarke and Cornish, 1983). In so doing, they grew closer to other criminologists working on the outside. And their influence has been considerable. With a staff of just over 45 in 1986, the Research and Planning Unit is the Goliath of the British criminological world.

One special decision was taken in the new phase. In 1981, the Home Office elected to follow the pattern of the United States Department of Justice and conduct victim surveys. Two sweeps have taken place in England and Wales in 1982 and 1984 (Hough and Mayhew, 1983; 1985) and a third is planned. A parallel sweep took place in Scotland in 1982. The surveys were intended chiefly to illuminate the "dark figure" of unreported crime, although there has been an additional baggage of questions about the fear of crime, attitudes to the police and "dealing with risk" (Home Office, 1981). Crime surveys have redefined policing, victimisation and the politics of crime. And they have engendered a spate of satellite projects bearing the mark of the new concerns about uncertain policing and public disquiet. There have been reports centred on the fear of crime (Maxfield, 1984), the victimisation of women (Worrall and Pease, 1986) and the social geography of offending (Smith, 1986). Significant segments of radical criminology have also responded to a new vision of crime as another intolerable affliction of the already vulnerable and suffering. Where once there were only offenders, working class victims have appeared to prompt analysis:

> There was a schizophrenia about crime on the left where crimes against women and immigrant groups were quite rightly an object of concern, but other types of crime were regarded of being of little interest or somehow excusable. Part of this mistake. . . stems from the belief that property offences are directly solely against the bourgeoisie and that violence against the person is carried out by amateur Robin Hoods in the course of their righteous attempts to redistribute wealth. All of this is, alas, untrue (Lea and Young, 1984).

The research staff of the Home Office Research and Planning Unit are now of much the same age and background as the academic sociologists of deviance. They passed through a similar cycle of growth and decline: their numbers also increased during the 1970s, rising from a total of 56 in 1973 to 61 in 1975. They also underwent a steady contraction between 1981 to 1985, when only 37 staff were in post. (The process of decline has been reversed of late, the complement at the end of 1986 being 45·5). They also seem to be members of the fortunate generation: only 24 per cent of the research staff being in their twenties and 7 per cent being older than fifty. The rest were in their thirties and forties in the winter of 1986 (Mayhew, 1986).

Staff of the Research and Planning Unit and the universities and polytechnics share a rough community of experience. There has been some considerable effort made by the Department to narrow the social, organisational and intellectual gulf between itself and the universities and polytechnics. Its

Research Programme for 1986–87 talks of the Research and Planning Unit's valuing "links with academic researchers, many of whom help the Unit in its day-to-day activities, for example in consultancies and seminars" (Home Office Research and Planning Unit, 1986). Academic criminologists have been invited to participate in the Unit's research planning process. They have been given novel access to research materials within the Unit, it becoming the practice to encourage outsiders to work on the British Crime Surveys and other data bases. Participants in such projects have included radical or critical criminologists who would not once have been invited and would probably have refused if they had been. Jock Young, Geoffrey Pearson and John Lea attended a Home Office Workshop on community initiatives in crime reduction in 1986. Jock Young took part in the public review of the Research and Planning Unit's research programme.

Home Office external funding has been steadily enlarged. External expenditure for law services by the Research and Planning Unit grew progressively from £185,000 in 1976–77 to £648,000 in 1985–86 (Mayhew, 1986), and an extra £500,000 has been added in 1986–87 to form a development fund for action projects and the like. However, the politics of research sponsorship have intervened to establish a rhetoric of relevance and utility. The Home Office has declared that "in the past it was possible to fund university studies whose relevance to current policy was somewhat limited. Now that resources are more constrained, more stringent criteria of relevance must be applied to the funding of research for the Home Office" (Home Office, 1985). The emergence of a more pronounced demand for "policy relevance" in externally funded research may well further accelerate the universities' movement away from the theoretical and contemplative.

A third sponsor is new and important. There has arisen in the United Kingdom a proliferation of radical local authorities staffed by people who had themselves passed through the universities of the 1960s and 1970s. They have constructed the new municipal populism of urban Britain, attempting to galvanise the more marginalised portions of society: organised groups of Blacks and Asians, homosexuals and Lesbians, women, trades councils and trades unions, unilateral disarmers, the more militant tenants' groups, travellers and squatters. As Campbell has argued, "the alliance around radical labourism has changed the contours of local and national politics, it set the new left agenda of the 1980s. For the first time, movements which lived their life outside the state and political parties found themselves moving in the same orbit" (Campbell, 1987). The dialectics of the new populism have tended to revolve around conflict with the police: the police being held to represent the central State to which the politicians of local councils are opposed; the police having given some practical definition to the marginalised groups (Holdaway, 1983); the police tending to focus much of their attention on the regulation of those groups; and, in David Downes' phrase, the police tending to over-control and under-protect the inner city. There is new money for research and a new response to radical criminological argument in the Police Committees and Monitoring Groups and Community Relations Councils and Women's Committees. Radical criminology has acquired powerful patrons.

66

In the wake of the British Crime Surveys, left-wing criminologists have mounted their own focused surveys of victims, examining sexual and racial assault, domestic violence and mundane working class crime in Merseyside, Islington (Jones, Maclean and Young, 1986) and Haringey. They have acquired a practical importance in the politics of the radical councils. Their words are taken seriously. They have become the new administrative crimin- ologists of the left, and they have experienced every incentive to address problems of policy. Pragmatic questions that had once been the sole preserve of others began to interest such radicals as Geoffrey Pearson, Jock Young, Richard Kinsey and John Lea. John Lea himself reflected, "the research techniques at our disposal in the development of crime prevention policy have progressed in leaps and bounds during the last decade. The importation of the victim survey gave us a qualitatively new type of data on which to base policy formation" (Lea, 1986). Some important radicals thus became applied criminologists at a time when applied criminologists turned towards the situated analyses of communal behaviour. And both seem able to work with the social anthropologists of deviance and control.

In all this movement there are the beginnings of an interesting convergence. It would be surprising if something of the sort had not taken place. Britain is geographically small and many of its universities are located in the South East. British criminology itself is the work of only two hundred or so scholars. It revolves around the doings of one pivotal generation and a smaller second generation who were trained principally in Cambridge and London and then in Sheffield and at much the same time. British criminologists know one another, they educate one another, they sometimes marry one another, they read each other's works and they gossip about each other. Criminologists must meet repeatedly in conferences, committees, seminars, pressure groups and in boards of examiners and editors. For practical purposes at least, it has become increasingly difficult to maintain a substantial distance between them. They form a social world. Politically, too, theorists and administrative criminologists collide with increasing frequency. As Hood remarked:

> There is a natural tendency (or so it seems) to draw criminologists, or rather criminological "experts" as practical advisers—or even as decision-makers—into the realm of policy-making or implementation....Furthermore, there is an equally strong tendency for those concerned with penal policy and practice to look to criminology for solutions to the many problems posed by crime and the operation of the agencies which exist to deal with it (Hood, 1987).

To be sure, the criminological world is composed of structures of activity which may never overlap: Merseyside Marxists and Exeter empiricists can bypass one another for long periods, and there are always some sociologists who will refuse to talk to one another. But quite strenuous efforts have been made to suppress the acrimony which once marked British criminology and, indeed, an unstable pattern of agreement has started to emerge. A common interest is not a consensus, and critical argument passes backwards and forwards, yet there is a central commitment to exploring a landscape defined by a few salient features: the new politics of victims, a recognition of the limitations of mundane policing and the problematics of social control, and agreement about the centrality of informal social control.

Conclusion

An intellectual and political generation in their late thirties and early forties dominates the sociology of crime and deviance. Its agenda was set largely in the 1960s and 1970s, focusing on problems of interactionism, feminism and Marxism but bent a little towards the investigation of matters touching on social policy. It has been joined by a younger generation of professional criminologists with empirical leanings. Together, they find themselves surrounded by a new and complicated web of dependencies and connections made possible by their own rise to maturity, the persistence of conventional sponsorship and the emergence of novel, somewhat unorthodox patrons with money and power. The work that is being done is marked by a decelerating rate of innovation, a drift towards normal science and a new pragmatism which addresses, above all else, the problems of victims, social control, the police, women and ethnic minorities in the communities of the inner cities.

Paul Rock

REFERENCES

BOTTOMS, A. (1987). "Reflections on the Criminological Enterprise". Unpublished inaugural lecture.

CAMPBELL, B. (1987). "Charge of the Light Brigade". *Marxism Today*. February 1987.

CLARKE, R. and CORNISH, D. (1983). *Crime Control in Britain*. Albany, State University of New York Press.

COHEN, S. (1971). Introduction to *Images of Deviance*. Harmondsworth, Penguin.

COHEN, S. (1974). "Criminology and the Sociology of Deviance in Britain". In P. Rock and M. McIntosh (eds.) *Deviance and Social Control*. London, Tavistock.

COHEN, S. (1972). *Folk Devils and Moral Panics*. London, Paladin.

COHEN, S. (1980). Preface to second edition of *Folk Devils and Moral Panics*. London, Paladin.

COHEN, S. and TAYLOR, L. (1976). *Prison Secrets*. London, National Council for Civil Liberties.

CRANSTON, R. (1979). *Regulating Business*. London, Macmillan.

ESRC (1984). "Research Grants: The Social Sciences and the Law Committee". Appendix I. November 1984.

GARLAND, D. (1985). *Punishment and Welfare*. Aldershot, Gower Publishing Company.

GARLAND, D. (1987). Private communication.

HAWKINS, K. (1984). *Environment and Enforcement*. Oxford, The Clarendon Press.

HEIDENSOHN, F. (1985) *Women and Crime*. London, Macmillan.

HOLDAWAY, S. (1983). *Inside the British Police*. Oxford, Blackwell.

HOME OFFICE (1981). *Public Surveys of Crime: Report of a Workshop*. London, Home Office.

HOME OFFICE RESEARCH AND PLANNING UNIT (1985). *Research Programme*. London, Home Office.

HOME OFFICE RESEARCH AND PLANNING UNIT (1986). *Research Programme*. London, Home Office.

HOOD, R. (1987). "Some Reflections on the Role of Criminology in Public Policy", Address to the British Society of Criminology, 28th January 1987.

HOUGH, M. and MAYHEW, P. (1983). *The British Crime Survey: first report*. London, HMSO.

HOUGH, M. and MAYHEW, P. (1985). *Taking Account of Crime: Key Findings from the 1984 British Crime Survey*. London, HMSO.

JONES, B. (1972). "Perspective". *Working Papers in Cultural Studies*. Spring 1972. 2.

JONES, T., MACLEAN, B. and YOUNG, J. (1986). *The Islington Crime Survey*. Aldershot, Gower.

LEA, J. (1986). "Towards Social Prevention". *Middlesex Polytechnic Centre for Criminology Working Paper*. November 1986.

LEA, J. and YOUNG, J. (1984). *What is to be Done About Law and Order?* London, Penguin.

MARTIN, B. and IRVINE, J. (1986). *An International Comparison of Government Funding of Academic and Academically Related Research. ABRC Science Policy Studies No 2*. Falmer, Science Policy Research Unit.

MAXFIELD, M. (1984). *Fear of Crime in England and Wales*. London, HMSO.

MAYHEW, P. (1986). Private communication.

NETWORK (1987) Newsletter of the British Sociological Association, January 1987.

PATEL, I. (1986). *Report by the Director 1985–86*. London, London School of Economics.

PHILLIPSON, M. and ROCHE, M. (1974). "Phenomenology, Sociology and the Study of Deviance". In P. Rock and M. McIntosh (eds.) *Deviance and Social Control*. London, Tavistock.

PLATT, J. (1981). "The Social Construction of 'Positivism' and its Significance in British Sociology, 1950–1980". In P. Abrams *et al.* (eds.) *Practice and Progress*. London, George Allen and Unwin.

REINER, R. (1985). *The Politics of the Police*. Brighton, Wheatsheaf.

ROCK, P. (1981). "Has Deviance a Future?" in H. Blalock (ed.) *Sociological Theory and Research*. New York, Collier Macmillan.

SMART, C. (1977). *Women, Crime and Criminology*. London, Routledge and Kegan Paul.

SMITH, S. (1986). *Crime, Space and Society*. Cambridge, Cambridge University Press.

TAYLOR, I., WALTON, P. and YOUNG, J. (1973). *The New Criminology*. London, Routledge and Kegan Paul.

UNIVERSITIES' STATISTICAL RECORD (1986). *University Statistics 1984–1985, Volume One, Students and Staff*. Cheltenham, Universities' Statistical Record.

WORRALL, A. and PEASE, K. (1986). "Personal Crime Against Women: Evidence from the 1982 British Crime Survey". *The Howard Journal of Criminal Justice*. **25,** 2.

YOUNG, J. (1971). *The Drugtakers*. London, MacGibbon and Kee.

BRIT. J. CRIMINOL.   Vol. 28   No. 2   SPRING 1988

METHODOLOGICAL DEVELOPMENTS

KEN PEASE (*Manchester*)

Method follows purpose. Innovations of method follow or create changed perceptions of issues. Innovations which have lasting significance are those which chime best with or generate new perceptions of which issues are important. The selection of methodological developments for mention in this note is necessarily subjective. The choice was informed by the writer's sense of where methodology produced or advanced new ways of thinking about patterns of crime and punishment. In looking at developments of method in this way, it is difficult not to be sidetracked by the extent of coverage of a topic. For example, coverage of the place of women in criminal justice has increased enormously. It is no necessary reflection on the methodological competence of that work to conclude that the innovation lies in the recognition of the importance of the topic reflected in the volume of research conducted. The methods used have tended to be relatively well-tried in other contexts.

In a review dealing largely with US work, Williams (1984) bemoaned "the demise of the criminological imagination". His analysis of the alleged demise suggested that "While there have been some imaginative theoretical works in the past decade, little of that work has become accepted by the criminological field. Instead, the focus has been on the development of methodological and technical tools, even to the extent that theory development itself has been tied to the general movement. The argument presented here is that more useful and insightful theories are products of imagination and speculation. Thus the current movement is largely useful for testing theories of the past, but not for developing theories of the future" (p. 90).

Perhaps one of the reasons for the state of affairs which Williams regretted is the change of audience of criminology. The perceptions with which criminological research now has to engage are very much more those of criminal justice practitioners than was the case even a decade ago. It is instructive now to read Downes' (1978) "Promise and performance in British criminology". In this, the major recent trend was perceived as being "a move from criminology to the sociology of deviance" (p. 483) followed by "growing variegation, fragmentation and schism within the sociology of deviance, between those favouring different perspectives and methods within it, increasingly differentiated by their practitioners into what Wiles has termed "new criminologies", drawing from different paradigms within the sociological tradition . . . united now only by a common antipathy to deterministic modes of discourse associated with traditional criminological approaches" (p. 484). This Tower of Babel of which Downes was writing only a decade ago is no more. It has been replaced by an (arguably excessive) emphasis on piecemeal and pragmatic approaches to particular crime problems with which *criminology* (not the sociology of deviance) deals in the 1980s. Against such a background, it is difficult to identify cases in which considerations of *method* can be said to have been innovative, and impossible to identify such cases in which there will be agreement.

Criteria for Inclusion and Sad Omissions

Two developments will be outlined which seem to the writer to meet the following criteria for inclusion
1. They advance or produce new perceptions of issues; the acid test of this is that they are apt to produce results which surprise.
2. The policy *relevance* of the changed perception is clear, even if the appropriate policy is not.
3. The work is extensively cited outside the United Kingdom.

It is crucial to avoid the impression that the third criterion claims primacy for the British work. It does not. It is merely asserted that the work is agreed to have a significance beyond the purely domestic. In the developments to be cited, it would be sometimes possible to refer to non-British contributions which predate the ones included, or to argue the relevance of European or American theoretical underpinnings for the British work.

There are two fundamental changes in perspective to which the developments included below have contributed. The first is the shift from a concentration on explanations to a concern with decisions under uncertainty. The second is the increased attention to event sequences in criminal justice. Thus stated, the changes do not seem earth-shattering. That their implications are profound will be asserted later in this paper.

The specific developments to be briefly reviewed are prediction studies and studies of birth cohorts. There were many other candidates for inclusion. There are no doubt several whose omission would have been less likely given a writer with a different background. There are others which the writer appreciates enough to regret their omission acutely. One such is the study of occupational crime. Richard Sparks (1983) wrote the entry on Britain in an international handbook of contemporary developments in criminology. In it, he opined that "sociological research on crime in relation to work done by Mars, McIntosh, Henry, Mack, Ditton and Levi is equal to the best research on that subject which has been done anywhere" (p. 96). Its methodological distinction is that a great deal of it is more "appreciative" of occupational crime than is the case in the Sutherland-inspired North American tradition, perhaps because of the greater prominence of social anthropologists within the British tradition. The British literature on occupational crime is one of the better legacies of the preoccupations of the 1960s. The approach leads to a clearer view of practical policy options in the tolerance or control of such crime (see, notably, Mars, 1982).

Another regretted omission is the work of Nigel Walker. It seems like a category error to call a person a methodological development, but Walker's work, spanning the discipline as it does, is yet united by an unerring ability to set out issues which an intelligent practitioner in criminal justice *should* wish to explore, and to cast them in a form which allows of empirical test, either using new or reinterpreting extant data. Walker is the criminological equivalent of the little boy who saw that the Emperor was naked—with the exception that he also conducts empirical tests of the nudity. The simplicity of many of the tests make Walker too easy to underestimate. In retrospect, what he has done

71

often seemed the obvious thing to do. That he has repeatedly been the first to do it is no accident. The work reported in Walker (1981a,b) and Walker and Marsh (1984) are three good examples of this which are sufficiently recent to retain current relevance. The change of the primary audience of criminology from the academic to the practitioner, which it is argued above has character- ised the last decade, is one which cannot fail to enhance Walker's already formidable reputation.

Prediction in Criminology

A new era in prediction in criminology can reasonably be said to have begun with Mannheim and Wilkins' (1955) Borstal prediction study. Sparks (1983) notes 'In Britain (as in California) the impetus for this kind of research, especially in the earlier years, came almost exclusively from the pioneering work of Leslie Wilkins. The methodological impact of the original Mannheim-Wilkins study on subsequent research has clearly been enormous" (p. 86). Clarke and Cornish (1983) go further, describing the study as "the most important single influence upon the subsequent progress of research within the Home Office" (p. 16) and "In practical terms, by delivering actual and potential administrative payoffs, the study had secured the future of a research capability within government" (p. 17). The Mannheim-Wilkins predictor broke new ground methodologically in three ways:
1. By addressing problems of multicollinearity among predictor variables.
2. By resolving the problems of shrinkage of predictive power in post- development applications of a measure.
3. By addressing the particular problem of the middle-range "unpredict- ables".

The most significant contribution of the Mannheim-Wilkins predictor lay outside the technical sphere. It was, as Sparks (1983) attests, in their demon- stration of the relevance of prediction methods to the evaluation of *decisions* as to penal treatment. It is along the lines laid down by Mannheim and Wilkins that many subsequent British prediction studies have developed. Notable among these was Frances Simon's (1971) attempt to identify criteria for success and failure on probation, in the context of a wider review of the prediction literature which remained an authoritative source for many years. Chris Nuttall's (1977) development of a parole predictor was developed as an aid to parole decision making. It was used, *inter alia*, to compare rates of reconviction of those released on licence with those of prisoners released at term. It remains at the heart of the operation of parole in England and Wales, by identifying those who should be seen by the Board, even though a local review committee has decided the prisoner to be unsuitable for release. That the Nuttall predictor has not been developed to coincide even more closely with policy aims in relation to parole represents a lost opportunity. The predictor itself was, and is, admirable.

It is not fanciful to see the guiding hand of the Mannheim-Wilkins tra- dition in more recent enterprises. Sparks (1983) sees echoes of its methods in the development of parole and sentencing guide-lines in the U.S.A. Less contentiously, its influence may be discerned in attempts to compare actual and expected rates of success (as however defined) of penal sanctions, although these attempts stop short of an explicitly developed predictor. Such designs tend to be termed "cross-institutional" designs in the British litera-ture. This is a misnomer, since it is not only institutions which may be com-pared by such designs. Clarke (1976) provides a statement of the advantages of designs which analyse naturally occurring variations. Notable among British studies of this kind is the classic work of Sinclair (1971) on probation hostels. His identification of the characteristics of successful probation hostels is arguably the saddest instance of neglected applicable research in the whole history of British criminology. This point is relevant to the claimed centrality of decision-making rather than evaluation. Research like Sinclair's, given the tradition from which it is derived, couches conclusions about institutions in terms which allow the estimation of how much is to be gained by making alternative decisions (in Sinclair's case, primarily alternative recruitment decisions).

Outside the Home Office, Farrington and Nuttall (1980) used discrepan-cies between actual and predicted reconviction rates to provide an index of institutional effectiveness. They find a high negative association between overcrowding and effectiveness in their analysis of nineteen prisons. The research also teases out the effects of prison size and prison crowding. Most recently, Farrington and Tarling's (1985) collection shows the liveliness of the British scions of the Mannheim-Wilkins line. The editors, taking the Borstal prediction exercise as a "landmark study", "expect prediction methods to be used increasingly in new areas—for example by the police in deciding how to allocate resources in crime investigation. Whereas prediction methods in the past have been used mainly in the area of treatment, we expect their use in prevention and in theoretical analysis to increase in the future" (p. 268).

Birth Cohorts

The Cambridge prospective longitudinal study of delinquent development is probably the best known of the few studies of its kind ever conducted anywhere. Perhaps it is so because of the range of issues on which its data have been brought to bear. The Cambridge study has clarified the value of self-reports of deviant behaviour (Farrington, 1973), provided the clearest available evidence of the effects of labelling on the progression into a criminal career (West and Farrington, 1977), and generated good evidence of the precursors of criminal careers (West, 1982) and of persistent criminality (Blumstein *et al.*, 1985). It has nailed more completely than any previous research the relationship between unemployment, school leaving and crime (Farrington *et al.*, 1986). This last paper provides a particularly good instance of the careful exclusion of possibilities through the imaginative conceptualis-ation of what could be happening allied to the technical ability to test the alternatives. It is the alliance of competence and imagination which has made the Cambridge study as influential as it has become. An example of the international importance of the Cambridge project was its use to assess the likely impact of the centralisation of criminal history records of all offenders in the *U.S.A.* (Langan and Farrington, 1983). The use occurred because the English study was not subject to the methodological criticisms to which otherwise relevant U.S. work was vulnerable (Langan and Farrington, 1983 pp. 531–2).

Coincidentally (?), at the time at which the Cambridge longitudinal research was being designed, Leslie Wilkins' (1960) research monograph *"Delinquent Generations"* was published. In the monograph, statistical analysis of crimes committed by different birth cohorts was undertaken. Wilkins found "the greatest crime proneness . . . to be associated with that birth group who passed through their fifth year during the war. . . Whether this means that distorted social conditions have their major impact on children between the age of four and five is not proved, but this is a likely hypothesis" (p. 8). The immediate effect of the Wilkins analysis was to spur comparative research in Denmark (Christiansen, 1964), Poland (Jasinski, 1966) and New Zealand (Slater *et al.*, 1966). Most recently Maxim (1985) has shown cohort effects associated with cohort size using Canadian data. That Wilkins' work has been criticised (Rose, 1968), is less important than that it provided a way of thinking about age-crime relationships which was seminal in the progression to more recent formulations of such linkages (see e.g. Greenberg, 1983).

The British studies cited provided one crucial stepping stone to the fuller consideration of time as a dimension in criminal justice. It is no accident that David Farrington's career reflects that development, from longitudinal study to a particular concern with criminal career research more generally. It now seems blindingly obvious that analysis of patterns within criminal careers are essential to sensible decisions in criminal justice. It is remarkable how recent the technically competent research in this area began.

Conclusions

It was argued earlier that there are two changes of perception to which the research cited has contributed. The first was the concentration on decisions rather than evaluation. The second was on event sequences. Both of these are crucial in a climate where policy relevance is demanded. British studies of prediction and of cohorts were influential in the progress towards a strategic vision of criminal justice. In a sense, they are both approaches to the understanding of criminal careers, and, rather differently, of careers of contact with the criminal justice process. They frame answers in ways which are usable by decision makers. Predictors can be used to enable decision-makers to assess the likely consequences of decisions—from the decision whether to report a crime to the decision whether to release a prisoner on licence. The parole predictor in current use can be employed by politicians to assess the impact on prison population of particular policy changes. In the fullness of time, data on criminal careers can inform prosecution and sentencing decisions, and can be used as pressure towards their consistency across area.

The original research approaches were unfashionable at the time or soon after the time at which they were first used. The Sturm und Drang of the 1960s did not conduce to their recognition as important. Yet in a pragmatic climate, their development, and the recognition of the possibility of strategy which that entails, have a chance of making real impact on the structure and the fairness of criminal justice. It is as always true that these methods must be located within a set of purposes. It is technically as easy to predict decisions of guilt of witchcraft as of burglary. There must be a climate of consistent questioning of underpinning principle (see Wilkins' contribution to Farrington and Tarling (1985)) for the techniques to find a defensible role in practice. Whether they do take their fullest place in criminal justice thinking must be open to doubt for reasons of political and other inertia. That they offer such possibilities, and have already changed perceptions, marks them out as methodological innovations of some importance.

REFERENCES

BLUMSTEIN, A., FARRINGTON, D. P. and MOITRA, S. (1985). "Delinquency careers: innocents, desisters and persisters". In M. Tonry and N. Morris (eds.) *Crime and Justice*. 6. Chicago, University of Chicago Press.

CHRISTIANSEN, K. O. (1964). "Delinquent generations in Denmark". *British Journal of Criminology*. **4,** 259–264.

CLARKE, R. V. G. (1976). "Cross-institutional designs and their place in evaluating penal treatments". In *Evaluation Research in Criminal Justice*. United Nations Social Defence Research Institute. Rome, Publication 11.

CLARKE, R. V. G. and CORNISH, D. B. (eds.) (1983). *Crime control in Britain: a review of policy research*. Albany, State University of New York Press.

DOWNES, D. (1978). "Promise and performance in British criminology". *British Journal of Sociology*. **39,** 483–502.

FARRINGTON, D. P. (1973). "Self-reports of deviant behaviour: predictive and stable?" *Journal of Criminal Law and Criminology*. **64,** 99–110.

FARRINGTON, D. P., GALLAGHER, B., MORLEY, L., ST.LEDGER, R. J. and WEST, D. J. (1986). "Unemployment, school leaving and crime". *British Journal of Criminology*. **26,** 335–356.

FARRINGTON, D. P. and NUTTALL, C. P. (1980) "Prison size, overcrowding, prison violence and recidivism". *Journal of Criminal Justice*. **8,** 221–231.

FARRINGTON, D. P. and TARLING, R. (eds.) (1985). *Prediction in Criminology*. Albany, State University of New York Press.

GREENBERG, D. F. (1983). "Age and crime". In S. H. Kadish (ed.) *Encyclopaedia of crime and justice*. London, Collier-Macmillan.

JASINSKI. J. (1966). "Delinquent generations in Poland". *British Journal of Criminology*. **6,** 170–182.

LANGAN, P. A. and FARRINGTON, D. P. (1983). "Two track or one track justice? Some evidence from an English longitudinal study". *Journal of Criminal Law and Criminology*. **74,** 519–545.

MANNHEIM, K. and WILKINS, L. T. (1955). "Prediction Methods in relation to Borstal Training". *Studies in the causes of delinquency and the treatment of offenders*. 1, London, HMSO.

MARS, G. (1982). *Cheats at work*. London, Unwin.

75

MAXIM, P. S. (1985). "Cohort size and juvenile delinquency: a test of the Easterlin hypothesis". *Social Forces*. **63,** 661–681.

NUTTALL, C. P. (1977). *Parole in England and Wales*. Home Office Research Study 38, London, HMSO.

ROSE, G. N. G. (1968). "The artificial delinquent generation". *Journal of Criminal Law, Criminology and Police Science*. **59,** 370–385.

SIMON, F. H. (1971). *Prediction methods in criminology*. Home Office Research Study 7, London, HMSO.

SINCLAIR, I. A. C. (1971). *Hostels for probationers*. Home Office Research Study 6, London, HMSO.

SLATER, S. W., DARWIN, J. H. and RICHIE, W. L. (1966). "Delinquent generations in New Zealand". *Journal of Research in Crime and Delinquency*. **3,** 140–146.

SPARKS, R. F. (1983). "Britain". In E. H. Johnson (ed) *International handbook of contemporary developments in criminology: Europe, Africa, the Middle East and Asia*. Westport Conn., Greenwood.

WALKER, N. (1981a). "Feminists' extravaganzas". *Criminal Law Review*. 379–386.

WALKER, N. (1981b). "A note on parole and sentence lengths". *Criminal Law Review*, 829–830.

WALKER, N. and MARSH, C. (1984). "Do sentences affect public disapproval?" *British Journal of Criminology*. **24,** 27–48.

WEST, D. J. (1982). *Delinquency: its roots, careers and prospects*. London, Heinemann.

WEST, D. J. and FARRINGTON, D. P. (1977). *The Delinquent Way of Life*. London, Heinemann.

WILKINS, L. T. (1960). *Delinquent generations*. Studies in the causes of delinquency and the treatment of offenders, 3, London, HMSO.

WILLIAMS, F. P. III (1984). "The demise of the criminological imagination: a critique of recent criminology." *Justice Quarterly*. **1,** 90–106.

BRIT. J. CRIMINOL. Vol. 28 No. 2 SPRING 1988

PSYCHOLOGICAL CONTRIBUTIONS TO CRIMINOLOGY

D. J. WEST

Introduction

Since the end of the Second World War mainstream criminology has tended towards increasing scepticism, even hostility, to psychological, and especially medico-psychological, ideas on criminal behaviour. Nineteenth century pioneers, such as Lombroso, who propounded theories suggesting that the common criminal is a biologically inferior creature, destined from birth to be an antisocial misfit, are continually cited as object lessons in dangerous fallacy and as warnings against the medicalization of social phenomena. Psychoanalytic concepts have become less and less acceptable, being arguably untestable and unscientific. Psychoanalytic theories about the defective character formation of the delinquent do not fit in with the fashionable view that criminal behaviours are socially determined reactions, natural expressions of the tensions existing between the powerful and the less powerful groups in society.

Empirical studies of personal characteristics predictive of recidivism are unpopular and have been challenged as self-fulfilling prophesies dependent upon arbitrary definitions of crime and a biased selection of candidates for prosecution. Moreover, the notion of criminal tendency being a persistent, individualised trait runs counter to modern research on the situational determinants of law breaking. The spectacle of dishonesty in high places seems to challenge the belief that deprivation leading to depravity is the only important source of crime. Penal regimes designed to modify deviant behaviour and attitudes during incarceration have failed conspicuously to influence criminal activity following discharge. This has provided yet another reason to doubt the relevance of psychological as opposed to social causes of crime.

Concern with just deserts and the unfair use of detention disguised as treatment have reinforced suspicion of penal measures founded upon a therapeutic model. Dubious penal practices, such as the detention on psychiatric grounds of political deviants in Russia and sexual deviants in America, the use of the ill-defined diagnosis of psychopathy and the even fuzzier antisocial personality disorder for the control of the rebellious young, or suspiciously expedient claims of insanity on behalf of politically motivated assassins, have provided critics of medical meddling with much ammunition.

Despite all the criticisms criminology remains a fruitful field for the psychological approach, in the study of offenders as individuals (some of whom are certainly peculiar), in the analysis of testimony, in socio-legal research, in the design and evaluation of penal regimes and in the practice of probation and social work. This paper can deal only with a few selected topics; tracing changes of method and outlook that have taken place over the last decades and noting the greater modesty and realism which confrontation with sociological perspectives has brought about.

Exploration of the Criminal Personality

On common sense grounds, if for no other reason, it is clear that the majority of offenders do not manifest any of the classic psychiatric syndromes and are not regarded by themselves or their associates as in need of therapy. Nevertheless, these apparently normal criminals may display characteristics deviating in degree or in kind from the norm of the general population. Psychologists have long been concerned to search for detectable differences which may have some causal connection with offending behaviour. Of course any sub-group of the population, whether selected by gender, ethnicity, social class or leisure pursuits, is to some extent special and likely to differ from average on measures of attitude, intelligence and personality. One would not expect professors and builders' labourers to have similar IQs or similar views. Deviances among criminal groups are of practical concern only if they antedate and appear to promote offending.

The work of Goring (1913) and others early this century helped lay to rest nineteenth century theories about the physically degenerate characteristics of criminals. Even the widely accepted belief in their mental inferiority came under critical scrutiny when the first tests of intelligence (which measured educational experience as much as problem solving ability) were applied to comparable social groups, such as black recruits to the American army. Nevertheless, the use of personality tests on offenders, to demonstrate differences rather than inferiorities, has remained popular, although it has provoked much criticism. One influential American review (Schuessler and Cressey, 1950) claimed that the results of such enterprises were meaningless, being so often negative or contradictory. That claim was exaggerated, failing to consider the possibility that different types of offender might have different characteristics, but undoubtedly there was much to criticise.

The characteristics of delinquents often described by clinical observers include aggressiveness, restlessness, poor attention span, under achievement, impulsivity, reluctance to postpone gratification in the interest of long term goals, intolerance of frustration and unreliability in personal relationships. Tests purporting to validate these characteristics were much in vogue in the fifties and sixties. Projection tests, such as the Rorschach ink blots and the Thematic Apperception Test (which called upon respondents to weave stories around a standard series of pictures of ambiguous situations) purported to deduce personality characteristics from observation of the working of subjects' imaginations. Such tests were the subject of much criticism on account of the large element of subjectivity in interpreting responses. Despite the introduction of standardised scoring systems, and despite the extensive use of the Rorschach in the famous American longitudinal delinquency surveys of Glueck and Glueck (1950), these approaches have not, in the long run, contributed much to criminological theory.

78

One projection device that showed promise was the Picture Frustration Test (Rosenzweig, 1945). This was related to the once very influential frustration-aggression hypothesis (Dollard *et al.*, 1939) according to which aggression is a learned response provoked by experiences of frustration. Subjects were required to fill in with appropriate words blank "balloons" issuing from the mouths of pictorial characters represented in embarrassing or frustrating situations. Responses that could be classed as extrapunitive (blaming others rather than blaming oneself or blaming no one—that is externalised aggression) were said to be characteristic of delinquents (Gatling, 1950). Attempts by Ruth Hanson and others to apply a rigorous scoring system to a modified version of the test, using forced choice responses, failed to discriminate delinquents and non-delinquents in a juvenile population in London (West and Farrington, 1973, 172 ff.)

One of the tests that has been most extensively applied in penal establishments, the MMPI questionnaire, successfully discriminates between criminals and non-criminals, but it includes items about police and lawyers which delinquents might well answer differently from others simply because of their particular experience. Moreover, insufficient attention has been paid to the possibility that the doleful circumstances in which tests are administered to offenders in custody may generate untruthful, depressive or anti-authoritarian answers by persons not usually so disposed. Demonstrations of the correlation between MMPI scores and risk of future offending (Hathaway and Monachesi, 1963) do not prove that the so-called psychopathic deviance scale is identifying a basic attribute of personality. Verbal anger and expressions of grievance (such as endorsing the statement "If people had not had it in for me I would have been much more successful") could be the consequence of life history and an indication of future antisocial intentions without necessarily being a measure of innate aggressivity.

In England, Hans Eysenck (1947), building upon pioneer work by Cyril Burt (1940) on the factor analysis of test scores, became the leading exponent of attempts to measure fundamental dimensions of personality. He identified variations that were said to be rooted in innate, inherited qualities of nervous system physiology. His original dimensions were extraversion-introversion (adapted from Jung's clinical typology) and "emotionality" or neuroticism. He developed questionnaires to assess both these traits in a single test. Scores on extraversion and neuroticism were uncorrelated and, on the model of two orthogonal dimensions, scores falling into the neurotic-extravert quadrant of the distribution were thought to indicate a predisposition to react with antisocial behaviour in the face of social pressure (Eysenck, 1964). Differences in arousal level in the cerebral cortex were postulated to explain differences in extroversion-introversion. The outgoing, socially active, stimulus-seeking extrovert was thought to have low arousal and to respond relatively poorly to conditioning situations, including disciplinary punishments. The introvert, more keyed up, with high cortical arousal, more reflective and self-examining, would react more sharply to punishments, actual or anticipated, and would therefore tend to be more conformist. Sedative drugs which decrease restraining cortical influences render introverts more extravert in their behaviour and test responses.

Eysenck and his collaborators reported correlations between extroversion and other psychophysical attributes, such as speed of conditioning, flicker fusion thresholds, psychomotor performance and even bodily configuration (mesomorphy). It was claimed that not only was an individual's position on the dimension relatively enduring, but that it was also an inherited characteristic, as shown by the concordance between the test scores of identical twins, even when separated at an early age. Such findings led Eysenck to unpopular and not very well supported conclusions about an inherited predisposition to criminality. In criminological researches his tests gave varied and sometimes contradictory results. Highly selected samples, such as incarcerated "psychopaths", tended to show neurotic-extravert characteristics, but with samples of more ordinary delinquents the correlations were sometimes insignificant (Little, 1963; West and Farrington, 1973, p. 113). Black (1972) reviewing nineteen different studies, concluded that neuroticism, but not extraversion, was sometimes a significant feature of offender samples.

A moderately phrased but somewhat devastating critique of the Eysenck theory appeared in a review by Farrington, Biron and LeBlanc (1982). They applied Eysenck's measures—including the dimension of "psychoticism" which had been added to the model at a later stage (Eysenck and Eysenck, 1976)—to samples in London and Montreal. They found some relationships between self-reported delinquency and the neuroticism and extraversion scales, but they were not very strong and not the same in the two samples. Examination of the correlations with individual items showed that the scales lacked homogeneity. None of the items was independently related to both official and self-report delinquency in the London sample. There was no tendency for items showing significant correlations in the London sample to do the same in the Montreal sample. All in all, Eysenck's approach has not provided the hoped for break through in specification of the criminogenic character.

Personality assessments derived from the MMPI have had rather more success when applied to extreme deviants such as homicide offenders. Megargee and Bohn (1982) identified contrasting types of over-controlled and under-controlled aggressors. The latter were prone to explosive outbursts at slight provocation. The former were individuals who usually kept their emotions rigorously in check, but exposed to persistent aggravation, such as might occur in chronic marital conflicts, they might suddenly erupt into extreme violence seemingly much out of character.

Analysis of actual behaviour has proved superior to formal testing, both for delineating the features of the typical delinquent and predicting the likelihood of developing or continuing involvement in crime. Teachers' observations of classroom behaviour have been especially effective predictors (Conger and Miller, 1966; Stott and Wilson, 1968; Wadsworth, 1979; West, 1982). In their London cohort study West and Farrington (1977) identified a cluster of youthful "antisocial" behaviours indicative of an impulsive, hedonistic life style which distinguished present and future delinquents from their non-delinquent peers who had attended the same schools. The relevant items included excessive fighting, verbal aggression, alcohol consumption, gambling, drug use and sexual promiscuity as well as a history of troublesomeness in the classroom. In an American survey by Lee Robins (1966) much the same cluster of behavioural items were found highly predictive of a multiplicity of social problems including crime in later adult years. Much the same items found their way into the criteria for diagnosing antisocial personality disorder in the American Psychiatric Association's Manual.

Although the stereotypical "criminal personality" is a gross oversimplification and generalisation, the evidence that intelligence and personality measures have some relevance is incontrovertible (Wilson and Herrnstein, 1985). It remains questionable, however, how far recognisable clusters of antisocial behaviours that appear consistent over time are intrinsic to the individual, or how far they reflect environmental pressures such as poverty or family criminality. Loeber and Dishion (1983), in a review of prediction data on juvenile delinquency found that the best predictors, better for example than social class, were parental child rearing techniques.

Unfavourable outcomes in the face of adverse predictors are not invariable. Little is known as yet about the effects of changing circumstances and life events. Over-enthusiasm for prediction as opposed to exploration and explanation, and realisation of the harm that may be done to individuals identified as a potential social menace, have attracted hostile criticism of long term surveys that seem based on too positivistic or fatalistic assumptions. Farrington's current follow-up of the most vulnerable group from our London cohort suggests that a proportion of them achieve a reasonable social adjustment by age thirty-two. Finally, nearly all published findings on the characteristics of delinquents have been based on samples dominated by poorly socialised common thieves and burglars who make up the bulk of penal populations. The relevance of these findings to white collar criminals and more sophisticated racketeers and fraudsters is doubtful.

Psychobiology

If studies of criminal personalities are viewed with suspicion, research into the biological components of behaviour, generally conceived as being innate, adverse and unalterable, arouse even more negative feeling, being linked in some minds with theories of mental, moral or racial inferiority exploited by Nazis and others to justify persecution. The concept of hereditary predisposition to crime ran counter to liberal social theories current after the last war and the evidence came under critical scrutiny. Methodological flaws in earlier twin studies were recognised, not least in the matter of identifying and defining "criminals", and more recent work yielded findings much more modest than the earlier claims. The great criminological twin research of Christiansen (1977) in Denmark, utilising a total population, suggested that heredity made only a slight contribution to the likelihood of criminality which was hardly of practical importance save in relation to the more extreme and unusual forms

of criminal behaviour. More recently, however, clearer evidence for a significant hereditary factor has come from adoption studies. Mednick *et al.* (1984),
in another Danish survey, found that recorded crime in male adoptees correlated more closely with criminality in their biological fathers than in their
adopting fathers. The effect held up against a variety of methodological
criticisms and tests of alternative explanations. Further confirmation came
from a similar Swedish survey (Bohman *et al.*, 1982), although the latter
also demonstrated the importance of intervening variables, notably alcohol
abuse.

Genes operate by influencing the development of bodily structures and
functions. Exceptionally, the cause of a gross disturbance can be traced to a
single gene locus, as in Huntingdon's Disease, which produces dementia,
paralyses and behavioural deterioration in early middle age. Another rare
condition, the XYY sex chromosome anomaly, made an appearance in criminological literature with the discovery of an over-representation of such cases
among special hospital inmates (Price and Whatmore, 1967). Yet another
Danish population survey (Witkin *et al.*, 1976) confirmed a raised incidence of
criminality among unselected XYY males. However since then criminological interest has waned with increasing awareness of the rarity of the
condition and the fact that interacting environmental factors are crucial to
the manifestation of behavioural effects.

Clinicians know that brain damage sometimes releases antisocial behaviour.
The connection makes criminological news whenever it is reported that some
irrational killing is the work of an offender found to have a gross brain lesion
(Martinius, 1983). Recent years have seen a recrudescence of interest in
evidence that lesser but much more common forms of brain malfunction,
whether due to injury or genetic causes may produce vulnerability to criminality through effects such as learning problems, emotional dyscontrol,
aggressivity and resistance to conditioning. Incidents liable to produce a
degree of brain damage, such as concussions, difficult or premature births
and infantile fevers with convulsions have been found unduly prevalent in
the histories of delinquents (Lewis, 1981). The exaggerated claims of some
enthusiasts (Mark and Ervin, 1970), who believe neurology can solve social
problems, may have distracted attention from the real significance of such
findings. In the United States psychiatrists have made liberal use of the diagnosis of hyperkinesis, the hypothetical result of subclinical and unmeasurable
"minimal brain damage", to explain the irritability and restlessness of
rebellious, delinquent-prone children (Offord, 1979). British psychiatrists
have tended to be more sceptical as to the physiological basis of overactivity
save in the minority of cases with definite physical signs of malfunction
(Rutter, 1982).

Electroencephalographic (EEG) tracings, although only a distant reflection of cerebral activity, have been useful in pin-pointing localised lesions and
in diagnosing epileptic tendencies. Hill and Pond (1952), pioneers in the study
of EEG anomalies in psychiatric patients and criminals, found a very high
proportion of abnormal records in a series of murderers referred for examination, particularly among those whose crimes were seemingly irrational.

82

Subsequent researches, while confirming a raised incidence of aberrant recordings among incarcerated offenders (Williams, 1969) have not fulfilled earlier expectations that electroencephalography would prove decisive in linking particular types of behaviour disorder with identifiable malfunctions. The EEG anomalies most often found are non-specific and of a kind present in substantial numbers in the ordinary population. Technical progress in artificially stimulated EEG responses, studies in brain lateralisation and the coupling of EEG findings with new methods of brain scanning, may change the picture.

The association of epilepsy and criminality, particularly violent crime, was thought to be close but is now recognised as relatively slight and indirect. John Gunn (1977) found a significant over-representation of epileptics among English prisoners, but it was still only a small percentage and could be accounted for at least in part by the tendency for prisoners to be drawn from sections of society most vulnerable to neurological impairments. A more recent American prison survey (Whitman et al., 1984) confirmed the raised prevalence but found no closer relationship with violent than with non-violent crime. Nevertheless there is strong clinical evidence for behavioural disturbances, both immediately following fits and in between attacks, in the case of temporal lobe epilepsy when the limbic system's control of emotional reactions is likely to be affected.

Deeper brain structures, notably the hypothalamus and its anatomically juxtaposed pituitary and pineal glands, are particularly closely concerned with stimulation and feed-back control over the levels of hormones which have a profound influence on aggressive and sexual responses. New information about the influence of hormone imbalance at the prenatal stage on the so-called sex differentiation of the human brain has led to biochemical explanations of individual variation in aggression (Meyer-Bahlburg and Ehrhardt, 1982) and sexual orientation (Gladue et al., 1984).

Some indication of individual variations in emotional responsiveness can be obtained from measures of autonomic nervous reflexes changes in heart rate, blood pressure, breathing and sweat secretion. On the assumption that socialization depends on successful avoidance learning, Hare (1970) has for many years been expounding the theory that psychopathic behaviour is linked to sluggish autonomic reflexes, slow reactions to electric shocks or other punitive stimuli and relative insensitivity to anticipatory cues. The experimental evidence for this remains uncertain and somewhat conflicting and the research has not as yet given reliable criteria for the classification or treatment of persistent antisociality.

It would be fair to conclude that although research into biochemical and neurological determinants of behaviour have not yet come up with explanations relative to the generality of deviance, and although pharmacological control of aberrant behaviour in non-psychotic criminals has not reached a stage that could properly be called treatment, the field is developing fast. One need not be put off by premature attempts to base legal argumentation on as yet poorly understood phenomena such as hyperkinesis and premenstrual tension.

Psychodynamic Approaches

In the late forties psychoanalysis had considerable influence on British criminology and on social work with offenders. Psychodynamic explanations
of delinquent character formation were widely read (Aichhorn, 1951;
Friedlander, 1947; Glover, 1960). It is impossible to review here the massive
accumulation of complex and often untestable theorising of the Freudian,
Neo-Freudian, Adlerian, Kleinian and Jungian schools, still less of their
numerous and more recent derivatives, such as the currently fashionable
school of Gestalt. None of this has any longer much impact on academic
criminology, although it still governs some therapeutic endeavours, such as
the analytically oriented treatments offered to offenders by the Portman
Clinic in London and the treatments described in the *Journal of Offender
Therapy* when it was under the editorship of the analyst Melitta Schmideberg.

Some of the ideas of the analytic schools have been taken over by experimental psychologists—displacement of aggression for example. Others, such
as the notion of repressed or unacknowledgeable motives, have been absorbed
into common wisdom and tend to be taken for granted. The theory that
intimate emotional interaction between the dependent infant and its all-
powerful parents determines the character of the child is highly relevant to
many criminological issues. A close, loving relationship with caring, attentive,
rule enforcing parents is said to inspire internalisation of standards and strong
guilt feelings for wrongdoing. Carried to excess the process may produce a
neurotic, guilt-laden character who tries to repress self-assertive and sexual
impulses that most people would consider normal and beneficial. Although
nervous, inhibited people are generally non-delinquent, some of them may
seek to express their suppressed impulses in oddly distorted antisocial ways,
such as persistent fire-setting or the seemingly purposeless magpie-like
accumulation of useless stolen articles. Motivational analysis of these
peculiar cases has proved instructive, although not necessarily helpful to
magisterial decisions or social control policy.

In contrast, chaotic upbringing by inconsistent, changing, uncaring, rejecting or erratic parental figures, with whom the infant cannot form close ties, is
said to lead to the development of an impulse–ridden character with a weak
conscience and noticeable absence of guilt about breaking social rules that
have never been properly absorbed.

The crucial importance of the early years for healthy psychological development was re-emphasised by John Bowlby (1946) in a celebrated study of
forty four juvenile thieves. This launched the theory that maternal bonding is
all-important and separation liable to produce permanent emotional damage
and an "affectionless', delinquent-prone adult. The theory became very
fashionable and influenced social work policies on fostering. Gradually,
however, more systematic researches showed the initial assumptions to be
simplistic and exaggerated. By the time Michael Rutter (1972) reviewed
the subject it was already clear that stressful circumstances associated with
the causes of separation and lack of adequate substitute care were as
important as the separation itself. Moreover the effects were variable, not

84

limited to the first two years as originally suggested and by no means irreparable.

It would be a pity if criticisms of the generalisability and epistemological basis of the schools of psychoanalysis were to lead to abandonment of motivational analysis. Psychoanalytic treatment, because it demands lengthy introspection and patient co-operation, is unsuited to many offenders, but inquiry into personal history, attitudes and reasons for offending behaviour is helpful in the understanding of particular cases. Incidentally, the social interactionist approach has much in common with psychodynamic exploration.

Experimental Psychology

Not so long ago experimental psychology seemed wedded to the notion that research should be limited to direct observation of behaviour, particularly the behaviour of the laboratory rat. Cognition and introspection was deemed irrelevant. Learning theories based on principles of animal conditioning were developed and applied to the explanation of delinquent behaviour. Gordon Trasler (1962) produced an explanatory system that endeavoured to account on conditioning principles for the connections between irregular upbringing and subsequent delinquency. For example, caring parents, by the sheer amount of time devoted to their children, might give them more opportunities for social learning.

Strict behaviourism has given way to explanations that take note of cognitive factors and verbal symbolism in interpreting the stimulus-response sequence. A rebuke from a "significant other" can be as powerful a negative reinforcer as a slap or an electric shock. Social psychologists have produced a large body of research showing how learning, for instance by imitation, modelling and the incorporation of attitudes, can be affected by the subject's situation and relationship with the source of information. The classic work of Milgram (1974) demonstrated that implicit encouragement from teachers could release in student subjects aggressive actions of unexpected ferocity.

Findings from experiments in the stimulation or suppression of aggressive responses have obvious implications for crime control. Frustration of goals or expectations, situations reminiscent of painful incidents from the past, threats to self-esteem, blocking of the means of escape from confrontation, facilitation through the rewarding results of previous violence, external reinforcement from aggressive models, victim conformity with adverse stereotypes and release from a build up of tension have all been found relevant to the likelihood of aggressive reactions (Bandura, 1969; Berkowitz, 1962, 1969; Green and O'Neal, 1976; Maier, 1949). The escalation of violence in confrontational situations, vividly portrayed in accounts of aggressive prisoners and policemen by Hans Toch (1969), has proved a fruitful area of study with results helpful in the training of police who have to handle threatening individuals and crowds.

The experimental manipulation of naturalistic situations helps expose the immediate determinants of the decision to commit a crime. The lost letter experiment was an interesting example (Farrington and Knight, 1980). The decision to steal an apparently abandoned stamped addressed envelope containing money was found to be influenced by the contents of the different letters which were enclosed with it giving indications of the circumstances—affluent or poor—of the supposed victims. The examination of victim-offender interaction has developed into a whole new subject—victimology. So-called victim precipitation of crime was first introduced in relation to homicide (Wolfgang, 1958) and rape (Amir, 1971), but it has much wider application.

Offenders' decision making processes have all too often been discussed at an abstract level, mostly on the cost-benefit model of temptation versus deterrence, rather than being subjected to empirical inquiry. A notable exception was the inquiry by Bennett and Wright (1984) into burglars' selection of premises to enter. The importance of research into the situational determinants of crime, in preference to the idiosyncratic motivations of individual offenders, has been emphasised by psychologists at the Home Office Research Unit in a spirited advocacy of "target hardening"—the locks and bolts strategy (Clarke, 1980).

Behaviour therapy is a form of treatment approved by experimentalists because it owes its theoretical justification to laboratory research in conditioning. Application to offenders has proved ethically problematic. Early attempts used aversive methods, administering electric shocks in conjunction with stimuli calculated to arouse disapproved thoughts (such as a whiff of gin for an alcoholic or the picture of a nude child for a paedophile). The aversive reaction built up by frequent repetition was intended to remove the temptation to disapproved behaviour. Such techniques have become unfashionable. They looked like thinly disguised coercion (Skinner, 1971), the aversive effects were unreliable and often temporary and the procedures were of no direct help in establishing substitute prosocial behaviours. Reinforcement by reward is more acceptable and has been used in penal institutions in the form of "token economies". Inmates earn privileges in return for approved behaviours such as cleanliness, industry, courtesy, co-operation in groups and avoidance of rule breaking (Kadzin, 1977; Laycock, 1979). Such regimes cannot tackle directly specific misbehaviours, such as housebreaking or thieving, which bring about incarceration and there is little evidence that on release habits acquired in prison generalise to the avoidance of crime.

Among the disciplines involved in criminology psychology has contributed most to the experimental testing of ideas, including the testing of effectiveness of treatment schemes. The result has been the development of extreme scepticism about efforts to divert individuals from criminal habits. Several influential reviews of treatment evaluations concluded that there was scant evidence of benefit (Brody, 1976; Lipton et al., 1975; Sechrest et al., 1979). Only a tiny proportion of the numerous interventions described in the literature incorporated valid control comparisons or used random allocation between treated and control groups. Few of those that did produced any significant reduction in offence rate; some actually seemed to make matters worse (McCord, 1978). These conclusions have had a stultifying effect on efforts to rehabilitate offenders and have been used to support policies based on classical ideas of punishment and suppression rather than training, welfare or psychological support.

The conclusion that "nothing works" in the treatment of offenders was never really fair. Nigel Walker (1971) has pointed out that many problems beset evaluations. Valid assessment calls for an adequately sized sample and a sufficiently long follow-up, a proper control group to provide a statistic of offending without treatment, a comparison of treated and control individuals over a similar span of time in freedom, and finally a clear and realistic difference between the treatment regime and the untreated cases. Many superficially promising treatment programmes have to be discounted because these exacting conditions are not met. However a more recent review by three prominent criminologists (Farrington, Ohlin and Wilson, 1986) concluded that good treatment experiments, especially those using the preferred method of random allocation, have not been entirely negative in outcome. Whereas counselling, guided group interaction and other "talking therapies" have not been shown to be effective with the generality of delinquents, pre-school coaching and exposure to prosocial peers, practical help for ex-prisoners (Shaw, 1974) and diversionary schemes for juveniles, based on instruction in coping skills and guidance to parents on the manipulation of rewards and sanctions, may be effective (Binder and Newkirk, 1977).

Miscellaneous Applications of Psychology

Space permits no more than passing reference to some of the numerous practical applications of psychology in penal affairs. The study of the reliability of courtroom testimony, of eye witness observations and recollections and their susceptibility to anticipation and suggestion, and examination of the fallible processes of identification are of particular importance since psychologists may be called as expert witnesses (Haward, 1979). Testing truthfulness with the aid of a polygraph, which can detect guilty knowledge by registering emotional reactions to key words, is a far from foolproof technique. It needs great discretion in interpretation and is less commonly used in Britain than in the United States, where some jurisdictions allow polygraph experts to give evidence at trials (Lykken, 1985). A Working Group of the British Psychological Society (1986) has concluded that "it is difficult to see how Members of the Society could engage in work as polygraph interrogators and claim that their conduct is consistent with the Society's current Code of Conduct".

On matters requiring clinical experience more than familiarity with tests of reliability, such as child custody decisions, the courts tend to call upon the psychiatric profession, and for some purposes, such as the imposition of treatment, they are statutorily obliged to do so. Court decisions on mental health grounds have been much affected by changes in psychiatric practice. The open door policy of mental hospitals, the gradual reduction of asylum beds in favour of supposed community care for the chronically disabled, and the limitations introduced in the 1983 Mental Health Act on enforced treatments and compulsory detention of psychopaths, have combined to make hospitals less willing or able to admit the obstreperous offender patient who is not acutely psychotic. Severe personality disordered individuals, addicts, neglected schizophrenics and sexual deviants are all increasingly susceptible to imprisonment rather than hospitalisation and are largely lost to medical research.

Studies of attitudes and decision making within the criminal justice system can be revelatory. The processes of sentencing (Hogarth, 1971) and of jury deliberation (Davis *et al.*, 1977) have been examined with interesting results, although the methods used have often depended on artificial devices such as mock trials or questionnaires based on hypothetical cases. The application of psychology in police studies is a rapidly developing field. Since actual and perceived even-handedness is important in the exercise of police work evidence of racial or class prejudice (Black and Reiss, 1970), the detection of unsuitable personality traits among prospective recruits (Adorno *et al.*, 1950) and studies of the effect of formal instruction on the attitudes of serving officers (Weiner, 1974) are among many examples of researches of interest to police.

Psychology is a continually expanding subject. Its principles and research methods are used more and more in management studies, in engineering optimal interactions between men and machinery, in job selection, in attitude manipulation, in communications and in education. Whilst not specific to criminology all of these applications are as relevant to criminal justice operations as to other spheres of employment and human endeavour.

Conclusion

Psychological research is so diverse, and fashions in criminology so changeable, it is hard to discern straightforward historical trends. Fundamental discoveries have been plentiful in the biological sciences recently and these must make their mark on behavioural studies, but they have only just begun to reach criminology. Progress has been made in reducing the isolation of the different disciplines and approaches to crime problems. Experimentalists now take note of psychodynamic hypotheses and humanistic concerns. Researches into offender characteristics no longer proceed without regard to the often overriding effects of environmental circumstances and social organisation. Specialised offences in which unusual psychological factors may be operating —such as violence towards children (Gardner and Gray, 1982), spouse battering (Roy, 1977), sexual offending (West, 1987) or shoplifting (Gibbens, Palmer and Prince, 1971)—are more frequently studied from a truly interdisciplinary standpoint in place of the one-time exclusive focus on individual psychopathology.

Gradually, crucial topics, such as the effectiveness of treatment systems and penal measures, are being subjected to methodologically sophisticated research, but there is a long way to go. Farrington, Ohlin and Wilson (1986) have pointed to the enormous gap in knowledge of how to reduce crime, rehabilitate offenders or intervene in the genesis of hard core offenders by socially deprived and deviant families. They plead for a new research strategy based on a determined experimental approach and more longitudinal studies.

The distinctive contribution of the psychological approach to criminology is its emphasis on systematic observation and measurement of criminal behaviour (Buckle and Farrington, 1984), testable theories, experimentation and repetition. For criminological research to prosper, this continuing psychological input is essential.

References

ADORNO, T. W., FRENKEL-BRUNSWICK, E., LEVINSON, D. J. and SANDFORD, R. N. (1950). *The Authoritarian Personality*. New York, Harper.

AICHHORN, A. (1951). *Wayward Youth*. London, Imago.

AMIR, M. (1971). *Patterns in Forcible Rape*. Chicago, Chicago University Press.

BANDURA, A. (1969). *Aggression: A Social Learning Analysis*. New York, Holt, Rinehart and Winston.

BENNETT, T. H. and WRIGHT, R. T. (1984). *Burglars on Burglary: Prevention and the Offender*. Aldershot, Gower.

BERKOWITZ, L. (1962). *Aggression: A Social Psychological Analysis*. New York, McGraw Hill.

BERKOWITZ, L. (ed.) (1969) *Roots of Aggression*. New York, Atherton.

BINDER, A. and NEWKIRK, M. (1977). "A program to extend police service capability". *Crime Prevention Review*, **4,** 26–32.

BLACK, D. J. and REISS, A. J. (1970). "Police control of juveniles". *American Sociological Review*, **35,** 63–77.

BLACK, W. A. M. (1972). "Extraversion, neuroticism and criminality". *Australian and New Zealand Journal of Criminology*, **5,** 99–106.

BOHMAN, M. *et al.* (1982) "Predisposition to petty criminality in Swedish adoptees". *Archives of General Psychiatry*, **39,** 1233–1247.

BOWLBY, J. (1946). *Forty-four Juvenile Thieves*. London, Baillière Tindall and Cox.

BRITISH PSYCHOLOGICAL SOCIETY (1986). "Report of the working group on the use of the polygraph in criminal investigation and personnel screening". *Bulletin of the British Psychological Society*, **39,** 81–94.

BRODY, S. R. (1976). *The Effectiveness of Sentencing*. London, H.M.S.O.

BUCKLE, A. and FARRINGTON, B. P. (1984). "An observational study of shoplifting". *British Journal of Criminology*, **24,** 63–73.

BURT, C. (1940). *Factors of the Mind*. London, London University Press.

CHRISTIANSEN, K. O. (1977). "Criminality among twins". In S. A. Mednick and K. O. Christiansen (eds.) *Biosocial Bases of Criminal Behavior*. Toronto, Wiley.

CLARKE, R. V. G. (1980). "Situational crime prevention: Theory and practice". *British Journal of Criminology*, **20,** 136–147.

CONGER, J. J. and MILLER, W. C. (1966) *Personality, Social Class and Delinquency*. New York, Wiley.

DAVIS, J. H., BRAY, R. M. and HOLT, R. W. (1977). "The empirical study of social decision processes in juries". In J. L. Tapp and F. J. Levine (eds.) *Law, Justice and the Individual in Society*. New York, Holt, Rinehart and Winston.

DOLLARD, J. *et al.* (1939). *Frustration and Aggression*. Newhaven, Yale University Press.

EYSENCK, H. J. (1947). *Dimensions of Personality*. London, Routledge and Kegan Paul.

EYSENCK, H. J. (1964). *Crime and Personality*. London, Routledge and Kegan Paul.

EYSENCK, H. J. and EYSENCK, S. B. G. (1976). *Psychoticism as a Dimension of Personality*. Hodder and Stoughton.

FARRINGTON, D. P., BIRON, L. and LeBLANC, M. (1982). "Personality and delinquency in London and Montreal". In J. Gunn and D. P. Farrington (eds.) *Abnormal Offenders, Delinquency and the Criminal Justice System*. Chichester, Wiley.

FARRINGTON, D. P. and KNIGHT, B. J. (1980). "Stealing from a 'lost' letter: effects of victim characteristics". *Criminal Justice and Behavior*, **7**, 423–436.

FARRINGTON, D. P., OHLIN, L. E. and WILSON, J. Q. (1986). *Understanding and Controling Crime*. Berlin, Springer-Verlag.

FRIEDLANDER, K. (1947). *Psychoanalytic Approach to Juvenile Delinquency*. London, Kegan Paul.

GARDNER, J. and GRAY, M. (1982). "Violence towards children" in P. Feldman (ed.) *Developments in the Study of Criminal Behaviour*. London, Wiley.

GATLING, F. P. (1950). "Frustration reactions of delinquents using Rosenzweig's classification system". *Journal of Abnormal and Social Psychology*, **45**, 749–752.

GEEN, R. G. and O'NEAL, E. C. (1976). *Perspectives on Aggression*. New York, Academic Press.

GIBBENS, T. C. N., PALMER, C. and PRINCE, J. (1971). "Mental health aspects of shoplifting". *British Medical Journal*, **(iii)**, 612–615.

GLADUE, B. A., GREEN, R. and HELLMAN, R. E. (1984). "Neuroendocrine response to estrogen and sexual orientation". *Science*, **225**, 1496–1499.

GLOVER, E. (1960). *The Roots of Crime*. London, Imago.

GLUECK, S. and GLUECK, E. T. (1950). *Unravelling Juvenile Delinquency*. New York, Commonwealth Fund.

GORING, C. (1913). *The English Convict*. London, H.M.S.O.

GUNN, J. C. (1977). *Epileptics in Prison*. London, Academic Press.

HARE, R. D. (1970). *Psychopathy: Theory and Research*. London, Wiley.

HATHAWAY, S. R. and MONACHESI, E. D. (1963). *Adolescent Personality and Behavior: MMPI Patterns of Normal, Delinquent, Dropout and other Outcomes*. Minneapolis, University of Minnesota Press.

HAWARD, L. R. C. (1979). "The psychologist as expert witness". In D. P. Farrington, K. Hawkins and S. Lloyd-Bostock (eds.) *Psychology, Law and Legal Processes*. London, Macmillan.

HILL, D. and POND, D. A. (1952). "Reflections on 100 capital cases submitted to electro-encephalography". *Journal of Mental Science*, **98**, 23–43.

HOGARTH, J. (1971). *Sentencing as a Human Process*. Toronto, University of Toronto Press.

KADZIN, A. (1977). *The Token Economy*. New York, Plenum.

LAYCOCK, G. (1979). "Behaviour modification in prisons". *British Journal of Criminology*, **19**, 400–415.

LEWIS, D. O. (1981). *Vulnerabilities to Delinquency*. Lancaster, MTP Press.

LIPTON, D., MARTINSON, R. and WILKS, J. (1975). *The Effectiveness of Correctional Treatment: A Survey of Treatment Evaluation Studies*. New York, Praeger.

LITTLE, A. (1963). "Professor Eysenck's theory of crime: an empirical test on adolescent offenders". *British Journal of Criminology*, **4**, 152–163.

LOEBER, R. and DISHION, T. (1983). "Early predictors of male delinquency". *Psychological Bulletin*, **94**, 68–99.

Lykken, D. T. (1985). "The probity of the polygraph". In S. M. Kassin and L. S. Wrightsman (eds.) *The Psychology of Evidence and Trial Procedure*. Beverly Hills, Sage.

McCord, J. (1978). "A thirty-year follow-up of treatment effects". *American Psychologist*, **33,** 284–289.

Maier, N. R. F. (1949). *Frustration: The study of Behavior without a Goal*. Ann Arbor, University of Michigan Press.

Mark, V. H. and Ervin, F. R. (1970). *Violence and the Brain*. New York, Harper and Row.

Martinius, J. (1983). "Homicide of an aggressive adolescent boy with right temporal lesion: A case report". *Neuroscience and Biobehavioural Reviews*, **7,** 419–422.

Mednick, S. A. *et al.* (1984) "Genetic influences in criminal convictions. Evidence from an adoption cohort". *Science*, **224,** 891–894.

Megargee, E. I. and Bohn, M. J. (1982). *Classifying Criminal Offenders; A New System based on the MMPI*. Beverly Hills, Sage.

Meyer-Bahlberg, H. L. F. and Ehrhardt, A. A. (1982). "Prenatal sex hormones and human aggression". *Aggressive Behavior*, **8,** 39–62.

Milgram, S. (1974). *Obedience to Authority*. London, Tavistock.

Offord, D. R. *et al.*.(1979). "Delinquency and hyperactivity". *Journal of Nervous and Mental Disease*, **167,** 734–741.

Price, W. H. and Whatmore, P. B. (1967) "Behaviour disorders and pattern of crime among XYY males identified at a maximum security hospital". *British Medical Journal*, **(i),** 533–536.

Robins, L. N. (1966). *Deviant Children Grown Up*. Baltimore, Williams and Wilkins.

Rosenzweig, S. (1945). "The picture-frustration method and its application in a study of reaction to frustration". *Journal of Personality*, **14,** 3–23.

Roy, M. (Ed.) (1977). *Battered Women*. New York, Van Nostrand Reinhold.

Rutter, M. (1972). *Maternal Deprivation Reassessed*. Harmondsworth, Penguin.

Rutter, M. (1982). "Syndromes attributed to 'Minimal brain dysfunction' in children". *American Journal of Psychiatry*, **139,** 21–33.

Schuessler, K. F. and Cressey, D. R. (1950). "Personality characteristics of criminals". *American Journal of Sociology*, **50,** 476–484.

Sechrest, L., White, S. O. and Brown, E. D. (1979). *The Rehabilitation of Criminal Offenders: Problems and Prospects*. Washington, D.C., National Academy of Sciences.

Shaw, M. (1974). *Social Work in Prison*. London, H.M.S.O.

Skinner, B. F. (1971). *Beyond Freedom and Dignity*. New York, Knopf.

Stott, D. H. and Wilson, D. M. (1968). "The prediction of early adult criminality from schoolage behaviour". *International Journal of Social Psychiatry*, **14,** 5–8.

Toch, H. (1969). *Violent Men*. Chicago, Aldine.

Trasler, G. (1962). *The Explanation of Criminality*, London, Routledge and Kegan Paul.

Wadsworth, M. (1979). *Roots of Delinquency*. Oxford, Martin Robertson.

Walker, N. D. (1971). *Crimes, Courts and Figures*. Harmondsworth, Penguin.

Weiner, N. L. (1974). "The effects of education on police attitudes". *Journal of Criminal Justice*, **2,** 317–328.

West, D. J. (1982). *Delinquency: Its Roots, Careers and Prospects*. London, Heinemann.

WEST, D. J. (1987). *Sexual Crimes and Confrontations*. Aldershot, Gower.

WEST, D. J. and FARRINGTON, D. P. (1973). *Who Becomes Delinquent?* London, Heinemann.

WEST, D. J. and FARRINGTON, D. P. (1977). *The Delinquent Way of Life*. London, Heinemann.

WHITMAN, S. *et al.* (1984). "Epilepsy in prison: Elevated prevalence and no relationship to violence". *Neurology*, **34,** 775–782.

WILLIAMS, D. (1969). "Neural factors related to habitual aggression". *Brain,* **92,** 503–520.

WILSON, J. Q. and HERRNSTEIN, R. J. (1985). *Crime and Human Nature*. New York, Simon and Schuster.

WITKIN, H. A. *et al.* (1976). "XXY and XXY men: Criminality and aggression". *Science,* **193,** 647–655.

WOLFGANG, M. E. (1958). *Patterns in Criminal Homicide*. Philadelphia, University of Philadelphia Press.

BRIT. J. CRIMINOL. Vol. 28 No. 2 SPRING 1988

FEMINISM AND CRIMINOLOGY IN BRITAIN

LORAINE GELSTHORPE (*Lancaster*) and ALLISON MORRIS (*Cambridge*)

The academic manifestation[1] of feminism is a recent development.[2] Indeed feminist work within criminology in Britain probably dates from the publication of Carol Smart's book *Women, Crime and Criminology* in 1976.[3] Frances Heidensohn (1977, 390) described its publication as a turning point and claimed that the issues raised by Smart were now "very firmly on the agenda for all criminologists" (1977, 392). Others were more sceptical. Paul Rock, in his review of Smart's book (1977, 393), doubted that "analytic losses" had been inflicted on criminological theories by not considering women. However, he acknowledged the *potential* value of feminism: "a feminist sociology would indeed be potent if it could indicate how much formal constructions should be modified to incorporate the female" (1977, 393) and "if it [criminology] can be proved to be analytically inadequate then a feminist criminology would be intellectually momentous' (1977, 394). Just over ten years later it seems appropriate to explore the extent to which these challenges have been met, the impact which feminism has had on mainstream debates in criminology and the significance of feminism for criminology. Consideration of these issues, however, demands first that we refer in brief to the development of feminism and its impact on other academic disciplines.

The Meaning of Feminism

Feminist critiques and perspectives on a range of topics—women's inequality, child care, social policy and the law—abound. However, the meaning of terms like "feminism" and "feminist" is not self-evident. For some, "feminism" conjures up a picture of women's liberationists of the 1960s; for others, it is an attitude, a way of seeing, a value commitment. Some locate the origins of feminism in the statements of Mary Wollstonecraft in the eighteenth century, others in the contemporary women's movement and the legislative changes achieved in the 1970s. Popular conceptions of feminists include references to women in the Greenham Common Peace Movement or in the women's movement generally, lesbian separatists and any groups or individuals who have tried to change the position of women or ideas about women. These disparate

Loraine Gelsthorpe is a Research Fellow in the Department of Social Administration, University of Lancaster, and Allison Morris is a lecturer at the Institute of Criminology, University of Cambridge.

[1] Feminism has also had an impact on policy and practice in the criminal justice system. We do not discuss that here, but obvious examples are rape law reform and changes in police policy on domestic violence.

[2] It is part and parcel of the re-emergence of the women's movement in the 1960s in the United States and in the 1970s in England. For a historical development of feminism, see Bouchier (1983) and Coote and Campbell (1987).

[3] There are earlier and important articles by Frances Heidensohn (1968 and 1970) but she describes (1985, 146) these as pre-feminist. There is also earlier research on women (for example, Smith (1962) and Cowie, Cowie and Slater (1968)), but these are not written from a feminist perspective.

views of the meaning of feminism are recognised within feminism. Indeed, the question of whether or not any unity can be assumed is one which perplexes many writers (Evans, 1977; Oakley, 1981; Bouchier, 1978 and 1983; Mitchell and Oakley, 1986). Olive Banks (1981) wrote about the *Faces of Feminism* and, more recently Rosalind Delmar (1986) referred to "feminisms". As women begin to speak about situations which they believe they share, they discover their differences from one another and from one another's perspective. Clearly, feminists inhabit different social, political and intellectual settings and do not necessarily share the same theoretical allegiances (Kuhn & Wolpe, 1978; Oakley, 1981, 335–338; Mitchell and Oakley, 1986).

This task of defining "feminism" is particularly difficult when it comes to identifying its essential characteristics. There is, in the literature, much discussion about whether or not feminist research is by, on, or for women (Stanley and Wise, 1983; Cain, 1986) and whether or not it necessarily involves political action. Feminists do commonly address gender relations, particularly the notion of male supremacy and the oppression of women, but this does not necessarily mean a shared understanding of the meaning of oppression (Barrett, 1980). However, despite these differences in theory, differences in practice are less significant.

At the very least, a feminist is someone who believes that women experience subordination[4] on the basis of their sex. Although this may not be the best or all-encompassing definition, we have to have a starting point and it provides that. Even those in the "I'm not a feminist but. . ." category would accept feminism in this broad sense and, as Janet Radcliffe Richards notes, there are good reasons for choosing a wide definition of feminism:

> All feminists, however firm their ideological commitments, must want as many people as possible to be willing to listen to arguments about the position of women rather than reacting with hostility whenever the subject of feminism comes up; it is in the interests of everyone who cares about justice to have as many people as possible thinking of themselves as feminists (1982, 15).

The essence then of feminist perspectives is that they reflect the view that women experience subordination on the basis of their sex, although they may differ on its origins and how it is institutionalised.

The Impact of Feminism on Academic Disciplines

Traditionally, men's studies have been passed off as "general knowledge". As Dale Spender puts it:

> Most of the knowledge produced in our society has been produced by men; they have usually generated their explanations and the schemata and then have checked with each other and vouched for the accuracy and adequacy of their view of the world (1981, 1).

---

[4] "Feminism" as a movement has been defined by Bouchier as "any form of opposition to any form of social, political or economic discrimination which women suffer because of their sex" (1983, 2).

Indeed, women have been excluded as both the producers and subjects of this knowledge. Feminism challenged this. It provided various possibilities: integrating women into existing theoretical perspectives, developing new theories and revitalising accumulated knowledge. However, feminist writers, first and foremost, placed at centre stage women's experience of the world.

We can see this in the changes in recent years within sociology, a discipline with close connections to criminology. In 1974, the British Sociological Association held a key conference on "Sexual Divisions and Society". Participants vehemently argued for more research on gender relations which they believed had been "consistently neglected by sociologists, and ridiculed and denigrated by some" (Barker and Allen, 1976, 2–3). Some of the contributions to this conference documented the inadequacy of existing research (for example, Frankenburg (1976) and Brown (1976)). But there were also papers on topics previously ignored by sociologists (like homework and housework) and on the use and development of theoretical concepts and models on which a more adequate understanding and explanation of gender relations might be built (for example, papers on the dual labour market, the political economy of domestic labour, and the deferential dialectic in relations between husbands and wives).

Since then, feminists within sociology have introduced new perspectives to research on education (Shaw, 1976; Clarricoates, 1980), health (Doyal and Pennell, 1979; Ruzek, 1986), motherhood (Oakley, 1979 and 1986; David, 1985), the State and women (McIntosh, 1978) and employment (Barker and Allen, 1976; Moroney, 1986). There is also some feminist work in the sociology of deviance (for example, Millman, 1975; Rodmell, 1981; Hutter and Williams, 1981) and in the sociology of law (O'Donovan, 1985; Smart, 1984; Cain, 1986). Feminists within sociology have in addition introduced a wider view of women and their activities, and have increased awareness of their position. In this way, they have provided important insights for understanding the importance of sexual divisions in society. But the key question is the extent to which these perspectives have influenced mainstream sociology.

While feminists have filled many gaps, there is little evidence to suggest that feminism has transformed the discipline. "Gender issues" are often seen only to relate to women, and although women and gender relations are well represented in discussions of the family, generally they are not in mainstream debates about community, power, work situations, class, politics, inequality and so on. Studies of social structure no longer actually ignore women but, as Ann Oakley writes, "there is frequently a lack of imagination about the contexts within which such studies may be seen as appropriate" (1981, 78).

Margrit Eichler (1980) has further questioned the impact and significance of feminist contributions by arguing that feminist literature in the social sciences has often itself used inappropriate conceptual tools and language, and has thus actually reinforced the sexual stereotypes which were so frequently the focus of feminist concerns. These criticisms are reiterated in the work of Roberts (1981), and Stacey and Thorne (1985) aptly refer to the "missing

95

revolution in sociology". They lament the fact that feminism seems not to have reconstructed basic paradigms. They argue that feminists working in sociology are merely "accommodated" and that feminist perspectives are 'ghettoised'.

The situation seems much the same in other academic disciplines.[5] Common themes which emerge from critical reviews are the continued dominance of men in the academic world and the dismissal of feminist modes of thought or analysis. Ruth (1981, 47), for example, argues that for women to be accepted they have to "think like men". Feminism is viewed as irrelevant, transient or trivial and feminists as biased. Feminist thought, its presuppositions, content and emphasis, is seen as an invalid enterprise. Those changes which have occurred tend to be described as token. For example, despite the attacks on psychology by major feminist writers (de Beauvoir, 1953; Millet, 1970; Greer, 1971; Firestone, 1971), Walker argues that:

> to a large extent the feminist critique has been co-opted by mainstream psy-
> chology without any widescale corresponding change in psychology's nature,
> theory or practice (1981, 111).

Mainstream has effectively remained "malestream".[6]

"Feminist Criminology?"

This brief review makes dismal reading. We need now to consider whether feminist perspectives have fared any better in criminology. The first task is to establish whether there is now a collective body of commentaries and concerns which can be termed "feminist criminology", for its existence cannot be taken for granted. Some writers have claimed that there is. Victoria Greenwood (1981), for example, defined "feminist criminology" as a collection of recent research, predominantly inspired and affected by influences from the women's movement, which illuminated the institutionalised sexism in the criminal justice process. More recently, Beverley Brown (1986, 355) suggested that it would be churlish to deny that "feminist criminology' existed, however diffi-cult it may be to define it. The critique of traditional theory and practice is the "unified package" (1986, 359) by which, she suggests, "feminist criminology" can be recognised. In contrast, Carol Smart (1981) has argued that neither the existence of feminist criminologists (self-appointed), female criminologists nor studies of women and crime constitute a "feminist criminology", for while some authors have conducted research from one theoretical position, others have adopted entirely different positions. Pat Carlen (1985) has also doubted whether attempts to establish a "feminist criminology" have been successful. She gives two reasons for this: first, many feminist writers have viewed crime as essentially a male activity and, secondly, their attempts to identify a global

---

[5] See Dale Spender's edited collection of essays *Men's Studies Modified* (1981) for a detailed discussion.
[6] This notion is borrowed from Maureen Cain. See also Stacey (1981).

theory of crime (which would apply to both men and women) or a special theory of women's crime are theoretically unsound.

There is no doubt that the term "feminist criminology" as currently used can create confusion. A concrete example of this is Frances Heidensohn's (1985) discussion of the association between the women's movement and crime which she presents as part of the contribution of "feminist criminology". She discusses the work of Freda Adler (1975) and Rita Simon (1975) who assert this association and then the critiques of their work by Steven Box (1983) and Darrell Steffensmeier (1978). It is not at all clear from Heidensohn's text who the "feminist criminologists" are, but she must mean Adler and Simon as she concluded: "in the least helpful way to women offenders. . . one branch of feminist criminology has at last made female crime visible" (1985, 160). However, we would not describe their work as feminist as it does not contain certain core elements. (We outline these later.) The point here is that to identify particular writers or work as part of a "feminist criminology" can confuse rather than clarify.[7]

We take the view that *a* "feminist criminology" cannot exist. To adopt any single definition would limit its development. Feminists who are criminologists reflect the tensions and differences which exist within each of these perspectives. Some argue that women and men should be dealt with equally in the criminal justice system (for example, Moulds, 1980); others believe that there are differences between men and women which justify differential dispositions (for example, Brophy and Smart, 1985; Heidensohn, 1986). Some reject the notion of fundamental differences between men and women in their potential or capacity to commit crime (for example, Adler, 1975); others argue that women's personality is different from men's (for example, Gilligan, 1982). For Carol Smart, the task of "feminist criminology" was initially to find "alternative modes of conceptualising the social world" (1976, 180); Mary McIntosh, on the other hand, saw it as bringing to the centre of the stage "the question of gross differences between male and female crime rates' (1977, 396). More recently, Maureen Cain (1986) suggested revealing the connections between 'policing' in everyday life and policing by and within official agencies as the appropriate agenda. Thus, just as we had to talk of "feminisms", we have to talk of feminist criminolog*ies*, or, better still, feminist perspectives within criminology.

However, we can identify certain core elements which we believe each would share. Feminist perspectives are, in essence, anti-positivist and critical of stereotypical images of women, and the question of women[8] is central. They share also an interest in using methodologies which are sympathetic to these concerns (Hanmer and Saunders, 1984). We believe the work which we discuss in the next sections meets these criteria.

[7] A simple demonstration of this is provided by the various responses of our immediate colleagues to the question "what does feminist criminology mean to you?" These ranged from consideration of "women's issues in the criminal justice system" and "making women visible in criminology" to "work by and for women" and a "a critical understanding of women, crime and the state". These are all very different enterprises, and, in isolation, do not constitute a "feminist criminology".

[8] We need to stress here that it is the question of *gender* which should be central, but most feminist work to date has primarily considered women.

Early Achievements in Criminology: Paradigms and Pitfalls

Early feminist writings focused on criminologists' "amnesia" of women.[9] To correct this, some writers appropriated existing criminological theories and "inserted" women. They assumed that women were hidden within the trajectory of theories developed to explain the criminality of men (Shacklady Smith, 1978; McRobbie, 1980). Other writers focused on the representation or, more accurately, the misrepresentation, of female offenders in conventional literature (Smart, 1976; Campbell, 1981). They developed a critique of "accumulated wisdom" about female offenders and attempted to determine why knowledge about them was shaped in the way it was, just as, on a more general level, feminists attempted to answer questions about the ways in which knowledge about women was sustained and mediated. These critiques demonstrated that theories of criminality developed from and validated on men had limited relevance for explaining women's crime. It was recognised that they were really only theories about men's crime. "Accumulated wisdom" was ambiguous, often flawed and, in many cases, simply untenable.

Much of the early feminist research consisted of exposés of discriminatory practices. Conventional criminology had assumed that women were dealt with more leniently than men in the criminal justice system (Mannheim, 1965; Walker, 1965). A whole generation of feminist researchers questioned this. They sought out and exposed the sexism which existed within the criminal justice system (Pearson, 1976; Carey, 1979; Casburn, 1979; Worrall, 1981; Eaton, 1983, 1985 and 1986; Carlen, 1983; Edwards, 1984) and, collectively, they demonstrated that the issue of women's treatment was complex. They highlighted the disparity between the rhetoric of leniency and the reality of practice. In addition, feminist researchers made visible women's victimisation, particularly in the area of sexual assault and domestic violence. Their work challenged many of the assumptions about and preconceptions of women who are victimised (Smart, 1976; Hanmer, 1978).

Each of these critical enterprises was important. Gender blindness is not a trivial oversight; it carries social and political significance. Moreover, theories which do not address gender are not merely incomplete; they are misleading.[10] But each of these enterprises has its limitations. First, the neglect of women in criminological theories cannot be viewed as systematic neglect, since the whole history of criminology's development is erratic. Women are not the only "blind spot": crimes of the powerful were also until recently ignored. Secondly, some writers seem to assume that "emptied of sexism" criminological theories would remain valid. This is patently not so (Greenwood, 1981, 73). Thirdly, feminist criticism assumes "sexism" in only those theories explicitly relating to women. This is an untenable assumption. Theories applied to men are also riddled with stereotypical images of men, masculinity, men's needs and desires and so on. The implicit assumption that men and boys have been dealt

---

[9] We need to acknowledge here the debt which British researchers owe to their North American counterparts. Much of the impetus for research here derives from their work in the 1970s. (See, for example, Klein and Kress, 1976; Klein, 1973; Datesman and Scarpitti, 1980; Chesney Lind, 1973 and 1978).

[10] Maureen Cain (1986, 258) describes such theories as "masculinist".

with "fairly" and in non-sexist terms is clearly wrong (Cousins, 1980). At the very least, such assumptions ignore differences in the treatment of men. They also ignore the fact that such factors as race, home circumstances, type of offence, demeanour and family commitments all clearly mediate the treatment of both female *and* male defendants. In fact, gender, in certain contexts, may not be as important as race or class (Greenwood, 1981). "Being a women" is obviously not a clear, single conceptual category; prospects, situations and experiences differ. It is surprising that many feminists writing on criminological topics ignore this.

Research has also suggested that sexist beliefs, where they exist, are mediated by administrative and organisational factors. Loraine Gelsthorpe (1986) has argued that simply to dismiss the criminal justice system and allied agencies as sexist obscures our understanding of the processing of offenders. What we need to know more precisely is how sexism works in practice. Thus in making sense of work in a police juvenile bureau, Gelsthorpe found that the need for officers to be seen to be "busy" and to be doing "real police work" had to be considered alongside any notion of sexism.

Feminists' claims about sexism also need to be examined at a theoretical level. Here too, considerable problems arise in attempts to follow through arguments that it is possible to identify, without equivocation, the "culprits" responsible for the treatment of women and for theoretical conceptions of them. In radical feminists' analyses, men are labelled as the key instigators of sexism, whereas socialist feminists promote the notion that the capitalist mode of production is instrumental in the exploitation of women. But neither men nor the capitalist mode of production can be singled out as chief conspirators in a plot against women. However ideas about women have been shaped, there is no one unified motivational force underlying that shaping (Kingdom, 1981; Cousins, 1980; Gelsthorpe, 1988).

More recent accounts of sexism have moved away from these reductionist explanations and have focused rather on ideological constructions of gender and on the concept of patriarchy (Kuhn and Wolpe, 1978; Barrett, 1980). But these new accounts have been generated, in the main, by women working outside mainstream criminology and, generally speaking, criminologists have been slow to assimilate them.

After the Critique

These critiques of existing accounts of women's crime and exposés of discriminatory practices were necessary enterprises but are not enough, *per se,* to shift the fundamental parameters and masculinity of criminology. A critique alone cannot constitute a theoretical approach. Indeed, Beverley Brown has argued that this critique has been responsible for "feminist criminology's" "failings and dead ends" (1986, 360). Earlier, Carol Smart (1982) had predicted that "feminist criminology" would "disappear into a theoretical cul-de-sac" or would be "resocialised into mainstream criminology unless feminists begin to re-assess the validity and purpose of their work so far". This takes us in two directions: consideration of more recent theoretical developments and examination of feminism's impact on mainstream criminology.

In 1976, Carol Smart discussed the possibility of formulating a "feminist criminology". By 1981, she viewed the task as redundant. There were, she wrote:

> more important goals to achieve than the one of constructing a sub-discipline to rank alongside other criminologies (1981, 86).[11]

Frances Heidensohn (1985) agrees with this. She concluded her text on *Women and Crime* by stating that the best way of understanding women and crime was not through "feminist criminology" but through:

> using insights into the role, position and social control of women which can be derived from other studies of women's oppression (1985, 197).

Thus one theme which has emerged in recent writings is a rejection of consideration of only those women who break the law. Instead discussion has centred on those who break the law, those who conform and the *relationship* between the two (see, for example, the edited collections of Smart and Smart, 1978 and Hutter and Williams, 1981). Bridget Hutter and Gillian Williams justify this in the following way:

> Examination of the explicit controls exercised over women who are seen as deviant because they act in ways beyond the bounds of "normal society" helps us to clarify (the) concept of "normal behaviour". Furthermore, it allows us to see more clearly the extent and nature of the covert controls employed to persuade all women to fit their behaviour into this normal pattern (1981: 9).

Heidensohn (1985, 197) views this approach as "ultimately the best way to understand women and crime".

This shift in emphasis is welcome, but it is important to be rather more specific. By focusing on general networks of control we may learn *who* fractures the boundaries of "acceptable behaviour and normal, natural trouble" (Gelsthorpe, 1985) and *how* they fracture them,[12] but we will not necessarily learn *why* women offend and we may thereby leave unchallenged models of crime causation which stress individual pathology. The difficulty is accommodating individual motivation within a broad context of structural constraints. In a different sphere, Carol Smart (1984) provides an illustration of how this can be done.[13] She points to the interactions between social institutions and every day life experiences which deepen our understanding of the pressures to

[11] Carol Smart's writings reflect this. They indicate a move away from criminology into issues within the sociology of law, family law, sexuality and reproduction and the construction of women's roles and identities as mediated through different social disciplines.

[12] This is not just a contemporary concern. Historical re-constructions of illegality are significant too (Sumner, 1980).

[13] See also Willis (1977) and Sharp, Green and Lewis (1975).

conform or deviate. Criminologists have not yet fully taken on the significance of this. Exploration of social control issues is essential to an increased understanding of *how* knowledge is sustained and mediated and *how* structural constraints affect our everyday lives. But the danger in this kind of approach is that generalisations are made about the success or failure of particular control mechanisms and we may inpute to individuals motives which are not theirs. Individual experiences are lost in the account.

Considering Feminism's Impact

We turn now to consider the impact of feminism on mainstream criminology. As Frances Heidensohn (1987, 21) succinctly put it:

> Has anyone . . . been listening? Have they taken it seriously? Have they changed their minds, their research studies or their institutional practices?

We noted earlier that it was not uncommon even in the 1970s for criminological textbooks, including critical reviews, to contain nothing at all on women. There are still examples of this in the 1980s. Frances Heidensohn (1987, 23) provides two: Stan Cohen's (1985) *Visions of Social Control* and David Downes and Paul Rock's (1982) *Understanding Deviance*. Heidensohn describes *Visions of Social Control* as "fundamentally flawed" as it takes no account of the gender dimensions of social control and is critical of Downes and Rock's failure to consider gender in their assessment of the validity of various deviancy theories.

   Some criminologists have attempted to take account of the criticism raised by feminists, but these attempts seem to us no more than token gestures. Stuart Hall and Phil Scraton (1981), for example, in a review article of current debates in critical criminology, refer to the emergence of a "feminist criminology" but thereafter ignore any significance that this might have for the issues raised. For instance, reference is made to the economic marginalisation of black youth (1981, 484), but not to the economic position of women generally or of black girls in particular. Similarly, they refer to the "poor taking advantage of the poor" (1981, 485); they take no cognisance of men taking advantage of women. The point is not that "women" should be discussed for the mere sake of it, but that their inclusion would have enriched theoretically the points being explored by Hall and Scraton. Another example is Jock Young's review of "models of criminology" in the same text, in which he systematically compares theories "on the central questions which any theory of order and criminality must tackle" (1981, 305). Young dutifully refers to he/she and him/her throughout. But the relevance or significance of gender for the theories reviewed is never explored. To borrow from Paul Rock (1977), the use of such language *is* a mere literary convention. It had no impact on Young's subject matter.

   A variant of this is what Frances Heidensohn (1987, 23) calls the "lean-to" approach. The contrast between the first (1971) and second (1981) editions of

Steven Box's *Deviance, Reality and Society* provides a demonstration of this. There is nothing at all on women in the first. In the second, about a page on self-report studies by girls is included in the chapter on the social distribution of criminal behaviour, two "caveats"—each no more than one and a half pages—are added to two further chapters and a small note on female inmates is added to another chapter. This is better than nothing. But women are presented as after-thoughts, not as integral to the arguments being developed in the chapters. Thus women appear as "by the way" and peripheral. For all intents and purposes, they are not really there.[14]

This is apparent in teaching and research too. Although most universities now include at least a few lectures on women and crime and some include whole courses, these highlight precisely the *failure* not the success of feminists to permeate the discipline (cf. Brown, 1986). The lectures are insertions, addenda and, therefore, marginal. There has undoubtedly been a tremendous increase in the amount of research on women and crime. Frances Heidensohn (1987, 16) describes this as a significant development in itself. But this research has primarily been the domain of women (often research students, at that) and small-scale.[15]

"Gender" has not become a critical issue on the criminological agenda.[16] Perusal of recent volumes of the British Journal of Criminology demonstrates this. These volumes contain titles which refer to "adult offenders", "abnormal offenders", "lifers", "black minority criminals", "children", "prisoners" and so on. On closer examination, these papers deal only with men. There are other articles which are clearly based on research which had mixed samples, but the significance of gender is rarely fully explored.

There is, arguably, an exception to this in what can broadly be called "victimology". Feminist thinking on violence against women has matured over the last ten years. In the 1970s feminists highlighted women as victims, particularly victims of sexual assault and domestic violence. However, each topic tended then to be treated in a discrete fashion. The emphasis in feminist research now has shifted. Male violence is more often treated as a "unitary phenomenon" along with other forms of male power (Edwards, 1987, 15). Examples of this are the work of Jalna Hanmer and Sheila Saunders (1984) and Ruth Hall (1985). Thus male violence is seen as socially constructed, socially produced and, to some extent, socially legitimated.

Roger Matthews and Jock Young (1986, 2) claim that it was feminist research on victims which brought home to them "the limits of the romantic

[14] See also McRobbie and Garber's (1976) critique.

[15] In recent years, the Home Office has funded one project on the effects of age-mixing in women's prisons (Genders and Player, 1986 and 1987) and is currently funding a project on mothers and babies in prison. The ESRC has funded one project on the transition of girls from school to work and a fellowship which enabled a female academic to carry out interviews with female prisoners and offenders (Carlen, 1987).

[16] We asked our immediate colleagues what impact they thought feminism had had on their work. Some acknowledged that it had none; they felt that it had no relevance for research on men or that they worked in areas in which there were "no gender issues". Others acknowledged a critical awareness. But the main theme which came across was that feminism was the property of a particular group or kind of woman. It was viewed as an exclusive, separatist activity.

conception of crime and the criminal".[17] And Trevor Jones, Brian Maclean and Jock Young (1986, 3) attribute "feminist victimology" with creating "enormous theoretical problems for the radical paradigm in criminology". Hence in the latter volume they examine gender differences in perceptions of risk, fears for personal safety, avoidance behaviours and victimisation and show not only that women are more fearful than men, but that they have good reasons for this. Yet there is a startling omission: they ignore the significance of gender relations as a central factor in understanding most crimes against women and make no reference to a key concept for a feminist understanding of these crimes: male power. It is never made explicit that women's fear of crime is women's fear of men. Their recommendations for change, for example, primarily focus on improving policing. As Betsy Stanko (1987, 123) succinctly puts it: "women's fear of criminal violence is reported ... but ... not their experience of violence".

In sum, then, the experience of feminism within criminology seems to us no different from that in other academic disciplines. There is undoubtedly an awareness of the existence of feminism—the invitation to write this paper demonstrates that—but feminism is viewed as the property of "others", "outsiders" even.[18]

The Significance of Feminism for Criminology

We agree with Frances Heidensohn (1987, 27) that "criminology is poorer in all its forms" because it has "not yet fully accepted and integrated" the importance of gender, let alone the interaction of gender with such factors as race and class.

Theories are weak if they do not apply to half of the potential criminal population; women, after all, experience the same deprivations, family structures and so on that men do. Theories of crime should be able to take account of both men's and women's behaviour and to highlight those factors which operate differently on men and women. Whether or not a particular theory helps us to understand women's crime better is of fundamental, not marginal, importance for criminology.

But the significance of feminism goes beyond this. For us, feminism is a mode of analysis; a perspective rather than a theory. This leads us to consider methodology. Sue Clegg (1985) has argued that there is no one coherent, unified set of methodological practices and principles which runs through feminist studies and we agree. However, there are methodological preferences within feminism and some writers have identified core elements in feminist approaches to research (Acker et al., 1983; Kelly, 1978).

---

[17] Young (1986, 27) later in the same volume suggests that feminist criminologists have forced radicals to re-examine their positions on punishment.

[18] It could be argued that feminists have identified certain areas as their own and have excluded men, but there are defensible reasons for this. In debates on pornography, for example, women may need to feel "safe" and this, at least in the short term, may mean excluding men for both emotional and practical reasons.

Liz Stanley and Sue Wise (1983) have usefully identified four main themes linking feminism and research in the social sciences: women should be made visible; research should be on, by and for women; non-sexist methodologies should be employed; and feminist research should have practical import and political impact. The research should, therefore, be useful to the women's movement.[19] In short, the "core elements" are "feminist consciousness" and "the personal is political". For some researchers, this has meant a preference for small-scale qualitative work which seeks to understand individuals' situations (Edwards, 1984) and which encourages subjects to participate in the research process (Roberts, 1981; Dobash and Gutteridge, 1986; Carlen, 1985 and 1987).

It might be easy enough to accept these dictates for research on women, but feminist perspectives have implications for research in criminology more generally. This leads us to re-examine the "on, by and for women" dictate more closely and, consequently, to question the exclusion of men from the feminist enterprise, both as research subjects and researchers. First, then, can men—for example, judges, police officers, prisoners or rapists—be the subjects of feminist research? Maureen Cain (1986) believes that they can if the requirement in feminist research that those investigated remain active subjects in the research process is altered slightly. Her revised version demands only that the subjectivity of those investigated should be taken into account. She explores this distinction through the hypothetical example of a feminist doing research on the Association of Police Officers.

A concrete example of a feminist approach to research on men is provided by the recent experience of one of us in carrying out research in men's prisons. The prime focus of that research was "to consider the concept of humane containment in a context of security and control. The research proposal made no mention of gender issues.[20] Despite this, the issue of gender had important consequences for the nature and structure of the research, particularly on the style of interviewing and on the content of discussions. There are four points to be made. Firstly, the two female researchers involved did not view those they spoke with as research "objects" or as "mere informants". Although their conversations with the prisoners involved an unequal balance of power—their clothes, tape recorders and freedom to walk round the prison gave them authority, much as they tried to resist it—their vulnerability as women enabled them to some extent to share the men's vulnerability as prisoners. Secondly, they did not restrict conversations to the research questions. Indeed, at times they dismissed the pre-designed questions and invited prisoners to redefine them so that between them they came up with the questions which were important to the prisoners. Thirdly, they tried to include in their discussions with the men, whether prisoners or prison officers, some reference to the impact of their life in prison on their wives, partners and children. Fourthly, they attempted to meet the women visiting men in prison and partners of

[19] This is an area in which many researchers fail, but there are studies, particularly on women as victims, which are linked with political action (Hanmer and Saunders, 1984).

[20] However, the Project Director did consciously set out to employ at least one woman for the field-work and, in fact, both field-workers were women.

prison officers and to learn from them directly something of their prison experiences. Thus the researchers tried to gain some insights into the meaning of imprisonment for the women who served out the men's sentences or worked out their men's shifts at home, for these affected men's experience of imprisonment. The point is that as feminist women the researchers felt it inappropriate to deny women's experiences. Gender awareness meant that they had to analyse men in relation to women as well as to other men. The general consensus of the research group was that feminism had in these ways added an important dimension to the project.

The question of whether or not men can engage in feminist research is more complex. Can men incorporate a feminist perspective, or do women have a monopoly of knowledge or understanding of feminist issues (Morgan, 1981)? It is possible to argue that women should be given the time and space to develop feminist perspectives in their own way, using their own language and not the categories and concepts provided for them by men and in traditional methodologies. At the same time, there is a strong argument for encouraging men to consider and make use of feminist perspectives. Men may not share women's oppression, but through research they may move to some comprehension of it. There is a distinction between feminism (and the emotional and political commitment which this entails) and feminist perspectives. Men may not be able to be truly involved in the former, but can share the latter.

In response to Paul Rock's challenges in the 1970s, it seems to us that feminism has much to offer women *and* men within criminological areas.*

REFERENCES

ACKER, J., BARRY, K., EASEVELD, J. (1983). "Objectivity and truth: problems of doing feminist research". *Women's Studies International Forum*. **6,** 423–435.

ADLER, F. (1975). *Sisters of Crime*. New York, McGraw-Hill.

BANKS, O. (1981). *Faces of Feminism*. Oxford, Martin Robertson.

BARKER, D. L. and ALLEN, S. (eds.) (1976). *Sexual Divisions and Society: Process and Change*. London, Tavistock.

BARRETT, M. (1980). *Women's Oppression Today*. London, Verso.

BOUCHIER, D. (1978). *Idealism and Revolution: New Ideologies of Liberation in Britain and the United States*. London, Edward Arnold.

BOUCHIER, D. (1983). *The Feminist Challenge*. London, Macmillan.

BOX, S. (1971). *Deviance, Reality and Society*. London, Holt, Rinehart and Winston.

BOX, S. (1981). *Deviance, Reality and Society* (2nd Edition). London, Holt, Rinehart and Winston.

BOX, S. (1983). *Power, Crime and Mystification*. London, Tavistock.

BROPHY, J. and SMART, C. (1985). *Women in Law*. London, Routledge and Kegan Paul.

*We would like to thank Maria Beleza, Tony Bottoms, Anne Bottomley, Maureen Cain, Janet Finch, Kathy McDermott, Lorna Smith, Colin Sumner, Nigel Walker and Warren Young for their helpful comments on an earlier draft.

105

BROWN, R. K. (1976). "Women as Employees: some comments on research in industrial sociology, in D. L. Barker and S. Allen (eds.), *Sexual Divisions and Society: Process and Change*. London, Tavistock.

BROWN, B. (1986). "Women and Crime: the dark figures of criminology". *Economy and Society*. **15,** 355–402.

CAIN, M. (1986). "Realism, Feminism, Methodology, and Law". *International Journal of the Sociology of Law*. **14,** 255–267.

CAIN, M. (1986). "Socio-Legal Studies and Social Justice for Women: Some Working Notes on a Method". Paper prepared for Australian Law and Society Association Conference, December 1986.

CAMPBELL, A. (1981). *Girl Delinquents*. Oxford, Basil Blackwell.

CAREY, K. (1979). "Police Policy and the Prosecution". Paper presented to British Sociological Association Conference (unpublished).

CARLEN, P. (1983). *Women's Imprisonment*. London, Routledge and Kegan Paul.

CARLEN, P. (1985). *Criminal Women*. Cambridge, Polity Press.

CARLEN, P. (1987). "Out of Care, into Custody: Dimensions and Deconstructions of the State's Regulation of Twenty-two Young Working-Class Women", in P. Carlen and A. Worrall (eds), *Gender, Crime and Justice*. Milton Keynes, Open University Press.

CASBURN, M. (1979). *Girls Will Be Girls*. London, Women's Research and Resources Centre.

CHESNEY-LIND, M. (1973). "Judicial enforcement of the female sex role: the family court and the female delinquent". *Issues in Criminology*. **8,** 51–69.

CHESNEY-LIND, M. (1978). "Chivalry re-examined: women and the criminal justice system" in L. H. Bowker (ed.) *Women, Crime and the Criminal Justice System*. Massachusetts, Lexington.

CLARRICOATES, K. (1980). "All in a day's work" in D. Spender and E. Sarah (eds), *Learning to Lose: Sexism and Education*. London, The Women's Press.

CLEGG, S. (1985). "Feminist Methodology—Fact or Fiction?", *Quality and Quantity*, **19,** 83–97.

COHEN, S. (1985). *Visions of Social Control*. Cambridge, Polity Press.

COOTE, A. and CAMPBELL, B. (1987). *Sweet Freedom: the Struggle for Women's Liberation* (2nd Edition). Oxford, Basil Blackwell.

COUSINS, M. "Mens Rea: a note on sexual difference, criminology and the law" in P. Carlen and M. Collison (eds.) *Radical Issues in Criminology*. Oxford, Martin Robertson.

COWIE, J., COWIE, V. and SLATER, E. (1968). *Delinquency in Girls*. London, Heinemann.

DATESMAN, S. and SCARPITTI, F. (eds.) (1980). *Women, Crime and Justice*. New York, Oxford University Press.

DAVID, M. E. (1985). "Motherhood and social policy—a matter of education?". *Critical Social Policy*. Issue 12, Spring, 28–43.

DE BEAUVOIR, S. (1953). *The Second Sex*, (Le Deuxième Sexe, Published in 1949) English translation published by Jonathon Cape.

DELMAR, R. (1986). "What is Feminism" in J. Mitchell and H. Oakley (eds.), *What is Feminism*. Oxford, Basil Blackwell.

DOBASH, R., DOBASH, R. E. and GUTTERIDGE, S. (1986). *The Imprisonment of Women*. Oxford, Basil Blackwell.

DOWNES, D. and ROCK, P. (1982). *Understanding Deviance*. Oxford, Clarendon.

DOYAL, L. with PENNELL, I. (1979). *The Political Economy of Health*. London, Pluto.

EATON, M. (1983). "Mitigating Circumstances: Familiar Rhetoric". *International Journal of the Sociology of Law*. **11,** 385–400.

EATON, M. (1985). "Documenting the Defendent" in J. Brophy and C. Smart (eds), *Women in Law*. London, Routledge and Kegan Paul.

EATON, M. (1986). *Justice for Women? Family, Court and Social Control*. Milton Keynes, Open University Press.

EDWARDS, S. S. M. (1984). *Women on Trial*. Manchester, Manchester University Press.

EDWARDS, S. S. M. (1987). "Prostitutes: Victims of Law, Social Policy and Organised Crime" in P. Carlen and A. Worrall (eds.), *Gender, Crime and Justice*. Milton Keynes, Open University Press.

EICHLER, M. (1980). *The Double Standard: A Feminist Critique of Feminist Social Science*. London, Croom Helm.

EVANS, R. J. (1977). *The Feminists Women's Emancipation Movements in Europe, America and Australasia 1840–1920*. London, Croom Helm.

FIRESTONE, S. (1971). *The Dialectic of Sex: The Case for Feminist Revolution*. London, Jonathon Cape.

FRANKENBERG, R. (1976). "In the production of their lives, men (?) ... sex and gender in British Community Studies", in D. L. Barker and S. Allen (eds), *Sexual Divisions and Society: Process and Change*. London, Tavistock.

GELSTHORPE, L. R. (1985). "Normal, natural trouble: girls and juvenile justice". *Lay Panel Magazine*. **13,** Northern Ireland Juvenile Courts Association.

GELSTHORPE, L. R. (1986). "Towards Sceptical Look at Sexism". *International Journal of the Sociology of Law*. **14,** 125–152.

GELSTHORPE, L. R. (1988). *Sexism, Crime and Justice*. (forthcoming), Gower.

GILLIGAN, C. (1982). *In a Different Voice*. Cambridge, U.S.A., Harvard University Press.

GREENWOOD, V. (1981). "The myths of female crime", in A. M. Morris with L. R. Gelsthorpe (eds.), *Women and Crime*. Cropwood Conference Series No. 13. Cambridge, Institute of Criminology.

GREER, G. (1971). *The Female Eunuch*. London, MacGibbon and Kee.

GREGORY, J. (1986). "Sex, class and crime: towards a non-sexist criminology", in R. Matthews and J. Young (eds.), *Confronting Crime*. London, Sage.

HALL, R. E. (1985). *Ask Any Woman: A London Inquiry into Rape and Sexual Assault*. Bristol, Falling Wall Press.

HALL, S. and SCRATON, P. (1981). "Law, class and control" in Fitzgerald, M., McLennan, G. and Pawson, J. (eds.), *Crime and Society*. London, Routledge and Kegan Paul.

HANMER, J. (1978). "Violence and the Social Control of Women" in Littlejohn, G. *et al.* (eds.) *Power and the State*. London, Croom Helm.

HANMER, J. and SAUNDERS, S. (1984). *Well Founded Fear*. London, Hutchinson.

HEIDENSOHN, F. M. (1968). "The Deviance of Women: A Critique and an Enquiry". *British Journal of Sociology*. **19,** 160–173.

HEIDENSOHN, F. M. (1986). "Models of Justice: Portia or Persephone? Some Thoughts on Equality, Fairness and Gender in the Field of Criminal Justice", *International Journal of the Sociology of Law.* **14,** 287–298.

HEIDENSOHN, F. M. (1977). Review Symposium on *Women, Crime and Criminology,* Smart, C. *British Journal of Criminology.* **17,** 390–392.

HEIDENSOHN, F. M. (1970). "Sex, crime and society" in G. A. Harrison and J. Perl (eds.), *Biosocial Aspects of Sex.* Oxford, Basil Blackwell.

HEIDENSOHN, F. M. (1987). "Women and Crime: Questions for Criminology" in P. Carlen and A. Worrall, (eds.), *Gender, Crime and Justice.* Milton Keynes, Open University Press.

HEIDENSOHN, F. M. (1985). *Women and Crime.* London, Macmillan and New York University Press.

HUTTER, B. and WILLIAMS, G. (eds.) (1981). *Controlling Women.* London, Croom Helm in association with the Oxford University Women's Studies Committee.

JONES, T., MACLEAN, B. and YOUNG, J. (1986). *The Islington Crime Survey.* Aldershot, Gower.

KELLY, A. (1978). "Feminism and Research". *Womens Studies International Quarterly.* **1,** 225–232.

KINGDOM, E. (1981). "Sexist bias and law" in edited volume *Politics and Power.* London, Routledge and Kegan Paul.

KLEIN, D. (1973). "The etiology of female crime: a review of the literature". *Issues in Criminology.* **8,** 3–30.

KLEIN, D. and KRESS, J. (1976). "Any woman's blues: a critical overview of women, crime and the criminal justice system". *Crime and Social Justice.* **5,** 34–49.

KRESS, J. (1979). "Bourgeois Morality and the Administration of Criminal Justice". *Crime and Social Justice,* no. 12, 44–50.

KUHN, A. and WOLPE, A. M. (eds.) (1978) *Feminism and Materialism.* London, Routledge and Kegan Paul.

McINTOSH, M. (1977). Review Symposium on *Women, Crime and Criminology.* Smart, C. *British Journal of Criminology,* **17,** 395–397.

McINTOSH, M. (1978). "The State and the oppression of women" in A. Kuhn and A. M. Wolpe (eds.), *Feminism and Materialism.* London, Routledge and Kegan Paul.

McROBBIE, A. (1980). "Settling accounts with subcultures: a feminist critique". *Screen Education.* 34, 37–49.

McROBBIE, A. and GARBEC, J. (1976). "Girls and Subcultures" in S. Hall and T. Jefferson, (eds.), *Resistance Through Rituals.* London, Hutchinson.

MANNHEIM, H. (1965). *Comparative Criminology.* London, Routledge and Kegan Paul.

MATTHEWS, R. and YOUNG, J. (eds) (1986). *Confronting Crime.* London, Sage.

MILLET, K. (1971). *Sexual Politics.* New York, Doubleday.

MILLMAN, M. (1975). "She did it all for love: a feminist view of the sociology of deviance" in M. Millman and R. Moss Kanter (eds.), *Another Voice: Feminist Perspectives on Social Life and Social Science.* New York, Anchor Books.

MITCHELL, J. and OAKLEY, A. (eds.) (1986) *What is Feminism?* Oxford, Basil Blackwell.

MORGAN, D. (1981). "Men, masculinity and the process of sociological enquiry" in H. Roberts (ed.), *Doing Feminist Research.* London, Routledge and Kegan Paul.

MORONEY, H. (1986). "Feminism at Work" in J. Mitchell and A. Oakley (eds.), *What is Feminism?* Oxford, Basil Blackwell.

MOULDS, E. (1980). "Chivalry and Paternalism: Disparities of Treatment in the Criminal Justice System" in S. Datesman and F. Scarpitti, (eds.), *Women, Crime and Justice.* New York, Oxford University Press.

OAKLEY, A. (1979). *Becoming a Mother.* London, Martin Robertson.

OAKLEY, A. (1986). "Feminism, Motherhood and Medicine—Who Cares?" in J. Mitchell and A. Oakley (eds.) *What is Feminism?* Oxford, Basil Blackwell.

OAKLEY, A. (1981). *Subject Women.* Oxford, Martin Robertson.

O'DONOVAN, K. (1985). *Sexual Divisions in Law.* London, Weidenfeld and Nicolson.

PEARSON, R. (1976). "Women defendants in magistrates' courts". *British Journal of Law and Society.* **3,** 265–273.

RICHARDS, J. R. (1982). *The Sceptical Feminist.* Harmondsworth, Penguin.

ROBERTS, H. Ed. (1981). *Doing Feminist Research.* London, Routledge and Kegan Paul.

ROCK, P. E. (1977). Review Symposium on *Women, Crime and Criminology.* Smart, C. *British Journal of Criminology.* **17,** 392–395.

RODWELL, S. (1981). "Men, Women and Sexuality: a feminist critique of the sociology of deviance". *Women's Studies International Quarterly.* **4,** 145–155.

RUTH, S. (1981). "Methodocracy, Misogyny and Bad Faith: The Response of Philosophy" in D. Spender (ed.), *Men's Studies Modified.* Oxford, Pergamon Press.

RUZEK, S. (1986). "Feminist Visions of Health: An International Perspective" in J. Mitchell and A. Oakley (eds.), *What is Feminism?* Oxford, Basil Blackwell.

SHACKLADY, SMITH, L. (1978). "Sexist assumptions and female delinquency: an empirical investigation" in C. Smart and B. Smart (eds.), *Women, Sexuality and Social Control.* London, Routledge and Kegan Paul.

SHARP, R., GREEN, A. and LEWIS, J. (1975). *Education and Social Control.* London, Routledge and Kegan Paul.

SHAW, J. (1976). "Finishing School: some implications of sex segregated education" in D. L. Barker and S. Allen (eds.), *Sexual Divisions and Society: Process and Change.* London, Tavistock.

SIMON, R. J. (1975). *Women and Crime.* USA, Lexington, D.C. Heath & Co.

SMART, C. (1986). "Feminism and Law: some Problems of Analysis and Strategy". *International Journal of the Sociology of Law.* **14,** 109–123.

SMART, C. (1981). "Response to Greenwood" in A. M. Morris and L. R. Gelsthorpe (eds.), *Women and Crime.* Cropwood Conference Series no. 13. Cambridge, Institute of Criminology.

SMART, C. (1982). Review, *Critical Social Policy.* **2,** 99–101.

SMART, C. (1976). *Women, Crime and Criminology: a Feminist Critique.* London, Routledge and Kegan Paul.

SMART, C. and SMART, B. (1978). *Women, Sexuality and Social Control.* London, Routledge and Kegan Paul.

SMART, C. (1984). *The Ties that Bind: Law, Marriage and the Reproduction of Patriarchal Relations.* London, Routledge and Kegan Paul.

SMITH, A. (1962). *Women in Prison.* London, Stevens.

SPENDER, D. ed., (1981). *Men's Studies Modified. The Impact of Feminism on the Academic Disciplines.* Oxford, Pergamon Press, The Athene Series.

STACEY, J. and THORNE, B. (1985). "The missing feminist revolution in sociology", *Social Problems*. **32,** 301–316.

STACEY, M. (1981). "The Division of Labour Revisited or Overcoming the Two Adams" in P. Abrams, R. Deem, J. Finch and P. Rock (eds.), *Practice and Progress: British Sociology 1950–1980*. London, George Allen and Unwin.

STANKO, E. A. (1987). "Typical Violence, Normal Precaution: Men, Women and Interpersonal Violence in England, Wales, Scotland and the USA", in J. Hanmer and M. Maynard (eds.), *Women, Violence and Social Control*. British Sociological Association. Hampshire, Macmillan.

STANLEY, L. and WISE, S. (1983). *Breaking Out: Feminist Consciousness and Feminist Research*. London, Routledge and Kegan Paul.

STEFFENSMEIER, D. J. (1978). "Crime and the Contemporary Woman, an analysis of changing levels of female property crime, 1960–1975". *Social Forces*. **57,** 566–584.

SUMNER, M. (1980). Prostitution and Images of Women: a critique of the Victorian Censure of prostitution. Unpublished M.Sc. *thesis*, University of Wales.

WALKER, B. M. (1981) "Psychology and Feminism—if you can't beat them, join them", in D. Spender (ed.), *Men's Studies Modified*. Oxford, Pergamon Press.

WALKER, N. D. (1965). *Crime and Punishment in Britain*. Edinburgh, University of Edinburgh Press.

WILLIS, P. (1977). *Learning to Labour*. London, Saxon House.

WORRALL, A. J. (1981). "Out of Place: Female Offenders in Court", *Probation Journal*. **28,** 90–93.

YOUNG, J. (1986). "The Failure of Criminology: the Need for a Radical Realism" in Matthews, R. and Young J. (eds.), *Confronting Crime, London, Sage*.

CRIMINAL JUSTICE AND THE CRIMINAL PROCESS

Andrew Ashworth (*Oxford*)*

"Criminal justice" is a term broad enough to encompass most of the concerns of penology, if not of criminology. By associating it with "the criminal process" in the title, the focus is fixed specifically upon the various decision-making stages through which a person suspected of crime is processed before, during or instead of court proceedings. The formal structure is provided by the criminal law, the law of criminal procedure and the law of sentencing. Significant actors involved in the process include not only the suspect/defendant and any legal adviser or representative for the defence, but also police, prosecutors, magistrates, judges, clerks and others.

Among the many and varied developments in this wide field, it is possible to discern four phases in British criminologists' approaches to criminal justice and the criminal process in the last fifty years. First, there was the positivist phase of the 1940s and 1950s; second, the empiricist phase, predominant in the 1960s and 1970s; third, the revisiting of the law in the late 1970s and early 1980s, characterised by the re-examination of legal rhetoric and by emergence studies; and fourth, the rise of "left realism" in the 1980s. It will be readily apparent that the phases have not been chronologically separate even if, in general terms, they reached their ascendancy one after the other. Moreover, there have been other currents of thought which have left their mark. On the other hand, the very notion of "criminal justice" rings a conceptual bell to which many British criminologists have not, for one reason or another, responded. Rather than attempting a stage–by–stage unfolding of the history, the aim here is to offer an assessment of the strengths and weaknesses of some of the main developments.

Whatever may now be thought of the positivism which prevailed in the years before and after the Second World War, the British criminologists of the time lost little opportunity to advance concrete proposals for reform of the legal structure. For them the most significant stage of the criminal process was sentencing, and the leading aim there should have been to find the most suitable and effective treatment for each offender. Thus the great works of Mannheim (1939, ch. VI) and Grünhut (1948, pp. 458–463) contain carefully argued cases for drawing experts and professionals more into the sentencing process, and show a willingness to discuss the details of law and procedure which is absent from most subsequent criminological writing. Even in this period, however, sentencing disparity was present as an issue (e.g. Mannheim, 1948, pp. 229–230), and it was not long before empirical studies of the phenomenon began to appear. Two studies of sentencing in juvenile

*Fellow and Tutor in Law, Worcester College; Associate, Centre for Criminological Research, University of Oxford.

courts sowed the seeds of an empirical phase which was to flourish in the next two decades (Grünhut, 1956; Mannheim, Spencer and Lynch, 1958). Yet variations in the use of sentences from court to court are not necessarily a cause for concern to the positivist, even if they offend popular conceptions of criminal justice, and these developments suggest that positivism never entirely replaced retributivism among British criminologists of the time.

What is striking about many of these works is that the early stages of the criminal process—the decision to prosecute, bail, charging, plea and so on—were hardly noticed, and were regarded as largely unproblematic in great enterprises such as the Cambridge study of sexual offences, which lavished considerable attention on the sentences given and on the law and its reform (Radzinowicz, 1956). One of the achievements of British criminology in the thirty years since then has been to reveal the extent to which the criminal process in practice differs from the law in the books. Perhaps the point was implicit rather than ignored in the earlier works. Sociologists would never assume that the law in the books is meticulously translated into practice in every respect. No practising lawyer would make this assumption either: for almost all purposes the law is what legal practice is, and any new statute or decision is soon surrounded and enveloped by working practices which push and pull, this way and that. This leaves those traditional law teachers who present the criminal law as a set of rules with its internal logic and dynamics—who engage in critical analysis within this structure but see no need to explain and evaluate the ways in which it actually impinges on citizens, and no need to relate the criminal law to the social structure. Fortunately this tradition is now receding from the law schools, although criminology still tends to have less influence there than in departments of sociology, psychology, social administration and so on.

There are few who would now propound the view that the centrepiece of the English criminal process is the trial, and that the few earlier procedures are merely designed to ensure that no one is put on trial unless there is a good case against them and that dangerous people are kept in custody before trial. This is because criminological research and criminologists have exposed aspects of the "real" criminal process. Perhaps the major discoveries were made in the sphere generally termed "plea bargaining", where three studies in the 1970s showed the significance of this in determining the outcome of cases, and its impact on defendants (McCabe and Purves, 1972a; Bottoms and McClean, 1976; Baldwin and McConville, 1977). The attempts of the legal establishment to marginalise and even to discredit (Napley, 1977) the findings of Baldwin and McConville failed: the researchers had indeed taken the word of convicted criminals, but a steady stream of cases coming before the Court of Appeal provided an embarrassing source of evidence of improprieties[1] and made the protestations of the legal profession seem too much. It could soon be asserted, on the basis of an official report (Fisher, 1978) and broader English research (McConville and Baldwin, 1981), that the whole construction of the prosecution case is often aimed from the outset at avoidance of a trial. A

[1] Most of these cases are discussed by Baldwin and McConville (1979b).

full-dress trial may be less of a centrepiece than a monument to the failure of the many pre-trial machinations to produce a guilty plea.

So the vast majority of criminal cases result in a guilty plea. There is no trial: the significant decisions are taken out of court. Maybe there has been a tendency to under-estimate the numbers of defendants who plead guilty because they accept their guilt,[2] and therefore voluntarily yield what some regard as their constitutional right. But an accurate description of the criminal process must now take account of the pressures towards the avoidance of the very adversary procedure which is said to characterise it—pressures to confess, to accept summary trial in many cases and to plead guilty to one or more charges. Many of these pressures have been exerted by the police from their position of great practical power over suspects and defendants. Research into the police is being discussed elsewhere in this special issue, but at least some mention of their influence must be made here. It has become a commonplace that early decisions in the criminal process seem strongly associated with and determinative of later decisions, and the power of the police in relation to police bail, court bail, the decision to prosecute and choice of charge has been considerable. To what extent this practical power will diminish in the wake of the Royal Commission on Criminal Procedure (1981) and the subsequent legal reforms remains to be seen. But to reform the procedures is not to alter the process, any more than the previous procedures determined the process. Will the procedures of the Police and Criminal Evidence Act 1984 constrain the police, or will it amount to pouring new wine into old bottles? Will the Crown Prosecution Service, with its potentially wide range of influence (decision to prosecute, choice of charge, mode of trial, plea negotiation), act independently of the police or identify with their concerns? Research already completed on prosecution practice in this country (Moody and Tombs, 1982; Sanders, 1985a, 1985b; Mansfield and Peay, 1986) suggests that the gap between rhetoric and reality will not easily be closed.

The body of research, then, makes it appear unlikely that the regular personnel of the criminal process—police, prosecutors, defence lawyers, court clerks, magistrates and judges—will forsake their predilection for the avoidance of trials. The adversary element in criminal justice will remain as the tip of the iceberg, with large numbers of cases processed in the murky world of exchange and barter beneath. It is worth reflecting that one of the few procedural innovations of recent years, the pre-trial review, involves a meeting of lawyers in the absence of the defendant (see Baldwin, 1985). The working routines of the various groups, their goals and the aspirations of individual members, become both a key to understanding practice and an identifiable restraint on the dynamics of change. To offer pressure of case-load as an explanation for many of these practices is unconvincing. There is often a subcultural understanding of what is good craftsmanship, what earns respect from colleagues, what assists working relationships with adversaries, what eases one's own job, what pays, and so on (Bankowski and Mungham, 1976;

---

[2] Bottoms and McClean (1976, p. 115) found that some two-thirds of their sample said that they pleaded guilty because they were guilty, but this does not rule out the possibility that behind the "get it over with" attitude lay a fear or mistrust of the criminal process.

McConville and Baldwin, 1981; Baldwin, 1985). Such sub-cultural under-
standings place defendants at a disadvantage in determining the course of
their case—almost a parallel with the alienation and confusion experienced
by some defendants in court, unfamiliar with the procedures, language and
geography of the courtroom (Carlen, 1976). Whether the spread of legal aid
and duty solicitor schemes will alter these experiences seems doubtful on past
evidence (Carlen, 1976; Bankowski and Mungham, 1976), but there may now
be more lawyers willing to break the mould rather than allow themselves to be
co–opted into a pattern of "professional" relationships.

Criminologists have, then, succeeded in dragging some low visibility practices into the arena of evaluation and appraisal. Yet visibility is more like a
necessary than a sufficient condition. Sentencing is visible, in that it takes
place in open court, but it is little trammelled by law or by legal accountability. There had long been laws which set maximum penalties and
empowered courts to impose certain types of sentence, but the development of
legal principles to guide the exercise of this vast discretion was slow. The
position in England has improved considerably in the last twenty-five years,
with regular reporting of sentencing decisions and academic commentaries
upon them (see Thomas, 1979), and a growing number of principles and
guidelines laid down by the Court of Appeal. Yet actual practice remains
elusive. The Lord Chief Justice has declared that the textbooks give a fairly
clear account of the factors which judges take into account in sentencing,
regarding this as a justification for prohibiting empirical research designed to
test the assertion.[3] Research on sentencing in magistrates' courts showed it to
be replete with and almost characterised by inter-court inconsistencies which
could only be explained by non-legal factors such as local bench tradition,
the nature of the local community, the influence of the clerk and the penal
philosophy of the magistrates (Hood, 1962, 1972; Tarling, 1979; Darbyshire,
1984). Discretion without guidance remains the predominant feature of
magistrates' court sentencing, since Court of Appeal judgements have little
relevance there. There are plenty of indications that, despite the appeal
system and the "judicial studies" programme, sentencing in the English
Crown Court suffers from the familiar dissonance between the law in the
books and the law in action.

Whereas police and lawyers in the pre-trial stages have been portrayed as
bending the rules and subverting the official processes, the reproach against
sentencers has been more one of disparity than of subversion—hardly surprising in view of the sparseness of relevant "law" or authoritative guidance of
any kind. One cannot subvert rules unless there are some. One can exercise
discretion inconsistently:[4] but is that a reproach if the lawmakers have
declined to create rules, principles or other forms of guidance? In the mid-
1960s the Magistrates' Association formulated its own "Suggestions for

---

[3] This was his view when banning the Oxford research on sentencing in the Crown Court: Ashworth,
Genders, Mansfield, Peay and Player, 1984, p. 64. The Home Office is currently conducting detailed
statistical research into Crown Court sentencing.

[4] For exploration of sentencing behaviour, see Fitzmaurice and Pease (1985) and Pennington and
Lloyd-Bostock (1987).

Traffic Offence Penalties'', a do-it-yourself response to the lawlessness of sentencing in magistrates' courts, and several local benches have now expanded this approach to other forms of crime. Crown Court sentencing is better served by principles laid down by the Court of Appeal, but there remains a wide and little-controlled discretion when dealing with the bulk of run–of–the–mill offences. Calls for decision stages in criminal justice (such as parole) to be "judicialised" ring strange when the very process of sentencing so conspicuously falls short of the principles of natural justice and the "rule of law". Not only is the factual basis of offence and defence subject to processes of construction and reconstruction with little legal control (Shapland, 1981; Wasik, 1986), but there is no coherent structure of sentencing rules and principles, and neither an obligation to give reasons for sentence nor a proper conception of what ought to count as a reason. Sentencing is clearly a part of the criminal process in which the law fails to incorporate its own rhetoric, and where criminologists might fruitfully dwell upon the deficiencies of the legal framework as much as upon the diverse strivings of individual judges and local courts. The general point has been made forcefully by McBarnet (1981) in relation to many earlier stages in the process: it may not be that police, lawyers and others adapt their behaviour so as to subvert the formal procedures, but that the law itself resembles at best a Gruyère cheese, with channels aplenty through which the *cognoscenti* can pass unhampered by rules. Legal rhetoric proclaims the right to silence, but the courts have introduced so many qualifications as to make the general proposition into a gross exaggeration. Legal rhetoric proclaims rights of privacy and freedom from unlawful intrusion, but the law gives the courts a discretion whether or not to admit evidence unlawfully obtained.[5] Legal rhetoric proclaims freedom of choice whether to plead guilty or not guilty and a "right" to be tried by one's peers, yet the law gives its approval to substantial sentencing discounts for those who plead guilty. Legal rhetoric proclaims a right to bail, and then the Bail Act provides a collection of vague exceptions without clear requirements of proof, which go far to undermine any serious concept of "right". Legal rhetoric proclaims the presumption of innocence as a "golden thread" running through English criminal law, yet the numbers of derogations from the principle now sanctioned by the legislature or the judiciary are legion. From the proposition that the law in action usually differs from the law in books, we have travelled to the proposition that the law in the books may not be what it is frequently said or assumed to be. The second phase has given way to the third. The prevalence of discretion within the legal structure, together with the lawyer's tendency to winkle out exceptions and qualifications even to clear rules, have buttressed the case for regarding the law as problematic and worthy of criminological attention.

The criminal law, then, may be not only an obstacle to be circumvented by police and lawyers, but also a resource upon which they can call occasionally to legitimate their actions (Chatterton, 1976), and an ally in protecting their

---

[5] See section 78 of the Police and Criminal Evidence Act 1984. For further theoretical discussion, see the criticism of McBarnet (1981) by McConville and Baldwin (1981), pp. 201–209.

actions from censure (abuse of discretion and "unreasonableness" are more difficult to establish than breach of a rule, and even rules can give way to exceptions). From uncovering the actual functions and effects of the criminal law, some criminologists have begun to tread the road back from deconstruction. The dangers are manifest. To call for reforms in a particular sphere such as bail or prosecutions may incur criticisms along the lines that any criminologist ought to recognise the impossibility of effective changes without a thorough re-structuring of the criminal process and certain aspects of the social system too. To dabble in liberal reformism is in substance to support existing power relations. On the other hand, to campaign for fundamental social reforms as the only way of making a real impact on the quality of criminal justice, whilst refusing to engage in dialogue on specific issues such as plea–bargaining or legal aid, is to run a high risk of total ineffectiveness.

However, the debate about means is at least more structured than the debate about ends. Of course there is no reason why "criminologists", however defined, should march in step along the road back from deconstruction. Indeed, many have fought shy of contemporary issues of public policy. Yet the fourth phase is characterised by a willingness to engage in current policy debates which has not been the prevailing approach among British criminologists since the first phase. The ground was cleared in the 1970s by work such as that of Hall (1979) on law and order campaigns. Since then a "left realist" movement has grown up, through writings such as those of Lea and Young (1984), Jones, Maclean and Young (1986) and Box (1987), which emphasises the impact of lawbreaking upon the most disadvantaged members of society and which proposes "realistic" measures to tackle this. This movement is not without its critics, but already it is turning some criminological attention back towards practical and moral issues which for too long have lain submerged (see de Haan, 1987). The years between the first and fourth phases saw great progress towards an understanding of how the criminal process works, yet without a corresponding development in concepts of criminal justice.

Consider the controversy over the jury. The legal rhetoric is that the jury constitutes a bastion of liberty, the individual's protection against oppressive laws and law enforcement, and the epitomy of people's justice. It concerns the right to be tried by twelve other citizens. Research in recent decades has raised doubts about the ways in which juries reach their decisions and about the accuracy of their decisions (McCabe and Purves, 1972b, 1974; Sealy and Cornish, 1973; Baldwin and McConville, 1979). There have also been major legal changes: on the one side stand the introduction of majority verdicts, restrictions on the range of offences for which jury trial is available, the approval of jury vetting by the prosecution in certain cases, and the reduction and proposed abolition of the defendant's right of peremptory challenge of potential jurors; on the other side stand the removal of most restrictions on who may serve as a juror, the reduction to eighteen of the minimum age for a juror, and the prohibition on questioning jurors about their religious or political beliefs. What benchmarks should be used to evaluate these changes? Should the restrictive measures be interpreted as a movement by the powerful to emasculate the one genuine fount of people's justice and therefore a source

·of challenge to the routine processing of cases? There were certainly worries that the abolition of the old qualifications for jurors had produced a higher acquittal rate, although the commissioned research did not bear this out (Butler, 1983). It is one thing to conclude that, despite its failings, trial by jury remains the ordinary citizen's best protection against oppressive prosecutions and unfair treatment (McConville and Baldwin, 1981, pp. 210–211). It is quite another thing to prescribe the kind of jury, for what types of case, at whose election, with what effects on the flow of cases, etc., in the context of an agenda for criminal justice. Will this be taken up in the fourth phase?

Research into the criminal process has, then, reached a high level of technical competence and generous coverage of most stages of decision-making, but without similar advances in theoretical frameworks which can be applied specifically to the problems of the criminal process. Some will reject this as a responsibility or even a legitimate aspiration of criminologists. Others may object that it all depends on what one regards as theory. Let me explain. Much of the research in previous decades was designed to assess whether a particular part of the criminal process was achieving its goals or operating as it was supposed to; some research was designed to investigate the effect of the process on defendants; belatedly, there has been research into the effects of the criminal process on victims (Shapland, Wilmore and Duff, 1985); some of the recent research is more openly motivated by administrative concerns about speed, economy and efficient management (e.g. Moxon, 1985). When criminologists have looked for external monitors of the process they are studying, the "Due Process" and the "Crime Control" models of Packer (1968) have often been invoked.[6] These models assist in interpreting trends and characterising systems, but they are not designed to be prescriptive either generally or specifically. In effect, they represent the conventional "on the one hand, on the other hand" of the academic. Perhaps it was assumed that criminologists would align with the Due Process model as a matter of course, but the writings of the left realists confirm that this is too sweeping and simplistic. Crime control and due process may both be desirable objectives and they may conflict, but the resolution of these conflicts is only one part of the task. To return to the jury, should it be every defendant's right to be tried by a jury, or is it proper to reserve this for serious cases? How should seriousness be determined for this purpose? It is facile to criticise every new legislative restriction on the right to jury trial for certain offences, since that assumes that in 1975 or 1935 the position was more satisfactory. Was it? According to what criteria is that judgement reached? Questions of this kind take us into the scantily charted waters of offence-seriousness. Research into what people's judgements on this are (e.g. Pease, Ireson and Thorpe, 1974; Sparks, Genn and Dodd, 1977, p. 184) provides a starting point, but the hard questions then begin. There is a need for a theoretical structure of social justifications, from which flows a new hierarchy among crimes of violence and sex offences, safety offences, environmental crimes, property crimes, public order offences and so forth. The issues lie on several levels—that of law enforcement, through the

---

[6] This is not to say that all criminologists have found them adequate: cf. Bottoms and McClean, 1976, ch. 9.

police or regulatory agencies; that of the use of the criminal process rather than some form of fixed penalty, diversion or administrative machinery; that of mode of trial, not forgetting the allied question of whether the choice of mode should be solely that of the prosecutor (as in Scotland) or should also be an option for the defendant in certain cases (as in England and Wales); and that of sentencing, where the level of criticisms has always outstripped the quality of constructive proposals. These questions will be answered differently by the liberal democrat, the conservative, the left realist, and others. But has any group taken social or criminological theory to the point at which it can yield a framework for answering these practical questions of criminal justice?

Perhaps criminologists as a whole have gone furthest in this direction when writing about sentencing policy. Criminologists appear to speak with one voice in arguing for less use of custodial sentences, but with two or more voices when arguing about what forms of sentence should replace them. The debate in which Cohen (1979, 1985) and Bottoms (1983)[7] have participated is richer in social theory than most of the modern policy-related criminological contributions, but has been bedevilled by shifting ground beneath. Part of Cohen's idea of the punitive city is that society is undergoing a dispersal of discipline and social control through the trend towards community-based corrections and "diversion". Among Bottoms' counter-arguments comes the point that between 1938 and 1979 both custody and probation-directed orders declined as a proportion of all sentences, with the rise of the fine and the suspended sentence as the principal features. This suggested that the trend was towards juridical punishments, but in the 1980s there have been strong movements in the opposite direction, with the fine declining in proportionate use and a corresponding increase in community service orders, probation and custody. Perhaps the clearest policy-related thesis here is Rutherford's "reductionist target" of a prison population of 22,000 by 1992 (1986, p. 174). This is supported by an elaborate working-out of the other features and effects of such a change of policy, although without the kind of thoroughgoing re-assessment of offence-seriousness which is practically essential if the sentencing system is to be reformed effectively.

Historians have made a theoretical contribution too, with Thompson's (1975) argument that the rule of law may be more than a grand-sounding apologia for the existing power structure raising possibilities which criminologists may have too lightly dismissed. Could not the ideology of the rule of law be mobilised in favour of a rather different distribution of benefits and burdens in society and in criminal justice? Would a Bill of Rights (Lacey, 1986) be a worthwhile step? All this depends on the notions of social and criminal justice which are treated as ideals. We have, as has been observed, moved away from the assumption that the rights of the individual defendant (whatever they may be) should be the paramount concern, never to be traded off for other gains. There are deep questions about the rights of victims, debated by criminologists at a level which includes wider conceptions of criminal justice (Shapland, Wilmore and Duff, 1985, ch. 10; Chambers and Millar, 1986; Miers 1987). Even notions such as social defence appear more

[7]See also the critique of Cohen by Morgan (1983).

118

persuasive when stripped of their social hygiene connotations and applied to the community's interest in law enforcement in poor neighbourhoods. Bills of Rights are more apt to protect individuals against the community and against unfair laws than to dictate the substantive content of the laws. It is that substance which is being sought. Once captured, the rule of law—with its virtues of the openness, certainty and predictability of legal regulation (Raz, 1979)—would promote and sustain the new criminal justice.

Or would it? One snag might be that the emphasis on the certainty of the law and the predictability of its effects on behaviour might militate strongly against crime control in some spheres. The flexibility of the common law, so beloved of judges as a tool for criminalising new varieties of wickedness (see Smith, 1984), would be curtailed, and this might be seen as a victory for individual rights. But corporations and wealthy individuals bent on neutralising the effect of a new law would be able to devise methods of circumventing it, in the sure knowledge that the rule of law would protect their activities. If criminologists are serious about "white–collar" and economic crime, then they must look at the habits of the supposedly law-abiding as well as the law-breakers, and must reconsider the social effects of adhering to the rule of law and thereby enabling "deviant" groups to stay one step ahead (McBarnet, 1987).

Another difficulty in setting too much store by the rule of law is that the laws and processes might be less important than the people who operate them. No operational system of criminal justice could exclude all discretion, and it would probably be unwise to attempt this. The focus then turns to the personnel who exercise the various discretions—the police, lawyers, the courts, probation officers and so on. It might be argued, for example, that reforms of legal education and entry into the legal profession, reforms of police recruitment and training, and reforms of methods for selecting magistrates could achieve far more than alterations of law which were not accompanied by major changes in personnel. The case for a career judiciary is little heard, perhaps because the might of the legal profession would quickly squash it, but there are European precedents and experiences to build upon. The democratisation of criminal justice through a working-class magistracy and juries (e.g. Taylor, 1982; Carlen, 1983) might necessitate minimum change in the legal framework of the criminal process whilst bringing considerable changes in practice. But there may be considerable dangers too: if these lay tribunals are not to dispose justice of a palm-tree kind, then there is a need to formulate policies, guidance and training programmes—to provide a basic structure, whilst leaving them discretion to deal with individual cases in the spirit of the general policies. We are back, then, to the question of how and by whom these general policy orientations should be determined.

One disturbing feature of the existing system is the extent to which defendants are dependent on the advice of legal experts. Defendants may find themselves excluded from pre-trial decision-making and reduced to the role of spectator at the trial, if one takes place, as the case is reconstructed by the lawyers. Just how necessary is it to have a criminal procedure which so profusely sprouts devices for circumventing it or minimising its significance?

Simplification and explanation are goals worthwhile in themselves and necessary if any real democratisation is to take place, and they would facilitate the re-entry of the defendant into decision-making in the criminal process. The present trend seems to be in the opposite direction. Having described how the pre-trial review is developing as an informal forum in which lawyers can "sort out" difficult cases before trial in a magistrates' court, Baldwin concludes by recommending that defendants should be entitled to be present at these reviews (1985, p. 165). Yet such a move might leave defendants no less confused than they are during court proceedings, and could so inhibit the lawyers as to drive the real discussions elsewhere. The defendant may therefore remain as a spectator whilst others decide upon his or her "best interests". Reforms which widen access to legal advice in police stations and legal representation in courts, desirable as they may be from one point of view, may run the same risk of heightening dependency on a group of lawyers who have their own concerns and aspirations.

What, then, may be seen as the strengths and weaknesses of the various movements in this sphere of British criminology in the last fifty years? The positivists of the first phase moved impressively in the sphere of public policy, but largely neglected the criminal process (the partial exception being the sentence of the court) as an object of study. The second phase has brought British criminology into its empirical pre-eminence, with a considerable volume of research which not only demonstrated on a wide scale that the law in practice often diverges from the law in the books and why, but also "discovered" many low-visibility pre-trial processes which had hitherto been starved of critical attention. Research of this kind remains essential as a basis for sound theorising and also for sound policy-making, although it is symptomatic of the present arrangements for Government funding of research that there have been instances of commissioning research in order to "legitimate" a policy which has been virtually decided upon. The achievements of this second phase are great, and the approach should be maintained. It is essential for a healthy criminology: the mistake would be to regard it as sufficient, and the weakness of this second phase is that the theoretical and conceptual aspects of criminal justice received far less attention in the welter of empirical projects. The balance was somewhat redressed in the third phase, as some criminologists turned their attention to the law itself and studied the extent to which the rules and rights embodied in legal rhetoric had a legal basis. Detailed examination often revealed more discretions than duties, and correspondingly fewer entitlements and less accountability. The study of discretion in criminal justice—its nature, exercise, structuring or elimination—is becoming a key area for criminologists (see Hawkins, 1986; Galligan, 1987). The fourth phase, like the first, is characterised by closer attention to the issues under current debate and to possible solutions. Many will regard it as a strength that more criminologists are entering public policy debates, but strength is liable to turn to weakness if there is insufficient understanding of the legal procedures of the pre-trial process or if concepts of criminal justice have been insufficiently developed to yield distinct lines of argument on the many detailed procedural issues.

There is bound to be uneasiness among criminologists about involvement in current policy debates. It is not so much that some criminologists take the narrow view that they have no business with devising specific solutions, or that there are no "solutions" as such. Rather it is that, too frequently, the issues are defined by the Government or by the mass media. And, even on those issues, the solutions which some criminologists may wish to propose range far beyond the particular problems of the day (be it sentencing, or diversion from the criminal process), so as to encompass underlying patterns in social organisation, housing policy, employment policy and so on. Arguments of this kind tend to be so productive of wider political disagreements as to be unattractive to those influential in formulating public policy, and they may fall by the wayside. That is no reason for abandoning them, but there are also other directions in which criminologists should move and which may bear greater fruit in the short or medium terms. Perhaps a recent call for a closer connection between criminology and the relevant literature of moral and legal philosophy points the way (de Haan, 1987): the conceptual and moral elements in criminal justice must be thoroughly ploughed over and drawn into criminological research and theory. The most obvious sphere for this is sentencing—questioning the rationale of punishment, the aims of sentencing, the criteria of offence–seriousness and the reasons for mitigation—but these elements also abound in the earlier stages of the criminal process. There is no shortage of questions of moral and social principle raised by prosecution policy, the right to trial by jury, advance disclosure of one's case to the other side, dropping charges and accepting pleas of guilty, the proper role of the victim, burden of proof, standards of criminal liability and so on. It is a tribute to British criminology of the last fifty years that we now understand much more about how the criminal process operates and how it relates to other aspects of the social and legal systems. We are better able to identify where the problems lie and what the dilemmas for policy are. Whatever shade of liberalism, conservatism, welfarism, socialism or other political outlook the criminologist adopts, there is no shortage of items on the agenda for a fifth phase.

REFERENCES

ASHWORTH, A., GENDERS, E., MANSFIELD, G., PEAY, J. and PLAYER, E. (1984). "Sentencing in the Crown Court", Occasional Paper no. 10, University of Oxford Centre for Criminological Research.

BALDWIN, J. (1985). *Pre-Trial Justice*. Oxford, Blackwell.

BALDWIN, J. and McCONVILLE, M. (1977). *Negotiated Justice*. Oxford, Martin Robertson.

BALDWIN, J. and McCONVILLE, M. (1979a). *Jury Trials*. Oxford, Oxford University Press.

BALDWIN, J. and McCONVILLE, M. (1979b). "Plea Bargaining and the Court of Appeal". *British Journal of Law and Society*. **6**, 200–218.

BANKOWSKI, Z. and MUNGHAM, G. (1976). *Images of Law*. London, Routledge.

BOTTOMS, A. E. (1983). "Some Neglected Features of Contemporary Penal Systems", in Garland, D. and Young, D. *The Power to Punish*. London, Heinemann.

BOTTOMS, A. E. and McCLEAN, J. D. (1976) *Defendants in the Criminal Process*. London, Routledge.

Box, S. (1987). *Recession, Crime and Punishment*. Basingstoke, Macmillan.

BUTLER, S. (1983). "Acquittal Rates", Home Office Research Bulletin no. 16.

CARLEN, P. (1976). *Magistrates' Justice*. Oxford, Martin Robertson.

CARLEN, P. (1983). "On Rights and Powers: Notes on Penal Politics", in Garland, D. and Young, D. *The Power to Punish*. London, Heinemann.

CHAMBERS, G. and MILLAR, A. (1986). *Prosecuting Sexual Assault*. Scottish Office Social Research Study. Edinburgh, HMSO.

CHATTERTON, M. (1976). "Police in Social Control", in King, J. F. S. (ed). *Control without Custody*. Cambridge, Institute of Criminology.

COHEN, S. (1979). "The Punitive City: notes on the dispersal of social control". *Contemporary Crises*. **3,** 339–364.

COHEN, S. (1985). *Visions of Social Control*. Polity Press, London.

DARBYSHIRE, P. (1984). *The Magistrates' Clerk*. Chichester, Barry Rose.

DE HAAN, W. (1987). "Fuzzy Morals and Flakey Politics: The Coming Out of Critical Criminology". *J. of Law and Society*. **14,** 321–333.

FISHER, SIR H. (1977). *Report of the Confait Inquiry*. London, HMSO.

FITZMAURICE, C. and PEASE, K. (1985). *The Psychology of Judicial Sentencing*. Manchester, Manchester University Press.

GALLIGAN, D. (1987). "Regulating Pre-Trial Decisions" in Dennis, I. (ed.) *Criminal Law and Criminal Justice*. Sweet and Maxwell.

GRÜNHUT, M. (1948). *Penal Reform*. Oxford, Oxford University Press.

GRÜNHUT, M. (1956). *Juvenile Offenders before the Courts*. Oxford, Oxford University Press.

HAWKINS, K. (1986). "On Legal Decision-Making". *Washington and Lee Law Review*. **43,** 1161–1311.

HOOD, R. G. (1962). *Sentencing in Magistrates' Courts*. London, Stevens.

HOOD, R. G. (1972). *Sentencing the Motoring Offender*. London, Heinemann.

JONES, T., MACLEAN, B. and YOUNG, J. (1986). *The Islington Crime Survey*. Aldershot, Gower.

LACEY, N. (1986). "The Case for a Bill of Rights". *New Society*. February 7.

LEA, J. and YOUNG, J. (1984). *What is to be done about law and order?* Harmondsworth, Penguin.

McBARNET, D. (1981). *Conviction: Law, the State and the Construction of Justice*. Oxford Socio-Legal Studies. London, Macmillan.

McBARNET, D. (1988). "The Limits of Criminal Law" in del Buono, V. (ed.), *Reform of the Criminal Law*. Toronto, Carswell.

McCABE, S. and PURVES, R. (1972a) *By-Passing the Jury*. University of Oxford Penal Research Unit, Occasional Paper no. 3.

McCABE, S. and PURVES, R. (1972b) *The Jury at Work*. University of Oxford Penal Research Unit, Occasional Paper no. 4.

McCABE, S. and PURVES, R. (1974) *The Shadow Jury at Work*. University of Oxford Penal Research Unit, Occasional Paper no. 8.

McCONVILLE, M. and BALDWIN, J. (1981). *Courts, Prosecution and Conviction*. Oxford, Oxford University Press.

122

MANNHEIM, H. (1939). *The Dilemma of Penal Reform*. London, George Allen and Unwin.

MANNHEIM, H. (1948). *Criminal Justice and Social Reconstruction*. London, Kegan Paul.

MANNHEIM, H., SPENCER, J. C. and LYNCH, G. (1958). "Magisterial Policy in the London Juvenile Courts". *Brit. J. of Delinq.* 8, 13 and 119.

MANSFIELD, G. and PEAY, J. (1986). *The Director of Public Prosecutions: Principles and Practices for the Crown Prosecutor*. London, Tavistock.

MIERS, D. (1987). "The Implications for the Criminal Justice System of Allowing Victims Greater Participation in Decision-Making".

MOODY, S. and TOMBS, J. (1982) *Prosecution in the Public Interest*. Edinburgh, Scottish Academic Press.

MORGAN, N. (1983). "Non-Custodial Penal Sanctions in England and Wales: a New Utopia?" *Howard Journal*, XXII, 148–167.

MOXON, D. (ed.) (1985). *Managing Criminal Justice*. London, HMSO.

NAPLEY, SIR D. (1977). "Alice in Zanderland". *Law Society's Gazette.* **74,** 830–831.

PACKER, H. (1968). *The Limits of the Criminal Sanction*. Oxford, Oxford University Press.

PEASE, K., IRESON, J. and THORPE, J. (1974). "The Development of a Scale of Offences Seriousness". *International Journal of Criminology and Penology*.

PENNINGTON, D., and LLOYD-BOSTOCK, S. (eds). (1987). *The Psychology of Sentencing*. Centre for Socio-Legal Studies, Oxford.

RADZINOWICZ, L. (1956). *Sexual Offences*. Macmillan.

RAZ, J. (1979). *The Authority of Law*. Oxford, Oxford University Press.

ROYAL COMMISSION ON CRIMINAL PROCEDURE (Chairman: Sir Cyril Phillips), Cmnd. 8092-1, London, HMSO.

RUTHERFORD, A. (1986). *Prisons and the Process of Justice*. Revised Ed. Oxford, Oxford University Press.

SANDERS, A. (1985a). "Prosecution Decisions and the Attorney General's Guidelines". *Criminal Law Review*. 4–19.

SANDERS, A. (1985b). "The Prosecution Process", in Moxon., D. (ed.) *Managing Criminal Justice*. London, HMSO.

SEALY, A. P. and CORNISH, W. (1973). "Juries and the Rules of Evidence". *Criminal Law Review*. 208–222.

SHAPLAND, J. (1981). *Between Conviction and Sentence*. London, Routledge.

SHAPLAND, J., WILMORE, J. and DUFF, P. (1985). *Victims in the Criminal Justice System*. Aldershot, Gower.

SMITH, A. T. H. (1984). "Judicial Law Making the Criminal Law". *Law Quarterly Review*. **100,** 46–76.

SPARKS, R., GENN, H. and DODD, D. J. (1977). *Surveying Victims*. London, Wiley.

TARLING, R. (1979). *Sentencing Practice in Magistrates' Courts*. Home Office Research Study no. 56. London, HMSO.

TAYLOR, I. (1982). *Law and Order: Arguments for Socialism*. London, Macmillan.

THOMAS, D. A. (1979). *Principles of Sentencing*. London, Heinemann.

THOMPSON, E. P. (1975). *Whigs and Hunters: the Origins of the Black Act*. London, Allen Lane.

WASIK, M. (1985). "Rules of Evidence in the Sentencing Process". *Current Legal Problems*. **38,** pp. 187–209.

BRIT. J. CRIMINOL. Vol. 28 No. 2 SPRING 1988

THE HISTORY OF CRIME IN ENGLAND
c. 1300–1914
An Overview of Recent Publications

J. A. SHARPE (*York*)

One of the most significant developments in British historical research over the last two decades has been a flowering of social history. Despite the prevalent conviction among the academic historical establishment that real history is about high politics, a growing corpus of scholarly publications attests to the presence of an alternative focus for historical study: that provided by past societies in their full complexity. Realisation of the potential inherent in this alternative focus has led to the exploration of a number of themes which might otherwise have been left to the popular historian, or relegated to a footnote by textbook writers. One of the most important of these themes is crime. Indeed, the point has now been reached when historians of crime are being described (or perhaps more properly accused) by historians in the mainstream of the discipline as working in a "fashionable" area. Work by historians of crime has assumed considerable proportions.[1] There are still many gaps, partial or total, in our knowledge, yet a number of broad themes have emerged from research into the subject, and it is now possible not only to put forward some methodological postulates, but also to make some fairly safe statements about broad developments between about 1300 and 1914.[2]

Reaching this conclusion should not, however, obscure the fact that work on the history of crime has been undertaken by scholars working from a number of positions. English historians (to the occasional despair of their continental colleagues) are not much given to theorizing, and thus there is comparatively little by way of arguing from ideological or theoretical positions among English historians of crime. Nevertheless, several intellectual currents, at times conflicting, at times interacting fruitfully, have flowed into current work on the subject. For the eighteenth century, perhaps the greatest initial impetus was provided by the broadly Marxist approach offered by Edward Thompson and his group at Warwick University (Thompson, 1975; Hay, *et al.*, 1975). Perhaps the most inherently hostile position to this approach was that held by a number of historians, notably J.S. Cockburn and J.H. Langbein, who worked outwards towards the history of crime from the technicalities of a

---

[1] The easiest way into this corpus of material is to read the review articles and collections of essays which have been written on the history of crime: among the former, see: Knafla, 1977; Bailey, 1980; Sharpe, 1982; Innes and Styles, 1986; among the latter: Hay, *et al.*, 1975; Cockburn, 1977a; Brewer and Styles, 1980; Gatrell, Lenman and Parker, 1980; Bailey, 1981; Rule, 1982; Jones, 1982; Fletcher and Stevenson, 1986. The field is now sufficiently developed to make writing works of synthesis a useful exercise: see: Sharpe, 1984; Emsley, 1987.

[2] Work on the history of crime and related matters after 1914 is not as developed as for some earlier periods, and hence has been excluded from this essay. The best short guide to statistical fluctuations is still McClintock and Avison, 1968. For an indication of where investigation of the social and community contexts of crime might lead, see Samuel, 1981.

more traditional legal history (e.g., Langbein, 1983). More generally, of course, a knowledge of legal history is essential to historians of crime, although, as some of the more sterile legal history suggests, they also have to confront a number of wider issues. For some, although not attracted by Thompson's ideological position, an awareness of these wider issues was provided by the new style of labour history which arrived in the 1960s. This, breaking away from labour history's traditional concern with trades unionism and early working—class movements, attempted to get to grips with a broad range of problems, of which crime was one (Jones, 1982). For historians working in periods before 1700, the biggest influence, in some cases subconsciously perhaps (e.g. Sharpe, 1983), was the approach to social history epitomized by the French journal *Annales*: a social history which was wide ranging, which made at least occasional nods at the social sciences, made heavy use of quantification, and also attacked the problem of popular mentalities. It is fair to say, however, that so far these various positions have not been defined with total clarity, and that the dialogue between them remains undeveloped.

For all historians working in this field, the initial problem is perhaps a definitional one. As criminologists will be aware, definitions of crime and other forms of deviant acts are subject to alteration, and are in any case likely to vary between the courts, law enforcement agencies, and various groups within society. These definitional problems acquire an even greater complexity when crime in the past is considered. The greatest difficulty, at least when dealing with periods earlier than the nineteenth century, is deciding what to leave out. Felonies, the serious offences which modern public opinion might describe as "real" crime, are easy enough to deal with, but historians of crime in the medieval and early modern periods have to consider offences tried before the local ecclesiastical or manorial courts (Marchant, 1969; Hair, 1972; Emmison, 1973; King, W. J., 1980). If the total picture of crime and law enforcement is being considered, such offences can hardly be ignored, but they add both to the numerical total and the definitional complexity of crime. Thus in one Essex village, Kelvedon Easterford, we find that between 1600 and 1640 there were twenty–four indictments at the assizes and quarter sessions for property offences committed in the parish, one for manslaughter, and two for infanticide. Over the same period 756 presentments were brought against Kelvedon inhabitants at the local archdeacon's court: 224 of them for being absent from church on Sunday or at Easter, 234 for various forms of sexual immorality, the remainder for a wide range of offences ranging from drunkenness to resistance to paying rates to the church (Sharpe, 1977). Such presentments were very often the outcome of pressures within the community, and fluctuations in them can provide the most subtle guide to shifts in local law enforcement: yet tracing them involves accepting a very broad definition of what "crime" was.

Most historians have, in fact, accepted an institutional definition: a crime is an act which can lead to suppression by a court or by legally accredited law enforcement agents, and which can be punished. Despite its flaws, accepting this definition left the way clear for what the first historians working in the field saw as their main task, counting such cases as surviving court records

125

have left to us (by period of interest: Given, 1977; Hanawalt, 1979; Samaha, 1974; Cockburn, 1977b; Sharpe, 1983; Beattie, 1986; Hay, 1982; Philips, 1977; Gatrell, 1980). Given appropriate documentation (and an enormous amount of material has been lost) the idea of studying long term trends in crime was an attractive one, as was the idea of setting the results of such an exercise against other socio-economic variables, demographic trends, harvest fluctuations, urbanisation, and so on. But as soon as such exercises were initiated, the problems became manifest. Any set of crime statistics poses questions of interpretation, a situation which is as true of statistics for felony in the fourteenth century as it is of crime in the modern inner city. On one hand come the problems inherent in the fact that most prosecutions in the past came "from below": study of early modern materials, in particular, demonstrated how offences often only entered the record as official prosecutions after a fairly complex filtering process within the local community (Curtis, 1977 and 1980; Herrup, 1984; Sharpe, 1980). On the other hand, complications arise from the implications for the crime statistics of pressure from above. It rapidly became apparent that "moral panics" could distort patterns of crime (Davis, 1980), and that "control waves" could be as significant a factor as "crime waves". Thus, in the period c. 1580–1640, the influence of what might broadly be described as Puritanism sent an ever expanding number of moral and regulative offenders to the courts (Wrightson, 1980). Historians have, therefore, become divided over the usefulness of counting. Even so, it is interesting to note that one of them has put forward the intriguing suggestion that a system depending on private prosecution rather than on the actions of police agencies in the modern sense was more likely to engender a situation where changes in prosecution levels were accurate measures of changes in the real level of crime (Hay, 1982).

Despite the difficulties, the efforts of a number of historians in the field of statistical studies has furnished us with at least a partial pattern of past prosecutions. Thanks to Hanawalt (1979) we now have a clear impression of levels of felony accusations in the early fourteenth century. There is then something of a lacuna for two centuries (to some extent filled by Bellamy, 1973 and 1984), but from about 1550 a fairly clear and rather unexpected pattern emerges. Over the period c. 1550–1630 felony, on the strength of surviving documentation, seems to have been prosecuted with increasing frequency, while over the same period, as we have noted, the number of petty offenders tried at the quarter sessions, ecclesiastical courts, and perhaps other local courts, also expanded. After the political upheavals of the mid seventeenth century levels of prosecution of felony, at least outside the London area, were low, and stayed low over the later seventeenth and much of the eighteenth centuries (Beattie, 1986; Cockburn, 1987; Marchant, 1969; Samaha, 1974; Sharpe, 1984; Wrightson, 1980; Wrightson and Levine, 1979). They rose again from the late eighteenth century, and reached a new peak in the first half of the nineteenth: yet from about 1850 the level of prosecution, and probably of actual crimes committed, fell, allowing one historian to talk of "the decline of theft and violence in Victorian and Edwardian England" (Gatrell, 1980: see also: Emsley, 1987; Radzinowicz and Hood, 1987). These two periods of rising prosecutions, c. 1560–1630, and c. 1780–1850, share some broadly similar characteristics. There were objective social problems in both: in the first period, demographic growth and consequent pressure at the base of society, in the second demographic growth again, this time coupled with the dislocations caused by urbanisation and industrialisation. Conversely, both periods also witnessed very marked respectable fears about the possibilities of social disintegration. Concern over the collapse of both the cosmic and the human order was central to late Tudor and early Stuart social comment, while in the late Hanoverian and early Victorian periods the spectre of revolution fused with acute worry over a crime problem which was now being highlighted by the publication of criminal statistics. Thus, taking very long term trends, a cyclical rather than a linear pattern emerges.[3] Even so, some linear trends can be traced: homicide, for example, seems to have fallen fairly steadily from the middle ages onwards (Stone, 1983 and 1985; Sharpe, 1985b; see also: Hammer, 1978; Macfarlane, 1981). Yet these should not be overstated: in particular, there is little evidence of a shift from a "feudal" criminality based on violence to a "capitalist" one based on property offences.

Despite the insights which counting offences provided, realisation of the social processes which preceded prosecution led a number of historians to examine the problems of law enforcement in the local community. So far, little work has been done in this area for periods after 1800, but a number of medieval and early modern villages have now been subjected to fairly close investigation (De Windt, 1976; Ingram, 1984a; Raftis, 1966; Sharpe, 1977; Wrightson, 1980; Wrightson and Levine, 1979). Such village studies have been revealing in a number of ways. Firstly, we must re-emphasise, they have shown the extent to which prosecution at the relatively distant courts of assize and quarter sessions would underrate actual criminal activity. To take an extreme example, twenty-three charges of assault were brought at the Lancashire quarter sessions against inhabitants of the manor of Prescott between 1615 and 1660. Over the same period, 1,252 accusations of assault were brought against Prescott inhabitants in the local manorial court (King, W. J., 1982). Secondly, research into individual communities has demonstrated that local law enforcement officers (parish constables, church-wardens, and manorial jurors) were drawn from the village elite of rich farmers and prosperous artisans, and has thus thrown new light on the nature of "policing" in eras which preceded the formation of a professional police. Thirdly, such research has made us more aware of the importance of the law and legal institutions at a local level. The law was something which even quite humble people were willing to use, and which was a more important normative force than might be imagined (Davis, 1984; Ingram, 1977; King, P., 1984; Sharpe, 1985c).

Study of crime on a local level also brings us into contact with that most elusive of issues, popular attitudes to crime and law enforcement. Awareness

---

[3] As we note at a later point, research on village communities c. 1250–1348 suggests that another local "control wave" occurred during those years, reinforcing this impression of the cyclical nature of law and order problems: for a discussion of the relationship between this period and the late Tudor and early Stuart one, see Spufford, 1986.

of exciting potential offered by such matters led to the formulation, especially among leftish historians of eighteenth- and nineteenth-century society, of the concept of "social crime" (Hay, *et al.*, 1975; Hobsbawm, 1972; Rule, 1979; Thompson, 1975). Social crime, according to one of the originators of the concept, represented "a conscious, almost a political, challenge to the prevailing social and political order and its values" (Hobsbawm, 1972, p.5). It can be identified when conflicting sets of official and non-official interpretations of the legal system exist, when an act of law-breaking contains manifest dimensions of social protest, or when a crime is unequivocally connected to wider social or political unrest. Poachers, smugglers, wreckers, writers of anonymous protest letters and rioters were all identified as social criminals, and their activities reinterpreted accordingly. Such reinterpretation opened up important areas of debate: but the concept of social crime is one which is vulnerable to a number of criticisms. Firstly, of course, it can lead to a romanticisation of certain types of criminal: nobody has been as fond of bandits as the left-wing historian. Secondly, and more seriously, the concept continues to defy precise definition. In the last resort, nearly every offender could be described as a social criminal: their actions presumably spring from other ideas about right and wrong than those held by officialdom, and, since this is so, are in a broad sense politically subversive. Conversely, eighteenth-century poachers or smugglers operating large organised networks aiming at supplying the growing consumerism of the period seem to reflect the spirit of an increasingly capitalist and market-oriented world rather than offering any challenge to it (Munsche, 1981; for a different view of poaching, see Jones, 1979).[4]

Nevertheless, the issues raised by the discussion of "social crime" have helped inform our appreciation of the possibility that some social groups had other ideas of legality and legitimate behaviour than those prescribed by authority, and that certain forms of action which officialdom held to be illegal were regarded as legitimate, or at least justifiable, by certain sections of the populace. One such manifestation of popular notions of proper standards which has recently been subjected to detailed research is the skimmington or riding, the English equivalent of the continental charivari (Ingram, 1984b). More familiar is that phenomenon where popular ideas of right and wrong so often came into conflict with those of officialdom, the riot. It is no longer possible simply to write riots off as the animalistic actions of a drink-sodden or loot-crazed mob: it is now accepted that riots and popular risings, from the Peasants' Revolt of 1381 to the inner city riots of the 1980s, can be interpreted in terms of the frustrations and aspirations of the lower orders (by period of interest: Hilton, 1977; Dobson, 1970; Slack, 1984; Sharp, 1980; Stevenson, 1979; Thompson, 1971). Both the riots and official reactions to them offer important insights into perceptions of law and order in the period in question.

Another crucial issue is that of identifying who was responsible for committing crimes. Generally, court records show that in all eras, a few offences (notably witchcraft, infanticide, and scolding) apart, most serious crime was

---

[4] A number of historians have attempted interpretative pieces attempting to examine the connection between changes in crime and other social or governmental developments. Among the more stimulating are: Langbein, 1974; Lenman and Parker, 1980; Philips, 1980; Soman, 1980.

committed by men (but see Beattie, 1975; and Wiener, 1975). Moving beyond this basic premise is difficult.

One important shift can be traced in violent offences. These were committed by a wide spectrum of society in the middle ages, and were not the prerogative of the poor until well into the eighteenth. Property offences, conversely, had always been committed mainly by the poor, from whose ranks other deviant types, notably vagrants and prostitutes, were also recruited. This last point, combined with the social dislocation of the period, was probably crucial to the construction of the notion of a "criminal class", or, following the term coined by the Frenchman H. A. Frégier, of a "dangerous class", over the first half of the nineteenth century (Emsley, 1987; for an earlier discussion of nineteenth-century developments, see Tobias, 1967). By the 1860s, it was an axiom of social debate that society was threatened not just by crime, but also by a "criminal class". Its members were distinguished from respectable society by their morality, dress, physiognomy, and argot. At their core stood a body of professional criminals who, as the *Times* put it in 1870, were "more alien from the rest of the community than a hostile army" (quoted in Emsley, 1987, p.63). The most recent research has tended to modify the reality of this alarming social construct: its real importance, is, perhaps, revealed in Emsley's comment that "the notion of a criminal class was, indeed remains, a convenient one for insisting that most crime in society is something committed on law abiding citizens by an alien group" (1987, p. 133).

The enduring significance of this Victorian concept of a "criminal class" should not obscure the possibility that an essentially similar entity existed in earlier periods. The Elizabethan concern over vagrancy, comparable in many ways to early nineteenth century fears of a criminal or dangerous class, was exaggerated (Slack, 1974; Beier, 1985). Yet study of archival materials suggests that around 1600 the poor were becoming not only more numerous, but also much more troublesome. Vagrants and the local poor (the two groups were far from mutually exclusive) coalesced into something like a "criminal class": by the early seventeenth century people accused of theft, witchcraft, drunkenness, bastard-bearing and infanticide were drawn almost entirely from their ranks. For earlier periods, the situation is more complicated. Work on medieval village communities, especially when the years 1250–1348, a period of mounting demographic pressure, are scrutinised, provides glimpses of a situation similar to that obtaining around 1600: there were attempts to discipline the disorderly poor, in this case through the manorial court (e.g., Razi, 1980). Conversely, and even making due allowance for the need to pare away legend, the middle ages also experienced relatively high-born bandits and leaders of outlaw bands (Keen, 1977; Stones, 1957): indeed, the decline of upper class violence in the century after 1550 is a subject in urgent need of further research, as is the need to investigate historical forerunners of "white collar" criminals (Hanawalt, 1975). More generally, the subject of organised and professional crime remains unstudied: certainly these existed in seventeenth-century London, while the emergence of England's first great criminal entrepreneur, Jonathan Wild, demonstrated how far these phenomena had developed by the 1720s (McMullan, 1984; Howson, 1970).

One area which is currently attracting considerable attention is the history of the police. The old approach, what is now thought of as "The Whig Interpretation of police history", is probably familiar enough (Reith, 1938 and 1943; Critchley, 1978). According to this interpretation, policing was pretty chaotic and ineffective before 1829, but then Pitt, true to the spirit of the Age of Reform, introduced the Metropolitan Police, and the way was opened for a natural progession to George Dixon. This view has now been challenged on a variety of levels. Work on the sixteenth and seventeenth centuries has shown that parish constables were not the inefficient nonentities as they have so often been portrayed (Wrightson, 1980; Sharpe, 1980; Kent, 1986). Study of eighteenth-century "police" agencies has suggested that they were not as inadequate as the apologists for the new police or their later historians have suggested (for pointers to work in progress, see Styles, 1982 and 1983). The new police were not universally accepted. Among local elites, urban and rural alike, there was widespread opposition, on both financial and ideological grounds, up to the mid nineteenth century. There was considerable lower class opposition over a somewhat longer period (Bailey, 1981; Emsley, 1983 and 1985; Jones, 1982; Storch, 1975 and 1976). The new police themselves took some time to develop into the paragons of professionalism and efficiency which subsequent historical myth was to make of them. The history of the police, more starkly than most other aspects of the subject, shows how a conventional wisdom about the history of crime breaks down when subjected to serious scholarly analysis.

If the introduction of the professional police in the nineteenth century marked a shift away from community values in law enforcement, roughly contemporaneous changes in punishment did even more so. Generally, historians of periods earlier than the nineteenth century have tended to devote little attention to punishment as a subject: although they have delineated quantitative changes in punishment, they have largely ignored the problems of underlying ideological changes (but see Sharpe, 1985a). One exception has been the development of transportation as a means of punishment, although even here the greatest body of writing has been devoted to transportation to Australia after 1787 (Hughes, 1987; Shaw, 1966; Smith, 1947). Of recent historians of seventeenth- and eighteenth-century crime, only John M. Beattie has really tackled the subject of punishment, in this case between 1660 and 1800, in detail (1986). His findings have done much to enrich our understanding of the subject. Perhaps his most original finding is that, despite the attention lavished by historians on the post 1688 "Bloody Code" of capital statutes, one of the most persistent themes of penal debate in his period was the search for effective forms of secondary punishment.

In the nineteenth century, this search seemed to have ended with the emergence of the prison as a major means of punishment. Yet here too there has been a disturbing tendency for pre–1800 developments to be flattened. Medieval prisons were rather more complex institutions than some have thought (Pugh, 1968), while from the middle of the sixteenth century the houses of correction, among whose functions was the punishment of petty offenders, represented something like a precursor of the modern prison. But despite these reservations, it is obvious that something new was taking place in the early nineteenth century. Before that time, debtors, a few political prisoners, and the inmates of the houses of correction apart, English prisons were intended primarily for the holding of suspected felons before trial, rather than as a means of punishment. With the early nineteenth century came the wide acceptance of the premise that, given that changing susceptibilities no longer accepted high levels of capital punishment, the prison would provide a handy means not only of punishing criminals, but also possibly of reforming them. England rapidly acquired a network of prisons under central government rather than local control, although the optimism about their reformatory potential rapidly waned (Evans, 1982; Ignatieff, 1978; Radzinowicz and Hood, 1986). This development was obviously connected to some wider societal and ideological changes, although their exact nature is still elusive. Michel Foucault argued that the shift in methods of punishment symbolised a much wider shift in values, not least in attitudes to the human body (1977). More conventionally, the rise of the prison has been associated with the shift towards an urban society and industrial capitalism: the fact that the modern prison attained prominence at about the same time as the modern factory is one of the most tired clichés in the history of punishment, yet it is difficult to dismiss it entirely (Rusche and Kirchheimer, 1977; Melossi and Pavarini, 1980).

But concentration on the rise of the prison in Victorian England, and of the concomitant dismantling of the "Bloody Code", should not obscure the importance of earlier trends. Once more, the medieval situation is obscure, although current research suggests that levels of capital punishment were low in the fourteenth and fifteenth centuries (Bellamy, 1973; Hanawalt, 1979). This situation altered rapidly from the mid sixteenth century onwards. As levels of prosecuted felonies rose in the Elizabethan period, so did levels of execution. National figures cannot be derived from the often fragmentary archival materials, but there is every indication that levels of execution were far higher, both absolutely and in relation to the number of accused, in the period c. 1590–1630 than in the eighteenth century (Sharpe, 1984). The calculations of one Victorian scholar, who estimated that the application of Elizabethan levels of execution to the London of the 1880s would result in 2,263 hangings annually in the capital (or, to continue the process, about 4,000 today) is instructive (Jeaffreson, 1887). Study of individual areas, the London region included, suggests that there was a massive drop in levels of execution over the seventeenth century. In Cheshire, to take the best documented case, the Court of Great Sessions sentenced an average of sixteen people to death annually in the 1620s, compared to one a year in the first decade of the eighteenth century. The increasingly severe legislation which followed the glorious revolution of 1688 was enacted in a period when hangings were less frequent than they had been for over a century. At the same time (although the process defies being charted other than impressionalistically) the old public shaming punishments for minor offences were less regularly resorted to: the pillory, the ducking-stool, the infliction of public penance by the ecclesiastical courts, the parading of brothel keepers and prostitutes through borough streets in a cart, all of these were felt to be increasingly inappropriate.

Consideration of punishment, and of the construction of the eighteenth-century "Bloody Code" and of the less familiar creation of capital offences in the Tudor period, leads to a final point: the importance to the history of crime of what might be termed official ideology. The history of crime was initially regarded as an excellent medium through which "history from below", the reconstruction of the lives and mentalities of groups who are often excluded from mainstream history, might be explored. Paradoxically, despite its contribution in this respect, it now seems that some of the most important insights to be gained from studying crime and law enforcement in the past are those bearing on the ways in which authority was maintained and controlling groups maintained their rule. This was, for example, the major theme of one of the earliest essays on the history of crime, Douglas Hay's "Property, Authority and the Criminal Law" (1975). This essay, despite the criticisms later made of it (Langbein, 1983; King P. 1984), raised debate over the importance of the history of crime to a new level, and it seems fair to suggest that historians of crime should turn away from their archives for a while and think of some of the broader implications of their subject. Certainly, to take a personal example, my work on early modern crime has convinced me that reflecting on the implications of the Reformation on law enforcement might at this stage in the development of the field be a more profitable use of time than constructing the next county's crime statistics.

What I hope to have done in this essay is to present an overview of work which has been completed on the history of crime in England up to the early part of the twentieth century. Obviously, in a short review essay of this type a number of important areas of research have been compressed, and a number of lesser themes have been virtually ignored. What I would emphasize, however, is that a number of themes, some already mentioned, others not, still await detailed research: the community and crime in the nineteenth and twentieth centuries; practically any aspect of the history of crime in the late fourteenth and fifteenth centuries; crime in provincial towns in most centuries before the nineteenth; crime among élite groups, whether upper class violence or the precursors of modern "white collar" crime; an historical victimology. These are just a few of the possibilities which come to mind. Even more exciting than these, however, are the possibilities offered by an interplay between criminological theory and historical materials. So far, historians have tended to shy away from confronting this problem: partly, because the sheer effort involved in establishing new areas of research leaves little time or energy for developing expertise in other people's disciplines; partly, because the British historical tradition is so hostile to social theory and social theorizing. Yet here, if anywhere, lies one of the most important future steps.

REFERENCES

BAILEY, V. (1980). "Bibliographical Essay: Crime, Criminal Justice and Authority in England", *Bulletin of the Society for the Study of Labour History*, **40,** 36–46.

BAILEY, V. (ed.) 1981. *Policing and Punishment in Nineteenth-Century Britain*. London, Croom Helm.

BEATTIE, J. M. (1975). "The Criminality of Women in Eighteenth-Century England". *Journal of Social History*, **8,** 80–116.

BEATTIE, J. M. (1986). *Crime and the Courts in England 1660–1800*. Oxford, Clarendon Press.

BEIER, A. L. (1985). *Masterless Men: the Vagrancy Problem in Britain 1560–1640*. London, Methuen.

BELLAMY, J. G. (1973). *Crime and Public Order in the Later Middle Ages*. London, Routledge and Kegan Paul.

BELLAMY, J. G. (1984) *Criminal Law and Society in Late Medieval and Tudor England*. Gloucester, Sutton.

BREWER, J. and STYLES, J. (eds.) (1980). *An Ungovernable People: the English and their Law in the Seventeenth and Eighteenth Centuries*. London, Hutchinson.

COCKBURN, J. S. (ed.). (1977a). *Crime in England 1550–1800*. London, Methuen.

COCKBURN, J. S. (1977b). "The Nature and Incidence of Crime in England 1559–1625: a Preliminary Survey", in Cockburn, J. S. (ed.). *Crime in England 1550–1800*. London, Methuen.

CRITCHLEY, T. A. (1978). *A History of Police in England and Wales*. (2nd ed.) London, Constable.

CURTIS, T. C. (1977). "Quarter Sessions Appearances and their Background: a Seventeenth-century Regional Study", in Cockburn, J. S. (ed.). *Crime in England 1550–1800*. London, Methuen.

CURTIS, T. C. (1980). "Explaining Crime in Early Modern England". *Criminal Justice History: an International Annual*, **1,** 117–38.

DAVIS, J. (1980). "The London Garotting Panic of 1862: a Moral Panic and the Creation of a Criminal Class in Mid-Victorian England", in Gatrell, V. A. C., Lenman, B. and Parker, G. (eds.). (1980). *Crime and the Law: the Social History of Crime in Western Europe since 1500*. London, Europa.

DAVIS, J. (1984). "A Poor Man's System of Justice: the London Police Courts in the Second Half of the Nineteenth Century", *The Historical Journal*, **27,** 309–35.

DE WINDT, A. (1976). "Peasant Power Structures in Fourteenth-Century King's Ripton". *Medieval Studies*, **38,** 236–67.

DOBSON, R. B. (1970). *The Peasants Revolt of 1381*. London, Macmillan.

EMMISON, F. G. (1973). *Elizabethan Life: Morals and the Church Courts*. Chelmsford, Essex County Council.

EMSLEY, C. (1983). *Policing and its Context 1750–1870*. London, Macmillan.

EMSLEY, C. (1985). " 'The Thump of Wood on a Swede Turnip': Police Violence in Nineteenth-Century England". *Criminal Justice History: an International Annual*, **6,** 125–49.

EMSLEY, C. (1987). *Crime and Society in England 1750–1900*. London, Longman.

EVANS, R. (1982). *The Fabrication of Virtue: English Prison Architecture 1750–1840*. Cambridge, Cambridge University Press.

FLETCHER, A. and STEVENSON, J. (eds.) (1985). *Order and Disorder in Early Modern England*. Cambridge, Cambridge University Press.

FOUCAULT, M. (1977). *Discipline and Punish: the Birth of the Prison*. London, Allen Lane.

GATRELL, V. A. C. (1980). "The Decline of Theft and Violence in Victorian and Edwardian England", in Gatrell, V. A. C., Lenman, B. and Parker, G. (eds.). *Crime and the Law: the Social History of Crime in Western Europe since 1500*. London, Europa.

GATRELL, V. A. C., LENMAN, B. and PARKER, G. (eds.) (1980). *Crime and the Law: the Social History of Crime in Western Europe since 1500*. London, Europa.

GIVEN, J. B. (1977). *Society and Homicide in Thirteenth-Century England*. Stanford, California, Stanford University Press.

HAIR, P. (1972). *Before the Bawdy Court: Selections from Church Court and Other Records Relating to the Correction of Moral Offences in England, Scotland and New England, 1300–1800*. London, Elek.

HAMMER, C. I. (1978). "Patterns of Homicide in a Medieval University Town: Fourteenth-Century Oxford". *Past and Present*, **78,** 3–23.

HANAWALT, B. (1975). "Fur Collar Crime: the Pattern of Crime among the Fourteenth-Century English Nobility". *The Journal of Social History*, **8,** 1–17.

HANAWALT, B. (1979). *Crime and Conflict in English Communities 1300–1348*. Cambridge, Mass, Harvard University Press.

HAY, D. (1975). "Property, Authority and the Criminal Law", in Hay, D., *et al.* Albion's Fatal Tree. London, Allen Lane.

HAY, D. (1982). "War, Dearth and Theft in the Eighteenth Century: the Record of the English Courts", *Past and Present*, **95,** 117–60.

HAY, D., *et al.* (1975). *Albion's Fatal Tree*. London, Allen Lane.

HERRUP, C. B. (1984). "New Shoes and Mutton Pies: Investigative Responses to Theft in Seventeenth-Century East Sussex". *The Historical Journal*, **27,** 811–30.

HILTON, R. H. (1977). *Bond Men Made Free: Medieval Peasant Movements and the English Risings of 1381*. London, Methuen.

HOBSBAWM, E. J. (1972). "Distinctions between Socio-Political and Other Forms of Crime", *Society for the Study of Labour History Bulletin*, **25,** 5–6.

HOWSON, G. (1970). *Thief-Taker General: the Rise and Fall of Jonathan Wild*. London, Hutchinson.

HUGHES, R. (1986). *The Fatal Shore: a History of the Transportation of Convicts to Australia, 1787–1868*. London, Collins Harvill.

IGNATIEFF, M. (1978). *A Just Measure of Pain: the Penitentiary in the Industrial Revolution 1750–1850*. London, Macmillan.

INGRAM, M. (1977). "Communities and Courts: Law and Disorder in Early Seventeenth-Century Wiltshire", in Cockburn, J. S. (ed.). *Crime in England 1550–1800*. London, Methuen.

INGRAM, M. (1984a). "Religion, Communities, and Moral Discipline in Late Sixteenth and Early Seventeenth-Century England: Case Studies", in Von Greyerz, K. (ed.). *Religion and Society in Early Modern Europe 1500–1800*. London, George Allen and Unwin.

INGRAM, M. (1984b). "Ridings, Rough Music and the 'Reform of Popular Culture' in Early Modern England". *Past and Present*, **105,** 79–103.

INNES, J. and STYLES, J. (1986). "The Crime Wave: Recent Writing on Criminal Justice in Eighteenth-Century England", *Journal of British Studies*, **25,** 380–435.

JEAFFRESON, J. C. (1887). *Middlesex County Records*, vol. 2. Clerkenwell, Middlesex County Records Society.

JONES, D. J. V. (1979). "The Poacher: a Study in Victorian Crime and Protest". *The Historical Journal*, **22,** 325–60.

JONES, D. J. V. (1982). *Crime, Protest, Community and the Police in Nineteenth-Century England*. London, Routledge and Kegan Paul.

KEEN, M. (1977). *The Outlaws of Medieval England*. 2nd ed. London,

KENT, J. R. (1986). *The English Village Constable 1580–1642: a Social and Administrative Study*. Oxford, Clarendon Press.

KING, P. (1984). "Decision Makers Decision Making in the English Criminal Law, 1750–1800", *The Historical Journal*, **27,** 25–58.

KING, W. J. (1980). "Leet Jurors and the Search for Law and Order in Seventeenth-Century England: 'Galling Persecution' or Reasonable Justice?" *Histoire Sociale: Social History*, **15,** 315–23.

KING, W. J. (1982). "Untapped Resources for Social Historians: Court Leet Records". *Journal of Social History*, **15,** 699–705.

KNAFLA, L. A. (1977). "Crime and Criminal Justice: a Critical Bibliography", in Cockburn, J. S. (ed.) *Crime in England 1550–1800*. London, Methuen.

LANGBEIN, J. H. (1974). *Prosecuting Crime in the Renaissance: England, Germany, France*. Cambridge, Mass, Harvard University Press.

LANGBEIN, J. H. (1983). "*Albion's* Fatal Flaws". *Past and Present*, **98,** 96–120.

LENMAN, B. and PARKER, G. (1980). "The State, the Community and the Criminal Law in Early Modern Europe", in Gatrell, V. A. C., Lenman, B. and Parker, G. (eds.) *Crime and the Law: the Social History of Crime in Western Europe since 1500*. London, Europa.

McCLINTOCK, F. H. and AVISON, N. H. (1968). *Crime in England and Wales*. London, Heinemann.

MACFARLANE, A. (1981). *The Justice and the Mare's Ale*. Oxford, Blackwell.

McMULLAN, J. L. (1984). *The Canting Crew: London's Criminal Underworld 1550–1700*. New Brunswick, N. J., Rutgers University Press.

MARCHANT, R. A. (1969). *The Church under the Law: Justice, Administration and Discipline in the Diocese of York 1560–1640*. Cambridge, Cambridge University Press.

MELOSSI, D. and PAVARINI, M. (1980). *The Prison and the Factory: Origins of the Penitentiary System*. London, Macmillan.

MUNSCHE, P. B. (1981). *Gentlemen and Poachers: the English Game Laws 1671–1831*. Cambridge, Cambridge University Press.

PHILIPS, D. (1977). *Crime and Authority in Victorian England*. London, Croom Helm.

PHILIPS, D. (1980). "'A New Engine of Power and Authority': the Institutionalization of Law–Enforcement in England 1780–1850", in Gatrell, V. A. C., Lenman, B. and Parker, G. (eds.) *Crime and the law: the Social History of Crime in Western Europe since 1500*. London, Europa.

PUGH, R. B. (1968). *Imprisonment in Medieval England*. Cambridge, Cambridge University Press.

RADZINOWICZ, L. and HOOD, R. (1986). *The Emergence of Penal Policy*. (vol. 5 of "A History of English Criminal Law"). London, Stevens & Sons.

RAFTIS, J. A. (1966). "The Concentration of Responsibility in Five Villages". *Medieval Studies*, **28,** 92–118.

RAZI, Z. (1980). *Life, Marriage and Death in a Medieval Parish: Economy, Society and Demography in Halesowen 1270–1400*. Cambridge, Cambridge University Press.

REITH, C. (1938). *The Police Idea*. Oxford, Clarendon Press.

REITH, C. (1943). *British Police and the Democratic Ideal*. Oxford, Clarendon Press.

RULE, J. (1979). "Social Crime in the Rural South in the Eighteenth and early Nineteenth Centuries". *Southern History*, **1,** 135–53.

RULE, J. (ed.). (1982). *Outside the Law: Studies in Crime and Order 1650–1850*. Exeter Papers in Economic History 15. Exeter University.

RUSCHE, G. and KIRCHHEIMER, O. (1939). *Punishment and Social Structure*. New York, Columbia University Press.

SAMAHA, J. (1974). *Law and Order in Historical Perspective: the Case of Elizabethan Essex*. New York and London, Academic Press.

SAMUEL, R. (ed.) (1981). *East-End Underworld: Chapters in the Life of Arthur Harding*. London, Routledge and Kegan Paul.

SHARP, B. (1980). *In Contempt of All Authority: Rural Artisans and Riot in the West of England 1586–1660*. Berkeley, California, University of California Press.

SHARPE, J. A. (1977). "Crime and Delinquency in an Essex Parish 1600–1640", in Cockburn, J. S. (ed.) *Crime in England 1550–1800*. London, Methuen.

SHARPE, J. A. (1980). "Enforcing the Law in the Seventeenth-Century English Village", in Gatrell, V. A. C., Lenman B., and Parker, G. (eds.) *Crime and the Law: a Social History of Crime in Western Europe from 1500*. London, Europa.

SHARPE, J. A. (1982). "The History of Crime in Late Medieval and Early Modern Europe: a Review of the Field". *Social History*, **7,** 187–203.

SHARPE, J. A. (1983). *Crime in Seventeenth-Century England: a County Study*. Cambridge, Cambridge University Press/Past and Present Publications.

SHARPE, J. A. (1984). *Crime in Early Modern England 1550–1750*. London, Longman.

SHARPE, J. A. (1985a). " 'Last Dying Speeches': Religion, Ideology and Public Execution in Seventeenth-Century England", *Past and Present*, **107,** 144–67.

SHARPE, J. A. (1985b). "The History of Violence in England: Some Observations". *Past and Present*, **108,** 216–24.

SHARPE, J. A. (1985c). "The People and the Law", in Reay, B. (ed.) *Popular Culture in Seventeenth-Century England*. London, Croom Helm.

SHAW, A. G. L. (1966). *Convicts and the Colonies: a Study of Penal Transportation from Great Britain and Ireland to Australia and Other Parts of the British Empire*. London, Faber and Faber.

SLACK, P. (1974). "Vagrants and Vagrancy in England 1598–1664", *Economic History Review*, 2nd Series, **27,** 360–79.

SLACK, P. (ed.) (1984). *Rebellion, Popular Protest and the Social Order in Early Modern England*. Cambridge, Cambridge University Press.

SMITH, A. E. (1947) *Colonists in Bondage: White Servitude and Convict Labour in America, 1607–1776*. Chapel Hill, University of North Carolina Press.

SOMAN, A. (1980). "Deviance and Criminal Justice in Western Europe 1300–1800: an Essay in Structure", *Criminal Justice History: an International Annual*, **1,** 1–28.

SPUFFORD, M. (1986). "Puritanism and Social Control?" in Fletcher, A. and Stevenson, J. (eds.) *Order and Disorder in Early Modern England*. Cambridge, Cambridge University Press.

STEVENSON, J. (1979). *Popular Disturbances In England 1700–1870*. London, Longman.

STONE, L. (1983). "Interpersonal Violence in English Society, 1300–1983", *Past and Present*, **102,** 206–15.

STONE, L. (1985). "A Rejoinder", *Past and Present*, **108,** 216–24.

STONES, E. L. G. (1957). "The Folvilles of Ashby—Folville, Leicestershire, and their Associates in Crime, 1326–1341", *Transactions of the Royal Historical Society*, 5th series, **7,** 117–36.

STORCH, R. D. (1975). "The Plague of Blue Locusts: Police Reform and Popular Resistance in Northern England 1840–57". *International Review of Social History*, **20,** 61–90.

STORCH, R. D. (1976). "The Policeman as Domestic Missionary: Urban Discipline and Popular Culture in Northern England 1850–80", *The Journal of Social History*, 481–509.

STYLES, J. (1982). "An Eighteenth-Century Magistrate as Detective", *Bradford Antiquary*, New Series **47,** 98–117.

STYLES, J. "Sir John Fielding and the Problem of Criminal Investigation in Eighteenth-Century England". *Transactions of the Royal Historical Society*, 5th series, **33,** 127–49.

THOMPSON, E. P. (1971). "The Moral Economy of the English Crowd in the Eighteenth Century". *Past and Present*, **50,** 76–136.

THOMPSON, E. P. (1975). *Whigs and Hunters: the Origins of the Black Act*. London, Allen Lane.

TOBIAS, J. J. (1967). *Crime and Industrial Society in the Nineteenth Century*. London, Batsford.

WIENER, C. Z. (1975). "Sex-Roles and Crime in late Elizabethan Hertfordshire". *The Journal of Social History*, **8,** 18–37.

WRIGHTSON, K. (1980). "Two Concepts of Order: Justices, Constables and Jurymen in Seventeenth-Century England", in Brewer, J. and Styles, J. (eds.) *An Ungovernable People: the English and their Law in the Seventeenth and Eighteenth Centuries*. London, Hutchinson.

WRIGHTSON, K. and LEVINE, D. (1979) *Poverty and Piety in an English Village: Terling, 1525–1700*. New York, etc., Academic Press.

BRITISH CRIMINOLOGY AND THE STATE

ROBERT REINER (*Bristol*)

"So we beat on, boats against the current, borne back ceaselessly into the past."
F. Scott Fitzgerald: *The Great Gatsby*

The standard legal textbook definition of a crime is "an illegal act, omission or event.... the principal consequence of which is that the offender, if he is detected and it is decided to prosecute, is prosecuted by or in the name of the State " (Cross and Jones, 1984, 1). All the current criminal law texts concur in the view that the only consistent distinguishing feature of a crime is that it "is a legal wrong that can be followed by criminal proceedings which may result in punishment" (Glanville Williams, 1983, 27).

The labelling-theory insight that "deviance is *not* a quality of the act the person commits, but rather a consequence of the application by others of rules and sanctions" (Becker, 1963, 5), may have been news to criminology, but it was platitudinous to criminal lawyers.[1] Lest it be thought that the definitions quoted mark some recent departure from a former legal absolutism, the textbooks all draw on a 1931 case in which Lord Atkin declared: "The domain of criminal jurisprudence can only be ascertained by examining what acts at any particular period are declared by the State to be crimes, and the only common nature they will be found to possess is that they are prohibited by the State." (*Proprietary Articles Trade Assn.* v. *Att. Gen. for Canada* [1931] AC at 324).

It would seem to follow that the concept of "the state" would be at the heart of criminology.[2] For as Hermann Mannheim puts it at the start of his 1965 textbook *Comparative Criminology*, "criminology.... means the study of crime", and crime, we have just seen, is a legal domain demarcated by the state. But Mannheim makes it clear that he is using criminology in a "narrower" sense, the study of criminal behaviour and criminals, not the "wider" sense which would encompass in addition issues of penology and prevention (Mannheim, 1965, 3).

The "science of criminology", as it sought to establish itself in the latter part of the nineteenth century as an independent and objective discipline, demarcated a distinctive object of knowledge: "what in fact *is* the criminal?" (Garland, 1985b, 122). Whereas the law denied any absolute basis for

---

[1] Indeed the concept of "crime" as an entity distinct from other wrongs develops only with the evolution of the modern, centralised, capitalist state (Jeudwine, 1917; Jeffrey, 1957; Kennedy, 1970; Lenman and Parker, 1980).

[2] These legal citations only establish a relationship between crime and the state in a descriptive, nominal way. It does not follow that the state is central to understanding or explaining the phenomena of crime and its control (Young, 1983, 87–9). The utility of notions of "the state" to criminology is the subject-matter of this essay, and is an open question unless one forecloses it by adopting a *functional* definition of the state, identifying it with particular purposes or consequences (Dunleavy and O'Leary, 1987, 3–4). Here I adopt an *organisational* definition, identifying the state with a specific configuration of governmental institutions, of relatively recent historical origin, marked by a separation of a "public", bureaucratic constellation of institutions claiming sovereignty and authority over a given territory (ibid., 1–3).

delineating the category of crime, criminology as the naturalistic science of "the criminal" *could* discern that he was "a being apart" (Marro, cited in Garland, op. cit., 124). Thus "the criminological positivists succeeded in what would seem the impossible, they separated the study of crime from the workings and theory of the state." (Matza, 1969, 143). As Matza goes on to suggest, the "lofty subject" of the role of the state, "unrelated to so seamy a matter as deviation', was implicitly demarcated by criminologists as the province of *political* science.

However, a parallel blindness occurred on the side of political theory. The "law and order" or "watchman" function of the state is seen by all political philosophies as its bedrock role (Held *et al.*, 1983, Part 1). Weber's definition of the state, probably the most influential in contemporary social science, points this way (even though it is explicitly couched as a statement of the *means* peculiar to the modern state, not the ends it pursues): "a state is a human community that (successfully) claims the *monopoly of the legitimate use of physical force* within a given territory" (Weber, 1919, 77). On the political left, whatever arguments there may be about the boundaries of the state, the Althusserian "repressive state apparatus" of army, police and prisons are pradigmatically within them (Althusser, 1971). Even on the libertarian right, Nozick's utopian "minimal state" would be a "protective agency" against force, theft, and fraud. (As well as the violation of contracts. Nozick, 1974, IX).

Yet until recently questions of law, order, crime and policing were never addressed in any detail in politics books (though nowadays no self-respecting text would be without a section on this area: Norton, 1984; Dearlove and Saunders, 1984; Drucker *et al.*, 1986). Indeed, in the heyday of its scientistic pretensions, political sociology (like criminology) eschewed any concern with the state (King, 1986, 2–3).

This paper will document and analyse British criminology's conceptualisation of, and relationship to, the state. For the century or so during which the positivistic conception of criminal science held sway, the exploration of its notion of the state matches Sherlock Holmes' celebrated non-barking dog (in *Silver Blaze*): how to interpret an absence.

An increasing concern with the state and the politics of crime was a keynote of the varieties of "new", "critical", "radical" and Marxist criminologies which began to flourish in the 1960s. Although these were often seen as totally fresh departures, consideration of crime in relation to wider questions of the state, legal order and political economy was commonplace before the blinkers of a specialised and technical criminal science rendered invisible what (with hindsight's 20:20 vision) seem obvious connections. For before this, during the late eighteenth and early nineteenth centuries, there had flourished on the Continent and in Britain "a science of police" (with connotations far broader than the present meaning of the term). This comprised a variety of projects for regulating crime and maintaining order which were part of the context within which what is characterised by histories of criminology as the "classical" school flourished. However this "science of police" is neglected in all the histories of criminological thought, with the sole exception of Radzinowicz's encyclopedic *History of English Criminal Law,* the third volume of which is largely taken up with an account of it. The work of this "police science", especially that of its foremost British exponent Patrick Colquhoun, is important for a proper understanding of "classical" criminology, and because it prefigures the broader conceptualisation of the problems of crime, order and justice which became the concern of radical criminology after the 1960s, (and most recently also of a notable revival of interest in criminal justice issues from the perspective of mainstream political thought: Dahrendorf, 1985; Berki, 1983; 1986; Norton, 1987).

The Science of "Police"

If we take "criminology" as a coterminous with self-avowed criminologists then, of course, it dates back only to the 1870s (Mannheim, 1960, 1). Similarly, if we restrict our concern not to the label, but to that particular conception of the domain of criminology derived from the naturalistic "human sciences" of the later nineteenth century. Indeed "to call the work of writers such as Beccaria, Voltaire, Bentham and Blackstone a 'criminology' is altogether misleading" (Garland, 1985, 14–15), and *a fortiori* to see them as "classical criminology". But this is to accept the perspective of the latter positivistic criminological "science" and its casting of its "metaphysical" ancestors into mere prehistory.

The main reason advanced for seeing the work of the earlier writers as not really a "criminology" is that they do not concern themselves with aetiological questions in an empirical way, (Vold, 1958, 23). Rather they take over from utilitarian psychology and mainstream jurisprudence a "voluntarist and rationalist theory of action" (Garland op. cit., ibid. 14–15.)[3] This picture comes from identifying a "classical criminology" what is only one strand in the spectrum of discourse about crime, order and control in the eighteenth and early nineteenth centuries. It arises from taking as paradigmatic Beccaria's *Dei Delitti e Delle Pene,* and its influence on Blackstone, Bentham and the movement for reform of the substantive criminal law and punishment. The latter reforms are, of course, widely recognised to be only part of a set of profound changes in the field of crime control, concompassing also the system of policing, the administration of justice, and more diffuse measures of "social control" (Donajgrodski, 1977; Phillips, 1980; Cohen and Scull, 1983). Although there is an extensive and sophisticated historical literature on the development of policing in this period (which I have summarised in Reiner, 1985a, Chapter 1), there has been virtually no consideration of it in writings on punishment or, more broadly, "penality" (Garland and Young, 1983)—nor vice versa in the police literature. This mutual blindness not only impoverishes our understanding of the complexity and range of different

[3] An apparently contradictory criticism is offered by Taylor, Walton and Young, 1973, 6–7, in relation to the "classical" explanation of the crime of the depraved poor as "the result of factors militating against the free exercise of rational choice". But this is only conceded as an exception to the over-arching conception of rational criminal man, and Taylor, Walton and Young's main line of attack on classicism is that "detailed discussion of the nature of criminal motivation is . . . avoided in most classical writings" (ibid., 5).

positions in the debate about crime and control. It also has led to the eclipse of an important body of thought, the "science of police", which had a close if ambiguous relationship to what is commonly called "classical criminology". When this array of partly competing, partly complementary discourses is excavated, it becomes clearer that while it advanced understanding by foregrounding questions of causation, positivism simultaneously excluded a set of broader issues which have only resurfaced recently.[4] In this sence the development of "criminology" bears the same relation to "police science" as "neo-classical economics" to "political economy" (Robbins, 1981).[5]

The "science of police" was a much broader intellectual enterprise than what has come to be understood as "classical criminology".[6] When the term "police" was introduced into England early in the eighteenth century it was viewed, usually with distaste, as a sinister and Continental, primarily French, conception (Radzinowicz, 1956, 1–8). The term had a much wider sense than the present-day one, Adam Smith defined "police" in 1763 as "the second general division of jurisprudence. The name is French, and is originally derived from the Greek 'politeia' which properly signified the policy of civil government, but now it only means the regulation of the inferior parts of government, viz: cleanliness, security and cheapness of plenty." (Smith, *Lectures on Justice, Police, Revenue and Arms*, cited in Radzinowicz, op. cit., 421.)

The "science of police" which flourished in Europe during the eighteenth century was a vast body of work[7] which encompassed the whole art of government in the sense of the regulation, management and maintenance of population, what Foucault has called "governmentality" (Foucault, 1979). In the eighteenth century the various discourses on government took the form of a science of police, the latter being a reference to the development and promotion of "happiness" or the "public good", rather than to the suppression of disorder, the surveillance of public space or the protection of private property, which is its contemporary reference." (Smart, 1983, 80). This narrower definition only begins to appear later in the eighteenth century in England (following the inspiration of the Fieldings) and on the Continent (Radzinowicz, 1956, 4; Pasquico, 1978, 45). Even then, the main English exponents—Bentham, Colquhoun; Chadwick all used the term in a much broader sense than the present day one, as did their European counterparts. As late as 1885 we find Maitland defining police as "such part of social organisation as is concerned immediately with the maintenance of good order, or the prevention or detection of offences," (Maitland, 1885, 105)—a usage connoting much more than stout men in blue coats.

[4] Interestingly Dahrendorf refers to himself in the Foreword to his lectures on *Law and Order* as "an unreconstructed eighteenth-century liberal" (Dahrendorf, 1985, xi). Beccaria was appointed to a Chair of "Political Economy and Science of Police" at Milan. In his lectures on *Elements of Political Economy* 1769 he included "police" as the "fifth and last object of political economy". (Cited in Pasquino, 1978, 45.)

[5] Let alone what is currently called "police science" i.e. the technical aspects of practical crime investigation (Walsh, 1985).

[6] Pasquino cites a bibliography which lists "for German–speaking lands alone and within the period from the start of the 17th century to the end of the 18th, no fewer than 3,215 titles under the heading of 'Science of police in the strict sense' ". (Pasquino, 1978, 48).

[7] Pasquino cites a 1760 book by Von Justi: *Foundations of the Power and Happiness of States, or an Exhaustive Presentation of the Science of Public Police (op. cit.,* 44).

This whole corpus of work, and especially the contribution of Colquhoun, merits attention as a precursor of criminology, especially in its latter-day newly rediscovered relationship with political economy and the state. It highlights the fact that what is taken to be "classical criminology" (the Beccaria tradition) represented only one pole in a complex network of debate about law, crime, order, punishment, control, the state, morals and "happiness". Beccaria and Von Humboldt were suspicious of strategies seeking to control crime through expansions of state power or police activity. In England an array of liberal and conservative opinion including Burke, Blackstone, Adam Smith and Paley all opposed the apostles of "police science". The Benthamite Utilitarian position which attempted to combine Beccaria's advocacy of reform of law and punishment, with a more positive strategy of prevention by policing and other interventionist social policies, was anything but predominant, and always faced considerable opposition and uneven political successes in such compromise measures as the 1839 or 1856 Police Acts.

The work of Colquhoun in particular is worthy of attention for a number of reasons.[8] He maps out his proposals for the prevention and control of crime on the basis of an attempt to investigate empirically and thereby to explain the pattern of crime.[9] But the phenomena of crime and criminal justice are not seen as independent realms which can be considered in isolation from a broader analysis of the social and economic structure. Like all his contemporaries, Colquhoun saw himself as engaged in political economy, not some specialist "criminology" asbstracted from the total project of governing (or "police"), yet Colquhoun was also very much alive to the symbolic as well as the instrumental aspects of policing.

This is not to suggest Colquhoun as a model for us. His staunch conservatism and lack of regard for civil liberties is unlikely to endear him to most present-day criminologists.[10] He did accept much of the "classical" argument for restricting the scope and severity of criminal sanctions on both humanitarian and instrumental grounds, and was an ardent advocate of after-care (Radzinowicz, 1956, 255–7). But he was an unsqueamish upholder of the political *status quo*, and as a magistrate "endeavoured with unflinching firmness to put down popular manifestations and disturbances" (Ibid, 213–4).

Colquhoun's criminology was one which located the ultimate causes of crime in the overall structure of economy and society. In addition to his better-known *Treatise on the Police of the Metropolis* and *Treatise on the Commerce*

[8] It has also been almost entirely neglected. The only lengthy consideration of this prolific writer's corpus of work is in Radzinowicz, 1956, 211–312. Apart from one article (Stead, 1977), he appears fleetingly in footnotes in most histories of the police, and virtually nowhere else. His contribution to the development of the police is underestimated, possibly because Peel slighted him (Radzinowicz, 1956, 230–1), but it was significant and acknowledged by many others (ibid.). But the importance of his work to criminology more generally is overlooked, perhaps because of an erroneous impression that it only concerned police reform.

[9] In his attempt to map quantitatively the contours of crime and social structure Colquhoun anticipates (albeit at a crude level) the French "moral statisticians" Quetelet and Guerry, and their more sociological approach, which was itself largely submerged later in the nineteenth century by individualistic criminal science (Morris, 1957, 44–8). The etymology of "statistics" as the "science of the state" ("political arithmetic" in Petty's usage) is worth noting (Pasquino, 1978, 50; Smart, 1983 79.)

[10] Or to some contemporaries. An anonymous pamphlet of 1800 spoke of his scheme as "a new engine of Power and Authority so enormous and extensive as to threaten a species of despotism". (Cited in Philips, 1980, 155.)

and Police of the River Thames, Colquhoun was the author of *A Treatise on Indigence* and numerous other works on political economy and the relief of poverty. Indigence was related to crime in a relationship of mutual inter-dependence,[11] and Colquhoun devoted much effort to mapping and measuring the class structure (primarily in *Treatise on the Wealth, Power, and Resources of the British Empire*). But Colquhoun's analysis was not a simple or reductionist economic determinism. The link between indigence and crime was "the character of the labouring people" (*Treatise on Indigenence*, 239). Poverty exerted a structural pressure to crime—"from a state of indigence, wretchedness and despair, the transition is easy to criminal offences"—and hence the relief of poverty was integrally related to the prevention of crime. But there were many links between objective structural condition and criminality, social and cultural processes which required specific analysis. The precise availability of legitimate opportunities had to be discovered.[12]

The link between ethnicity and crime, for example, was explored in these terms. Colquhoun addressed what he saw as the "system of fraud and depradation" among Jews of German–Dutch extraction. This was not a racial issue—it was not due to "any actual disposition on their parts to pursue these nefarious practices," a point evident in the contrast with the respectable Portuguese Jewish community. It was "generated in a greater degree by their peculiar situation in respect to society", in particular lack of training. The remedy was utilising internal community resources: better integration with the Portuguese Jews and the influence of the synagogues, with state inter-vention (in the form of compulsory apprenticeship) only as a last resort (Radzinowicz, 1956, 273–4).

Overall, though the link between structural economic conditions and crime was constituted by a variety of factors which in modern jargon would be seen as aspects of "control theory" (Downes and Rock, 1982, Ch. 9). The basic problem was that "the morals and habits of the lower ranks in society are growing progressively worse". This was the product of the erosion of positive influences such as religion, and the flourishing of malign influences, such as bawdy ballad-singers and pubs. Rather than prohibiting such leisure pur-suits, they should be turned to good effect, for example by distributing uplift-ing literature for the use of ballad-singers (Radzinowicz, op. cit., 275). In addition, there was invoked a free-floating variable of "the thoughtless improvidence of this class of labouring people, that they are generally the first who indulge themselves by eating oysters, lobsters and pickled salmon etc., when first in season, and long before these luxuries are considered accessible to the middle ranks of the community; whose manners are generally as virtuous as the others are depraved". (Ibid., 235.)

Formal and negative social control in the specific sense of criminal justice and punishment was only a relatively minor element in the reduction of crime,

---

[11] The *Treatise on Indigence* was subtitled *Ameliorating the Condition of the Poor. . . .by the Diminution of Moral and Penal Offences, and the Future Prevention of Crimes.*

[12] Illegitimate opportunities and the sheer volume of goods available to steal were also relevant: crime was "the constant and never-failing attendant on the accumulation of wealth" (*Treatise on the Commerce and Police of the River Thames*, 155–6).

and their role was conceived more in terms of prevention through the restriction of temptations and the bolstering of mortality than through deterrence and fear (though these were important for the hard-core delinquent). Colquhoun's distinctive advocacy of a professional police force must be located within this overall analysis and strategy, but its role was to be much broader than merely enhancing the certainty of detection (and thus the deterrent efficacy of the precisely calculated penalties of the classical criminological schema). The explanation of crime was not in terms of a classical "rational man" model, nor even "the rational choice within social constraints" model attributed to the "moral statisticians" (Garland, 1985a, 110). For all its crudity and bourgeois snobbery, it was a complex (if sometimes unsubtle) unravelling of a network of cultural and social processes and influences interplaying with moral choice. The answer lay more in the field of welfare than penality, and even the police were conceived primarily in these terms. A more effective police would not only benefit the respectable, but "all those whose vices and enormities it tends to restrain". Its terrain of operation was to be "upon the broad scale of General Prevention—mild in its operations—effective in its results; having justice and humanity for its basis, and the general security of the State and Individuals for its ultimate object". (*Treatise on the Commerce and Police of the River Thames*, 38.)

This brief consideration of the late eighteenth early nineteenth century "science of police" has demonstrated that alongside the "classical" school of criminology there flourished, in Britain as well as Europe, a conception of crime, order and control which was more alive to the interpretation of politics, law and social justice with criminality than was the later science of the criminal. It also operated with a more sociological notion of the aetiology of crime than the standard picture of classical criminology's "economic man". For all the gains of the later positivist school in the direction of understanding criminal psychology (cf. West's essay in this volume), it eclipsed the relationship between state, social and legal order which has only been re-addressed in the last three decades.

Positivist Criminology

The content, conditions of existence and implications of the programme of positivist criminology have been so definitively analysed recently (Garland, 1985a and b; Radzinowicz and Hood, 1986) that no more is needed here than a brief summary of its relationship to the state.

Garland identifies as "the heart of the criminological enterprise ... the dual concepts of *individualisation* and *differentiation*" (Garland, 1985b, 115). The individualism of "classical criminology" insisted "that all men are equal, free and rational" and this liberal humanism "put definite limits upon the operation and presentation of regulatory forms" (ibid, 130). The location of crime in particular social classes—the indigent or the dangerous—by Colquhoun and the "science of police" laid bare the links between crime, politics and morality. It led either to demands for social reform or outright clashes between class cultures or both. What scientific criminology offered was relief of this "legitimatory deficit" . . . The existence of a class which was constantly criminalised—indeed the very existence of an impoverished sector of the population—could now be explained by reference to the natural, constitutional propensities of these individuals, thereby excluding all reference to the character of the law, of politics or of social relations." (Ibid., 131.)

While the analytic relationship between the state and crime slipped out of the frame, underlying the project of scientific criminology was "the constant figure of the State as the presumed subject of this enterprise. . . criminology's arguments were explicitly directed towards an increased interventionism on the part of the State . . . But this assumption that the central State is indeed the proper subject of this process (and not private organisations, or more localised administrations), and the political arguments and ideologies which might justify such a position, are so entrenched in this programme that they go mostly unspoken . . . the issue is passed over in the silence of self-evidence. However . . .not only the politics but also the practical ambitions of criminology necessitate the State as their subject." (Ibid., 129–30.) Thus criminological science, while dropping the relationship of crime and the state from its field of vision, nonetheless promoted "an extended statism" (ibid., 134) through demands for public support of the caring and controlling professions who delivered the new scientific expertise and policies.

The changing conceptions of the state and its strategies for social regulation within which criminology was embedded are usually interpreted as a response to "crisis" (Garland, 1985a, 59–66). It is important, however, to recognise exactly what constituted the sense of crisis in this period. Crime in general was *falling* not rising in the latter part of the nineteenth century (Gatrell, 1980), and this was widely recognised by contemporaries who puzzled about the causes of this "English miracle" (Radzinowicz and Hood, 1986, Ch. 5).[13] The Metropolitan Police Commissioner's Report for 1882 spoke of London as "the safest capital for life and property in the world", while the criminal statistics at the dawn of the new century were said to exhibit our "exceptional immunity from crime" (ibid., 116–7). The last quarter of the nineteenth century was "a period of unfaltering optimism" concerning crime, following on the mid-century decades of "qualified optimism"—and a far cry from the "unrelieved pessimism" of the first four decades of the nineteenth century (ibid., 113–5).

Where then was the "social and penal crisis of the 1890s' which is often seen as a precondition of the criminological programme? (Garland, 1985b, 117). The fundamental root of the feeling of anxiety which many commentators have identified in the last two decades of the nineteenth century was Britain's reduced and threatened economic dominance, undermining confidence in the old liberal notions of self-adjusting social equilibrium. "Confidence waned and prospects clouded over, as the last quarter of the nineteenth-century saw Britain slipping from the sunny uplands of mid-Victorian liberal capitalism towards the valley of the shadow of socialism and war." (Porter, 1987, 13.) The response of the governing classes was divided. Some saw the remedy in a

---

[13] At the same time there were panics about specific kinds of crime, for example a supposedly new strain of juvenile violence (Pearson, 1983).

tougher marshalling of the state's forces of order. Others advocated increasing state intervention in the economic and social arena to secure the long-term allegiance of the working-class as the necessary precondition for safeguarding the core of the free-enterprise system and the rights of property. (Ibid., 20–1). Unevenly and patchily to be sure, but nonetheless steadily, it was the latter position which prevailed. The consequences for the state's "repressive apparatuses" of the long-term strategy of stability through incorporation and winning the consent of the mass of the working-class were complex. Deprivation, crime, public order and political subversion were separated out into differentiated problems for state policy, not the integrated image of the indigence/dangerousness couplet which had been perceived by the "science of police". The coincidence of wider social anxiety with the growth of Fenian and anarchist terrorist incidents was the precondition for the radical departure from British tradition of establishing the Special Branch in the 1880s as the first specifically political police (Porter, 1987). The continuing concern with demarcating and elucidating the political as distinct from the ordinary (i.e. abnormal) offender, although it had a long history in England, was sharpened and accentuated in this period, (Radzinowicz and Hood, 1986, Ch. 13; Bottomley, 1979, 10–20).

The latter part of the nineteenth century saw many disturbances and riots, arising out of industrial or political conflict. (Stevenson, 1979; Richter, 1981). However the conception of these, and the strategy for dealing with them, altered as mid-Victorian ruling-class confidence receded. The police had been established in part as a way of supplanting brute coercion with a more complex combination of moral co-option and surveillance of the masses, with finely-tuned delivery of legitimate "minimum force" as the ultimate back-up (Silver, 1967). This became accentuated with the rise of the more inter-ventionist state towards the end of the nineteenth century. By the early years of this century the police had almost completely taken over from the army for purposes of riot control. Police strategy itself became part of a virtuous circle of declining levels of violence as the state and those involved in political or industial conflict accepted constitutional parameters for resolving disputes and the prime battle became one over public opinion rather than immediate physical control of particular spaces, (Geary, 1985). This more subtle strategy for controlling disorder went hand-in-hand with the growing involvement of the central state, concerned more with long-run social stability than short-term suppression (Reiner, 1985b; 140; Geary, 1985, Chs. 3, 4, 6). Police ability to tread the tightrope between premature or excessive shows of force and the threat of being overwhelmed due to inadequate preparation was crucially dependent on adequate political intelligence, gathered through the political police whose birth had been contested for so long (Porter, 1987; Khan et al., 1983, 94–5).

As far as mundane crime is concerned the twin themes of individualisation and differentiation which Garland has identified as the core of positivist criminological science continued to underpin theory, research and penal policy throughout the first five decades of this century. Criminals were dis-tinguished not only from "normal" conformists or political dissidents, but in increasingly complex ways from each other. Distinctions between habituals, the feeble-minded, vagrants, drunkards, juveniles, and young adults proliferated in penal theory and practice (Radzinowicz and Hood, 1986). Right down to the post-Second World War "Welfare State" penal policy developed as one aspect of an increasingly interventionist state. The state's task was seen stretching beyond negative crime-control measures to a broader responsibility for reducing criminogenic features of the social structure by a panoply of social and welfare policies. Offenders, especially juvenile ones, were hopefully to be reclaimed by rehabilitative interventions shaped by scientific research and advice (Bailey, 1987). This approach also underlay the state's sponsorship of criminological research, falteringly in the inter-war years, but with a strong institutional base after the 1957 creation of the Home Office Research Unit and the establishment of the Cambridge Institute of Criminology two years later. These developments were made possible by s.77 of the Criminal Justice Act 1948 which authorised the Home Secretary to conduct, or support financially, research into "the causes of delinquency and the treatment of offenders, and matters connected therewith". (See papers by Morris and Martin in this volume. Also: Butler,1974; Lodge, 1974; Sparks, 1983; Clarke and Cornish, 1983; Bottoms, 1987; Hood, 1987). Thus in the century after the birth of a self-conscious and self-labelled criminological movement, the state became increasingly involved in sponsoring it, as well as supporting a panoply of experts in penal treatment. This was all part-and-parcel of the generally more interventionist state, promoting an array of social and welfare policies and responsible for economic management, partly, although by no means only, as a way of sustaining the preconditions of order and conformity. Down to the 1950s this programme was broadly successful in achieving a more crime-free, orderly and integrated society. The project of the original "science of police" as an interrelated set of policing, legal and social measures, was implemented, even though the criminal science that replaced it in theory blocked out overt recognition of the role of the state which nourished it. The state only came back into criminological awareness following the "epistemological break" engendered by the variety of radical criminologies which flourished after the 1960s.

Radical criminology and the state

During the late 1960s British criminology began to experience a proliferating babble of critiques and proposed new programmes for theory and research. As one commentator remarked: "The danger of experiencing too great a succession of so-called paradigmatic revolutions, without any concomitant intervals of normal science, is a sense of toppling into a metaphysical swamp." (Downes, 1978, 498.) At first the National Deviancy Conference constituted a kind of organisational umbrella.Mutual opposition to "establishment criminology" and its institutional denizens the Home Office Research Unit and the Cambridge Institute (both barely ten years old despite being perceived as hoary monoliths) provided some ideological glue. But by the early 1970s theoretical and political schisms began to proliferate, and by

1976 it was necessary to speak of "the new criminolog*ies*" (Wiles, 1976). The history of these developments and controversies has been well documented elsewhere (for example in Cohen, 1971, 1983; Rock and Mackintosh, 1974; Sparks, 1980, 1983). Consequently I will restrict myself to the way that the new departures all involved a rediscovery of the state. Indeed one of the key unifying themes was a generally oppositional stance to the state and its works, for all the divergent ways in which these might be analysed. Roughly we can distinguish three main stages in the treatment of the state in recent radical British criminology.

(a) Radical conflict theory

One of the key British works of Marxist criminology has claimed that: "Most criminological theories—including much of 'radical criminology'—have no concept or theory of the state." (Hall *et al.*, 1978, 194). It is true that, in so far as they used the term at all, the new criminologies of the late 1960s and early 1970s operated with a hazy and amorphous image of the state as "Leviathan" (Matza, 1969).[14] Mostly they did not use the concept of the state explicitly in referring to the collectivity of official control institutions. These were given some vaguer label, such as "societal control culture" (Lemert, 1951) or "social reaction" (Taylor, Walton and Young, 1973).

The official control institutions of the state became problematic for British criminologists in a variety of ways, "Labelling theory" emphasised that the origins and application of deviant labels required analysis, both because these constituted the categories of deviance, and because they were able causally implicated in "secondary deviation", which was supposedly more significant socially than initial "primary" deviant acts (Becker, 1963; Lemert, 1967).[15] Control institutions were also morally and politically problematic for the "new" criminologists' "underdog" sympathies (Becker, 1967). Gouldner's influential 1968 critique of Becker pointed the way towards a more macro-structural analysis of the operation of control institutions.

The culmination of this plea was Taylor, Walton and Young's 1973 *The New Criminology*, which was both the most controversial and the most seminal work of radical criminology in this period. What is striking in the light of the subsequent development of radical criminology is the virtually complete absence of discussion of the state. In their sketch of the "formal requirements" of "a fully social theory" of deviance, the state figures fleetingly in the call for analysis of how "the political economy of the state" must play a part in elucidating the "wider origins of deviant reaction" (pp. 273–4). *The New Criminology* has a problematic relationship to Marxist theory, as the authors' well-known debate with Hirst indicated (Taylor, Walton and Young, 1975, Chs. 8–10).[16]

---

[14] "Matza's discussion is so abstract and ahistorical as to provide little guidance to understanding the operation of the state in a particular society at some given historical moment." (Pearce, 1976, 48).

[15] Studying the development of categories of crime as well as of criminal behaviour had already been urged by some writers within a more conventional criminological framework e.g. Jeffery, 1960.

[16] Though a debate about whether there could be an authentically Marxist theory of law and crime was to appear ironic a few years later when the issue had become rather "whether a Marxist framework can and should replace all others" (Nelken, 1980, 197).

The absence of an elaborated analysis of the role of the state is a key to what is probably the central weakness of *The New Criminology* (and the radical criminologies of which it is the ultimate embodiment): its totally oppositional stance. This was pin-pointed not only by mainstream "bourgeois" critiques (e.g. Inciardi, 1980; Sparks, 1980) but also by more explicitly Marxist writers. Their castigation of the "correctionalism" of traditional criminology meant a failure to "distinguish the destructive or demoralising aspects of some kinds of deviance from the potentially liberating ones. . . . An approach to deviance that can't distinguish between politically progressive and politically retrogressive forms of deviance doesn't provide much of a basis for real understanding or political action". (Currie, 1974, 112). This would require "a political philosophy and a theory of history within which to assess the deviant act" (ibid., 111). That is, a more articulated and rounded notion of the state and its functions is needed. Hirst makes this explicit: "The operation of law or custom, however much it may be associated in some societies with injustice and oppression, is a necessary condition of existence of any social formation. Whether the social formation has a State or not, whether it is communist or not, it will control and coerce in certain ways the acts of its members. . . One cannot imagine the absence of the control of traffic or the absence of the suppression of theft and murder, nor can one consider these controls as purely oppressive." (In Taylor, Walton and Young, 1975, 240). A similar conclusion about the one-sided, simplistically oppositional treatment of moral and political issues by the "new" deviance theory was also reached through a different route, via symbolic interactionism. "Rather than convey a model of moral life as densely textured and intricate, they have constructed a kind of sociological Flatland. . . . Not only is there a denial of complexity and ambiguity, there is a failure to differentiate between *kinds* of value. It seems to be assumed that notions concerning, say, murder, clothing, marihuana and chocolate are all interchangeable analytic units." (Rock, 1974, 154–6).

The central weakness in the radical criminologies culminating in *The New Criminology* was this absence of a systematic analysis of the concepts of the state, law and order (political and moral). In the years after *The New Criminology*, three reactions are discernible. Business as usual continued for conventional "mainstream" work, side-stepping the issues posed by the new theoretical critique (Sparks, 1983, 89). Theoretical analysis moved predominantly into some kind of Marxist direction, explicitly foregrounding the concepts of law and state. At the same time, problems with Marxist approaches were broached by critiques from a number of other theoretical traditions (notably in Downes and Rock, 1979).

(b) Marxist criminology and the state

The first phase of an overtly Marxist criminology primarily involved erstwhile radical conflict theorists altering the language and tone, rather than the conceptual structure of their theories. This is vividly shown in an American example by a detailed comparison of two versions of Chambliss' article on the law of vagrancy (Klockars, 1980, 100–2). The jargon of pluralist conflict theory is consistently swapped for Marxist terms in the later version but the structure remains the same. (E.g. in "The Statutes served a new and equally important function for the social order" the word "ruling class' replaces "social order.") An English example is Taylor, Walton and Young's more explicitly Marxist reworking of *The New Criminology,* the 1975 collection *Critical Criminology.* The former book's advocacy of "human diversity" which would not be subject to control in socialist society should have been discussed in terms of "the withering away of the state" according to the later book (Taylor, Walton and Young, 1975, 20). The result of these changes in the development of a criminology built around an *instrumentalist* theory of law and state as straightforward tools of ruling-class interests. (E.g. Pearce, 1976, 58–66.) As Young put it: "Radical criminological strategy is not to argue for legality and the rule of law but it is to show up the law, in its true colour, as the instrument of a ruling class, and *tactically* to demonstrate that the State will break its own laws, that its legitimacy is a sham, and that the rule-makers are also the greatest of rule-breakers." (Young, 1975, 89).[17] This is a succinct instance of what Young in his later "realist" incarnation would call "left idealism".

The instrumentalist notion of law and state has many obvious problems. Above all it cannot readily or plausibly interpret laws which on the face of it operate to control members of the ruling-class or to advance the welfare of the working-class. Nor can it explain why there is clear cross-class consensus about the most central aspects of criminal law and criminal justice (Levi, 1987, Ch. 3). A reading of Marx on the origins of the Factory Acts in *Capital* (Vol. 1, Ch. 10) shows clearly that Marx's own analysis of the relationship between class, law and state was not an instrumentalist one.

The reaction to the perceived inadequacies of instrumentalism amongst many Marxist criminologists was "back to the classics". Nor so much to Marx himself because of the lack of an elaborated theory of law and the state in his mature work, as to later Marxist theorists. Thus in the joint National Deviancy Conference/Conference of Socialist Economists' 1979 *Capitalism and the Rule of Law: From Deviancy Theory to Marxism,* there are papers exploring the possibilities of such early twentieth century Marxists as Renner or Pashukanis.

The apogee of the attempt to develop an analysis of law, crime and the state within the Marxist tradition is the ambitious and complex 1978 book *Policing the Crisis* by Stuart Hall *et al.* This is an impressive marriage of concepts derived from "new" deviance theory (moral panic, folk-devils, deviance amplification, labelling) with modern Marxist theory of the state, particularly as developed by Gramsci, Althusser and Poulantzas. Starting with the analysis of the "mugging" scare of 1972–3 (and in particular one particular

[17] In so far as it argues that dominant state-defined conceptions of crime neglect much anti-social behaviour, Box's claim that "there is more to crime and criminals than the state reveals" (Box, 1983, 15) is a recent example of this position. It is not clear what is gained by encompassing all evils under an amorphous category of "crime" (Bottomley, 1979, 10). Box's book does, however, valuably underline most criminology's neglect of offending (against ordinary rules of criminal law) by agents of the state itself and "the powerful" more generally.

robbery in Handsworth in 1972), the authors "go behind the label to the contradictory social content which is mystifyingly reflected in it" (Hall *et al.*, 1978, vii). From the study of the "mugging" panic the authors are led to analyse "the general 'crisis of hegemony' in the Britain of the 1970s". This involves both the elaboration of a theoretical framework for understanding crime, law and state, and a breakdown of post-war British social history, centring on how economic and political crises pave the way for the mobilis-ation of fears and anxieties, and legitimate the development of an exceptional form of authoritarian "strong state" and "law and order society".

Policing the Crisis is undoubtedly an intellectual *tour de force* in its bold attempt to synthesise a diversity of approaches, and gives a fascinating spectacle of "the epistemological dilution of structuralist Marxism through its confrontation with the nasty business of empirical reality" (Sumner, 1981, 277–8). The complex theoretical edifice seems, however, to be built on a rather cursory brush with this "nasty business".

Two critiques, from opposing ideological positions (and different percep-tions of "empirical reality"), have converged on the problem of identifying the central concept of moral panic. When is concern, and public policy directed towards it, to be analysed as a "panic", as distinct from a reasonable response to a problem? Hall *et al.* speak of "panic" when "the official reaction to a person, groups of persons or series of events is *out of all proportion* to the actual threat offered"? (p. 16). But this reference to "proportion" makes the concept an arbitrary value judgement unless it is solidly anchored in both agreed criteria of proportionality and convincing evidence about the scale of "the threat". Subsequent research has shown that contrary to the implication of Hall *et al.* the mugging scare was preceded by substantial increases in crime in general, as well as crimes of violence and "robbery and assault with intent to rob" more specifically (Pratt, 1980; Waddington, 1986). From an opposing perspective, it has been pointed out that the evidence for a general public panic about mugging in 1972–3 is itself flimsy (Sumner, 1981, 281–5). It is inferred from a top-down reading of the state's reaction to mugging, with the only direct evidence about *public* opinion being dubiously representative "letters to the editor". The more general point is the lack of grounding of even more sophisticated Marxist analyses of state and crime in empirical research, especially on the inside workings of state institutions.[18] (The sole exception is a recently published volume on the police by members of the *Policing the Crisis* team: Grimshaw and Jefferson, 1987. Although primarily focused on patrol work this does mark an important advance in giving some empirical data on the decision-making process within a police force.) There are still no criteria developed for demarcating the oppressive from other aspects of the functioning of the state, as is indicated by the unanalysed notion of the "proportionality" of "panic" to "problem".[19]

[18] A partial exception to this is the burgeoning "revisionist" historical literature on policing and punish-ment (Brogden, 1982; Philips, 1983; Ignatieff, 1981; Reiner, 1985: Ch. 1). This is mostly "bottom-up" history, however, revealing little about state institutions from the inside.

[19] One exception is Jefferson and Grimshaw, 1984 and its discussion of "socialist justice" principles.

Post-Marxist criminology and the state

In recent years a number of strands of criminological discussion have emerged which recognise the political context of crime and law but reject or qualify a Marxist approach. There are two primary roots of these developments. The first is the magnitude of the crime problem as a public issue, and the re-appearance of public disorder with clear political implications, both after a century of apparent decline (Reiner, 1985c; Gatrell, 1987; Lea *et al.*, 1987; Dunning *et al.*, 1987). The second is the fragmentation of the class context for radical perceptions of crime and disorder, and the growing salience of other dimensions: race, gender, age, generation and location.

Three main post-Marxist strands can be discerned in current debate about the state, law, order, crime and politics. The first reflects the influence of Foucault, in particular his seminal work on the history of punishment (Foucault, 1977, 1979). This has sensitised many British criminologists to the integral links of power and knowledge, the complex and subtle weaving of relations of power throughout the social sphere as distinct from a concen-trated locus of state power, and the disciplinary face of apparently liberating movements towards relaxing formal social controls (Cohen, 1979, 1984, 1985; Abel, 1982; Garland and Young, 1983; Scull, 1979; Cohen and Scull, 1983). The price of this analytic subtlety is a lack of clear implications for policy or politics, beyond rather vague gestures towards "anarchism" or "progressive penal politics", which indicate little more than one's heart is in the right (or left?) place (Young, 1983, 100; Garland, 1985; 262; Cohen, 1985, 272).

The second strand is the development of what Young calls a new "left realism" (Young, 1979, 1986; Lea and Young, 1984; Kinsey, Lea and Young, 1986; Taylor, 1981). This starts from the recognition that crime ought to be an important political issue for the left, but that hitherto the right has succeded in "stealing" it to their political advantage (Downes, 1983). Victimisation surveys, especially those conducted on a local basis, reveal that crime is a major problem in reality precisely for the most socially deprived and vulnerable sections of the population, the left's traditional heartland (Kinsley, 1985; Jones *et al.*, 1986). Viable policies for preventing or alleviating crime can be pursued as immediately practical reforms, with-out waiting for a socialist millenium or succumbing to the tough "law and order" placebos of the right (Morison, 1987). At the same time these policies would be compatible with, if not presuppose, a wider agenda of progressive democratisation of local and central state structures and an empowerment of the deprived. This analysis has been subject to severe criticism, questioning its realism and its socialism (Scraton, 1985; Gilroy and Sim, 1985). But it has been widely welcomed for taking the issue of crime seriously while still recog-nising its broader political dimensions, (and it influenced Labour's 1987 General Election Campaign (Reiner, 1987b). The analytic side of "left realism" has not developed in pace with its empirical research and policy recommendations. In particular there has been little discussion of the concept of, and relationship to, the state. (Apart from some parts of Taylor,

1981).[20] Interestingly the empirical research by "left realists" has been sponsored by parts of the "local state", radical councils such as Merseyside or Islington (Reiner, 1987a).

The final strand of recent work on crime and the state, perhaps the most noteworthy of all, is the appearance of liberal and conservative analysis of "law and order" which recognise its political aspects. In a sense this returns to the problematic of "the science of police", locating the crime and order issue within the broader project of governance.[21] Traditionally the liberal and conservative stance has been to see problems of crime control as merely technical matters, or as straightforward moral confrontations of good and evil. But in recent years a number of important works have appeared, developing sophisticated analysis of "law and order" from within the traditions of liberal or conservative political philosophy (Berki, 1983, 1986; Dahrendorf, 1985; Norton, 1985, 1987).

One of the key aspects of this has been the attempt to distinguish between different facets of state activity. This has also been a keynote of a significant American contribution to Marxist analysis of crime and the state, which could potentially provide a theoretical underpinning to "left realism" (Marenin, 1982, 1985). This distinguishes between the role of the state in preserving "general order, the interests of all in regularity", from "specific order, that is the use of state power to promote particular interests" (Marenin, 1982, 258–9). This points to a theoretical rationale for the "left realist" stance of perceiving the issue of crime and order at least partly from *within* the state, as contrasted with radical criminology's erstwhile totally oppositional perspective. There is here the prospect of some convergence of hitherto conflicting positions, with a measure of consensus stemming from a more complex analysis of the state's functioning. One novel fall-out from this might be the development of empirical research on, and a more grounded understanding of, the working's of the state's institutions for crime control.[22] The state would thus become not only part of criminology's conceptual field but also of its research agenda.

REFERENCES

Abel, R. (ed.) (1982). *The Politics of Informal Justice*. New York, Academic Press.
Althusser, L. (1971). "Ideology and ideological state apparatuses," in *Lenin and Philosophy*. London, New Left Books.

[20] This has been facilitated partly by left realism's implicit conception of the "law and order" issue in terms of mundane property and personal crime, as distinct from questions of public disorder, large-scale professional crime, or white-collar offences. There is a parallel with the way that labelling theory's concentration on "nuts, sluts and perverts" permitted the flourishing of sympathy with the deviant and hostility to social control.
[21] Significantly the Home Office Research Unit's work is now much more concerned with studies of the police and other aspects of the state, as distinct from its earlier concentration on penal technique (Reiner, 1987a).
[22] Empirical research on state control apparatuses has hitherto been restricted to the lower-levels of police organisations or the under-life of prisons. Work on the more overtly political and policy levels has been mainly within a public law framework, focusing on the accountability issue, (Lustgarten, 1986; Maguire, Vagg and Morgan, 1985). What empirical research there has been on higher-level functioning has been either historical or based on official statistics. It is only recently that empirical field-work on higher levels of state control organisations has been attempted, as by Rock, 1987 (and forthcoming) on the development of victim policy in Canada and the U.K., and my own current research on chief constables.

BAILEY, V. (1987). *Delinquency and Citizenship*. Oxford, Oxford University Press.

BECKER, H. (1963). *Outsiders*. New York, Free Press.

BECKER, H. (1967). "Whose side are we on?". *Social Problems*, **14,** 239–247.

BERKI, R. (1983). *Considerations on Law and Order*. Hull Papers in Politics 35, University of Hull.

BERKI, R. (1986). *Security and Society: Reflections on Law, Order and Politics*. London, Dent.

BOTTOMLEY, A. K. (1979). *Criminology in Focus*. Oxford, Martin Robertson.

BOTTOMS, A. E. (1987). "Reflections on the Criminological Enterprise". *Cambridge Law Journal*, 240–263.

BOX, S. (1983). *Power, Crime and Mystification*. London, Tavistock.

BROGDEN, M. (1982). *The Police: Autonomy and Consent*. London, Academic Press.

BUTLER, Lord R. A. B. (1974) "The Foundation of the Institute of Criminology in Cambridge", in Hood, R. (1974), 1–11.

CLARKE, R. and CORNISH, D. (1983). *Crime Control in Britain*. Albany, State University of New York Press.

COHEN, (ed.) (1971). *Images of Deviance*. London, Penguin.

COHEN, S. (1974). "Criminology and the sociology of deviance in Great Britain," in Rock, P. and Mackintosh, M. (1974), 1–40.

COHEN, S. (1979). "The Punitive City". *Contemporary Crises*, **3,** 339–363.

COHEN, S. (1981). "Footprints in the sand," in Fitzgerald, M. *et al.* (1981), 220–247.

COHEN, S. (1984). "The deeper structures of the law or 'Beware the rulers bearing justice' ". *Contemporary Crises*, **8,** 83–93.

COHEN, S. (1985). *Visions of Social Control*. Cambridge, Polity Press.

COHEN, S. and SCULL, A. (eds.) (1983). *Social Control and the State*. Oxford, Martin Robertson.

COLQUHOUN, P. (1797). *Treatise on the Police of the Metropolis* 4th ed.

COLQUHOUN, P. (1800). *Treatise on the Commerce and Police of the River Thames*.

COLQUHOUN, P. (1806). *Treatise on Indigence*.

COLQUHOUN, P. (1814). *Treatise on the Wealth, Power and Resources of the British Empire*.

CROSS, R. and JONES P. (1984). *Introduction to Criminal Law*, 10th ed. by R. Card. London, Butterworth.

CURRIE, E. (1974). "The New Criminology". *Crime and Social Justice*, 109–113.

DAHRENDORF, R. (1985). *Law and Order*. London, Stevens.

DEARLOVE, J. and SAUNDERS, P. (1984). *Introduction to British Politics*. Cambridge, Polity Press.

DONAJGRODSKI, A. P. (ed.) (1977). *Social Control in Nineteenth Century Britain*. London, Croom Helm.

DOWNES, D. (1978). "Promise and performance in British Criminology". *British Journal of Sociology*, 483–502.

DOWNES, D. (1983). *Law and Order: Theft of an Issue*. Fabian Society/Labour Campaign for Criminal Justice.

DOWNES, D. and ROCK, F. (eds.) (1979). *Deviant Interpretations*. Oxford, Martin Robertson.

DOWNES, D. and ROCK, P. (1982). *Understanding Deviance*. Oxford, Oxford University Press.

DUCKER, H., *et al.* (eds.) (1986). *Developments in British Politics 2*. London, Macmillan.

DUNLEAVY, P. and O'LEARY, B. (1987). *Theories of the State*. London, MacMillan.

DUNNING, E., *et al.* (1987). "Violent disorders in twentieth century Britain," in Gaskell, G. and Benewick, R. (eds.) *The Crowd in Contemporary Britain*. London, Sage, 19–75.

FOUCAULT, M. (1977). *Discipline and Punish*. London, Allen Lane.

FOUCAULT, M. (1979). "On governmentality". *Ideology and Consciousness*, **6**, 5–23.

FOUCAULT, M. (1980). "Prison talk", in Gordon C. (ed.) *Michel Foucault: Power/Knowledge*. Brighton Harvester.

GARLAND, D. (1985a). *Punishment and Welfare*. Aldershot, Gower.

GARLAND, D. (1985b). "The criminal and his science". *British Journal of Criminology*, **25**, 109–137.

GARLAND, D. and YOUNG, P. (eds.) (1983). *The Power to Punish*. London, Heinemann.

GATRELL, V. (1980). "The decline of theft and violence in Victoria and Edwardian England", in Gatrell, V., *et al.* (1980); 238–338.

GATRELL, V. (1987). "Crime, Authority and the Policeman—State 1750–1950," in Thompson, F. (ed.) *The Cambridge Social History of Britain 1750–1950*. Cambridge, Cambridge University Press.

GATRELL, V., LENMAN, B. and PARKER, G. (eds.) (1980). *Crime and the Law*. London, Europa.

GEARY, R. (1985). *Policing Industrial Disputes 1893–1985*. Cambridge, Cambridge University Press.

GILROY, P. and SIM, J. (1985). "Law, Order and the State of the Left". *Capital and Class*, **25**, 15–55.

GOULDNER, A. (1968). "The sociologist as partisan: sociology and the welfare state". *The American Sociologist*, 103–116.

GRIMSHAW, R. and JEFFERSON, T. (1987). *Interpreting Policework*. London, Allen and Unwin.

HALL, S., *et al.* (1978). *Policing the Crisis*. London, Macmillan.

HELD, D., *et al.* (eds.) (1983). *States and Societies*. Oxford, Martin Robertson.

HIRST, P. Q. (1985). "Marx and Engels on law, crime and morality," in Taylor, I., Walton, P. and Young, J. (1985), 203–244.

HOOD, R. (ed.) (1974). *Crime, Criminology and Public Policy*. London, Heinemann.

HOOD, R. (1987). "Some reflections on the role of criminology in public policy", *Criminal Law Review*, 527–538.

IGNATIEFF, M. (1981). "State, Civil Society and Total Institutions: A critique of recent social histories of punishment," in Cohen, S. and Scull, A. (1983), 75–105.

INCIARDI, J. (ed.) (1980). *Radical Criminology: The Coming Crises*. Beverly Hills, Sage.

JEFFERSON, J. and GRIMSHAW, R. (1985). *Controlling the Constable*. London, Muller.

JEFFERY, C. R. (1957). "The development of crime in early English Society". *Journal of Criminal Law, Criminology and Police Service*, **47**, 647–666.

JEFFERY, C. R. (1960). "Historical development of criminology," in Mannheim, H. (1960), 364–394.

JEUDWINE, J. W. (1917). *Tort, Crime and Police in Medieval Britain*. London, Williams and Norgate.

JONES, T., MacLEAN, B. and YOUNG, J. (1986). *The Islington Crime Survey*. Aldershot, Gower.

KAHN, P., LEWIS, N., LIVOCK, P. and WILES, P. (1983). *Picketing*. London, Routledge.

155

KENNEDY, M. (1970). "Beyond Incrimination". *Catalyst,* reprinted in Chambliss, W. and Mankoff, M. (eds.) (1976) *Whose Law, What Order?* New York, Wiley, 34–64.

KING, R. (1986). *The State in Modern Society.* London, Macmillan.

KINSEY, R. (1985). *Merseyside Crime Survey.* Liverpool, Merseyside County Council.

KINSEY, R., LEA, J. and YOUNG, J. (1986). *Losing the Fight Against Crime.* Oxford, Blackwell.

KLOCKARS, C. (1980). "The contemporary crises of Marxist criminology," in Inciardi, J. (1980), 92–123.

LEA, J. and YOUNG, J. (1984). *What is to be done about law and order?* London, Penguin.

LEA, J., MATTHEWS, R. and YOUNG, J. J. (1987). *Law and Order: Five years On.* London, Middlesex Polytechnic.

LEMERT, E. (1951). *Social Pathology.* New York, McGraw-Hill.

LEMERT, E. (1967). *Human Deviance, Social Problems and Social Control.* Englewood Cliffs, Prentice-Hall.

LENMAN, B. and PARKER, G. (1980). "The State, the community and the criminal law in early modern Europe," in Gatrell, V., *et al.* (1980), 11–48.

LEVI, M. (1987). *Regulating Fraud.* London, Tavistock.

LODGE, T. (1974). "The founding of the Home Office Research Unit," in Hood, R. (1974), 11–24.

LUSTGARTEN, L. (1986). *The Governance of the Police.* London, Sweet and Maxwell.

MAGUIRE, M., VAGG, J. and MORGAN, R. (eds.) (1985). *Accountability and Prisons.* London, Tavistock.

MAITLAND, R. (1985). *Justice and Police.* London, Macmillan.

MANNHEIM, H. (ed.) (1960). *Pioneers in Criminology.* London, Stevens.

MANNHEIM, H. (1965). *Comparative Criminology.* London, Routledge and Kegan Paul.

MARENIN, O. (1982). "Parking Tickets and Class Repression: The Concept of Policing in Critical Theories of Criminal Justice". *Contemporary Crises,* **6,** 241–266.

MARENIN, O. (1985). "Police Performance and State Rule". *Comparative Politics,* 101–122.

MATZA, D. (1969). *Becoming Deviant.* Englewood Cliffs, Prentice-Hall.

MORRISON, J. (1987). "New strategies in the politics of law and order". *Howard Journal of Criminal Justice,* 203–216.

MORRIS, T. (1957). *The Criminal Area.* London, Routledge and Kegan Paul.

NATIONAL DEVIANCY CONFERENCE/CONFERENCE OF SOCIALIST ECONOMISTS (1979). *Capitalism and the Rule of Law.* London, Hutchinson.

NELKEN, D. (1980). "Capitalism and the Rule of Law: Review Article". *International Journal of the Sociology of Law,* **8,** 193–199.

NORTON, P. (1984). *The British Polity.* London, Longmans.

NORTON, P. (ed.) (1985). *Law and Order and British Politics.* Aldershot, Gower.

NORTON, P. (1987). " 'Law and Order' in Perspective", paper to British Society of Criminology, May.

NOZICK, R. (1974). *Anarchy, State and Utopia.* Oxford, Blackwell.

PASQUINO, P. (1978). "Theatrum politicum: the genealogy of capital, police and the state of prosperity". *Ideology and Consciousness,* 41–54.

PEARCE, F. (1976). *Crimes of the Powerful.* London, Pluto.

PEARSON, G. (1983). *Hooligan*. London, Macmillan.

PHILIPS, D. (1980). "A new engine of power and authority," in Gatrell, V., *et al.* (1980), 155–189.

PHILIPS, D. (1983). "A just measure of crime, authority, hunters and blue locusts," in Cohen, S. and Scull, A. (1983), 50–74.

PORTER, B. (1987). *The Origins of the Vigilant State*. London, Weidenfeld.

PRATT, M. (1980). *Mugging As A Social Problem*. London, Routledge and Kegan Paul.

RADZINOWICZ, L. (1956). *History of the English Criminal Law*, Vol. 3. London, Stevens.

RADZINOWICZ, L. and HOOD, R. (1986). *History of the English Criminal Law*, Vol. 4. London, Stevens.

REINER, R. (1985a). *The Politics of the Police*. Brighton, Wheatsheaf.

REINER, R. (1985b). "Policing strikes". *Policing*, 138–148.

REINER, R. (1985c). "Policing, Order and Legitimacy," in Spitzer, S. and Scull, A. (eds.) *Research in Law, Deviance and Social Control 1:8*. Greenwich, Connecticut, JAI Press.

REINER, R. (1987a). "The Politics of Police Research," in Weatheritt, M. (ed.) *Police Research*. London, Croom Helm.

REINER, R. (1987b). "Law and Order," in *Channel 4 Election Brief*, 17.

RICHTER, D. (1981). *Riotous Victorians*. Ohio University Press.

ROBBINS, L. (1981). "Economics and Political Economy". *American Economic Review*, reprinted in *Essay on the Nature and Significance of Economic Science 3rd. ed*. London, Macmillan, xi–xxxiii.

ROCK, P. (1974). "The sociology of deviancy and conceptions of moral order". *British Journal of Criminology*, reprinted in Wiles, P. (1976) 145–158.

ROCK, P. (1987). *A View From the Shadows: The Ministry of the Solicitor General of Canada and the Justice for Victims of Crime Initiative*. Oxford, Oxford University Press.

ROCK, P. and MACKINTOSH, M. (eds.) (1974). *Deviance and Social Control*. London, Tavistock.

SCRATON, P. (1985). *The State of the Police*. London, Pluto.

SCULL, A. (1977). *Decarceration*. Oxford, Martin Robertson.

SILVER, A. (1967). "The demand for order in civil society," in Bordus, D. (ed.) *The Police*. New York, Wiley.

SMART, B. (1983). "On discipline and social regulation," in Garland, D. and Young, P. (1983), 62–83.

SMITH, A. (1763). *Lectures on Justice, Police, Revenue and Arms*. (Published as *Lectures on Jurisprudence*, Oxford University Press, 1978).

SPARKS, R. (1980). "A critique of Marxist criminology," in Morris, N. and Tonry, M. (eds.) *Crime and Justice 2*. Chicago University Press, 159–210.

SPARKS, R. (1983). "Britain," in Johnson, (ed.) *International Handbook of Contemporary Developments in Criminology Vol. 2*. Westport, Conn., Greenwood Press, 79–105.

STEAD, P. J. (1977). "Patrick Colquhoun" in Stead, P. J. (ed.) *Pioneers in Policing*. New Jersey, Patterson Smith, 48–63.

STEVENSON, J. (1979). *Popular Disturbances in England 1700–1870*. London, Longman.

SUMNER, C. (1981). "Race, crime and hegemony". *Contemporary Crises*, **5**, 277–291.

TAYLOR, I. (1981). *Law and Order: Arguments for Socialism*. London, Macmillan.

TAYLOR, I., WALTON, P. and YOUNG, J. (1973). *The New Criminology*. London, Routledge and Kegan Paul.

157

TAYLOR, I., WALTON, P. and YOUNG, J. (1975). *Critical Criminology*. London, Routledge and Kegan Paul.

VOLD, G. (1958). *Theoretical Criminology*. New York, Oxford University Press.

WADDINGTON, P. A. J. (1986). "Mugging as a moral panic". *British Journal of Sociology*, 245–259.

WALSH, D. (1985). *A Dictionary of Criminology*. London, Routledge and Kegan Paul.

WEBER, M. (1919). "Politics as a vocation," in Gerth, H. and Mills, C. W. (eds.) *From Max Weber*. London, Routledge and Kegan Paul, 1970.

WILES, P. (ed.) (1976). *The Sociology of Crime and Delinquency in Britain; Vol. 2: The New Criminologies*. Oxford, Martin Robertson.

WILLIAMS, GLANVILLE (1983). *Textbook of Criminal Law*. London, Stevens.

RADICAL CRIMINOLOGY IN BRITAIN: THE EMERGENCE OF A COMPETING PARADIGM

JOCK YOUNG (*London*)

To some of the technicians of the Welfare State, Alvin Gouldner has applied the appellation "zoo keepers of deviance". The term is less attractive than the role, but I am bound to admit that twenty years ago I and many of my generation might not have been greatly bothered by it, since we had been nurtured in a positivistic cocoon with the belief that applied social science held the key to a better world. Some of us have emerged from that position in the intervening years and consequently share many of the moral concerns of the new generation of sociologists of deviance even if not all of the views of society upon which their positions depend. . . If what has been termed "Fabian criminology" has failed, it has done so, I suspect, in consequence of its failure to recognise in the moral nature of Man the Mark of Cain (Terence Morris, 1976, pp. 11–12).

Leaving aside the existence of . . .interesting disputes and division, it is clear that the new perspective overall has now become established and institutionalised. In the same way initially criticisms art movements (such as Dada and Surrealism) eventually become respectable, so too has the new deviancy and criminology become part of the accepted order of things. Its practitioners are ensconced in orthodox academic departments, journals, examining boards and publishing companies. No booklist would be complete without one (Stanley Cohen, 1981, p. 241).

British criminology in the late 1960s was at a cross roads. The social democratic positivism which had been dominant in the post-war period entered into a period of prolonged crisis, out of which emerged the two major contending paradigms: radical criminology and administrative criminology. Of course, parallel processes occurred in other Western countries, but the exceptional success of radical criminology in this country, together with the particular flair of the state-centred administrative criminology, are a product of specific political and social conditions in Britain. It goes without saying that criminology does not occur in a vacuum. The central problem for social democratic or Fabian positivism was that a wholescale improvement in social conditions resulted, not in a drop in crime, but the reverse. I have termed this the aetiological crisis, and it was, of course, accompanied by grave problems in the prisons and within policing (Young, 1986).

Social policies which had a fairly bipartisan support were rendered suspect. And of course the ability of the Welfare State in a situation of high employment and affluence to solve problems across the spectrum was a theme for wide discussion. There were for example, grave doubts in housing policy about high-rise blocks, abuse of urban planning and its destruction of community, in education about ability testing, IQ and the efficacy of comprehensivisation, in mental health with regards to the reductionists basis of much psychiatry and the deleterious effects of mental hospitals and in the inability of State medicine to equalise health care, etc. In particular, nagging doubts about the whole philosophy of Welfarism, of throwing money at problems without demonstrable social gains. It was the persistance, perhaps even of growth, in a wide spectrum of social problems within the Welfare State. Thus the crisis in criminology did not, of course, come out of the blue, it was part and parcel of the particular crisis in politics and culture in the late sixties which was refracted in the internal problems of criminology itself.[1]

First of all, however, let us examine the tenets of radical criminology.

What is radical criminology?

It is that part of the discipline which sees the causes of crime as being at core the class and patriarchial relations endemic to our social order and which sees fundamental changes as necessary to reduce criminality. It is politically at base socialist, libertarian/anarchist, socialist or radical feminist. It quarrels amongst itself—as such a radical mix has throughout history—but it is quite distinct from those parts of the discipline which see crime as a marginal phenomenon solvable with technical adjustments by control agencies which are, in essence, all right and in need of no fundamental changes. If there is a convergence in recent years between radical and establishment criminology, as Paul Rock correctly argues, it is because there has been a large-scale conceptual influence across each side of the divided and a genuine argument about the "facts" of crime. In the jargon of the philosophy of science, whereas in the early years the paradigms of radical and establishment criminology were simply incommensurable, they are now competing and incompatible. (See Lakatos and Musgrave, 1970.)

Let us look at the major tasks of the new criminology.

(1) *To Situate Theory*

The first job of the new criminology was, as Al Gouldner pointed out, an act of "excavation", it was:

> to demonstrate that all studies of crime and deviance, however deeply entrenched in their own technical traditions, are inevitably also grounded in larger more general science theories which are present (and consequential) even as unspoken silences (1973, p. ix).

---

[1] There are, of course, parallels in other social sciences, particularly the sociology of education which, of course, shares many joint authors with criminology (e.g. Paul Willis, Howard Becker, Cyril Burt). See, for example, the discussion in V. Furlong, 1985.

It was to situate different types of criminological work within their specific paradigms and underlying philosophies and then to engage in a critique. This was significant because criminologists were unaware that they were writing from a particular social and political perspective. Positivism saw itself as having transcended the past debates so that "scientific" criminology represented the correct understanding of human nature and criminal behaviour. The establishment that there *was* a debate going on in criminology over human nature and social order and that this was an on-going part of the twentieth century sensibility was of great importance.

(2) *Centrality of the Study of Disorder*

That theoretical task of radical criminology was to recover the study of crime and disorder as a central focus of concern for social scientists. This involved demonstrating, not only that disorder could be understood in terms of the whole society, but that it could also illuminate that whole.

The study of crime and disorder were thus not of peripheral concern to the study of society but rather order and disorder were two sides of the same coin, and both were intimately and causally related—that order concealed disorder and was maintained by it. The non-marginal status of criminology and the sociology of deviance was thus a central plank in their platform. It was necessary to combat what Stan Cohen called:

> that sort of philistine distrust which greets Durkheim's *Suicide* and the whole of the work of Freud. How can looking at suicide explain how society work "normally"? How can the interpsychic conflicts of a few middle class Viennese Jews explain how the "normal" mind works? (1981, p. 231).

Thus similarly, the new deviancy theory and radical criminology attempted to bring the study of crime and disorder out of the intellectual ghetto in which positivism had placed it.

Out of this came a sense of irony: crime related not to that which was peripheral to the society, but, both in its material causes and in the values evoked, it related to those central to social order. And activities, whether they were thieving, rape or violence, were part of a continuum of behaviour rather than being apart from "normal" behaviour.

(3) *The Political Nature of Crime and Deviancy*

A central task was to undo the notion of false objectivity which positivism had created in its pursuit of a mistaken scientificity. As David Matza put it in a famous passage:

The scholar's or scientist's way of becoming partially blind is, inadvertently
perhaps, to structure fields of inquiry in such a way as to obscure obvious connections or to take the connections for granted and leave the matter at that. The
great task of disconnection—it was arduous and time-consuming—fell to the
positive school of criminology. Among their most notable accomplishments,
the criminological positivists succeeded in what would seem the impossible. They
separated the study of crime from the workings and theory of the state. That
done, and the lesson extended to deviation generally, the agenda for research and
scholarship for the next half-century was relatively clear, especially with regard
to what would *not* be studied. Scientists of various persuasion thereafter wandered
aimfully, leaving just a few possibilities uncovered, considering how deviation
was produced. Throughout, a main producer remained obscure, off-stage due to
the fortunate manner in which fields of inquiry were divided. The role of the
sovereign, and by extension, instituted authority was hardly considered in the
study of deviant behaviour. That lofty subject, unrelated to so seamy a matter as
deviation was to be studied in political science. There, as in the curriculum in
government or political sociology, Leviathan had little bearing on ordinary
criminals. And in criminology, the process of becoming an ordinary criminal was
unrelated to the workings of the state. It was, it must be granted, a pretty neat
division, (1969, pp. 143–4).

Crime and deviance were a product of human action and social reaction they
have at core this dyadic structure. Thus the problem of crime is a definitional
problem as much as it is a behavioural problem. And the definitional problem
is a political problem, whether it is the assessment of the limits of permissible
violence or the nature of theft.

(4) *Against Reductionism*

Radical criminology was the main torch carrier against reductionism. It was
critical of any attempt to see the offender as a denatured, determined creature
without conscious will and was insistent on granting meaning to the act of
deviancy. It was in the vernacular, *appreciative* of the deviant act. The particular brand of positivism to which it was whole heartedly opposed, was biological reductionism. That is the explanation of a social event (crime or deviancy)
in terms of biology (e.g. XYY chromosomes, an inadequate autonomic
nervous system). Clarence Jeffrey, 1978 President of the American Society of
Criminology, spotted this feature of radical criminology, and denounced it
with characteristics aplomb, when he wrote: "The communist ideology of
anti-positivism, anti-bourgeoisism, radical sociology/criminology is frankly
challenged by any notion of the biological foundations of behaviour (1980,
p. 119). Quite so; although he is probably unaware that such opposition to
biological reductionism was shared by all the great sociological thinkers, not
merely Marx and the Marxists.

I have spelt out the four characteristics of radical criminology with some
care, particularly as there have been numerous attempts to marginalise it by

defining it, for example, as identical to Marxist criminology. As I have indicated, the above characteristics are held by a variety of radical currents, including Marxism, albeit with different emphases.

British criminology and the United States

It is difficult to understand British criminology without writing about the United States. American criminology is a powerhouse of ideas, research techniques and interventions which understandably dominate Western thinking about crime. The expenditure on the National Crime Survey alone far surpassed the combined expenditure of all European research projects. There is also a hint of creative desperation: for the United States has quite an exceptional crime rate, particularly with regards to crimes of violence. And here is the paradox: an exceptional capitalist state, with a crime rate reminiscent of a Third World country and with—perhaps relatedly—a very restricted Welfare State and the absence of clearly demarcated socialist politics (see E. Currie, 1986), is by far the major producer of criminological ideas. Yet these ideas are extraordinarily influential and very often brilliant. It was the impact of the West Coast labelling theory centring around Howard Becker which set the creaking chariot of radical criminology off on its course and it was the subcultural theory of Albert Cohen, Richard Cloward and Lloyd Ohlin which set off our own versions at the London School of Economics and the Centre for Contemporary Cultural Studies at Birmingham. With regards to the new administrative criminology centring around the Home Office and its academic affiliates it is the victim survey work of the U.S. National Institute of Justice and the ideas thrown up by Wilson and Kelling, which have been extremely influential, whilst the situational crime prevention strategy, however original, has its roots in the work of Oscar Newman and the Westinghouse Corporation Environmental Design Programme. The more creative of these processes, whether in radical or establishment criminology, involve a transformation of American ideas which, rather like popular music, play back to America the culture of Europe. What is most important is they do not involve the *translation* of American ideas to a British context but, so to speak, a *transposition*. That is, they have to travel a considerable distance politically, culturally and, indeed, in terms of the contours of crime itself. It is with this in mind that, if I am criticised for drawing the parameters of radical criminology so wide as to embrace a large part of British criminology one should note that radical criminology, by this definition, is in the United States a distinctly minority phenomenon. (See J. Inciardi, 1980).

The Impact of Radical Criminology in Britain

The birth of radical criminology in this country in an organisational form was the National Deviancy Conference (NDC) formed in July 1968 as a breakaway from the Third National Conference of Teaching and Research on

Criminology at the University of Cambridge. A gauge of the productivity of this generation of new criminologists can be made by looking at the output of speakers at the NDC between its inception in 1968 over a five year period to 1973. Of course, it continued for quite a while after that date, but let us look at this sample of the first five years. During this period there were sixty-three speakers from Britain at the conference who have produced between them just under 100 books on crime, deviancy and social control. I have not included books out of this area and there are, of course, some very distinguished contributions to other branches of sociology–and I have not the time or the patience to count the vast array of articles and research reports produced. And, of course, many of these people continue to write in the field. Among many radical luminaries Steve Box, Phil Scraton and Pat Carlen, for example, gave papers later on. The term "mainstream criminology" has become rather a misnomer for establishment criminology. Radical criminology, after all, in Britain has become at least an equal partner in the criminological enterprise and is, in many areas, the majority tendency. It was radical criminology which led the critique on the social democratic positivism which was the mainstay of British criminology in the post-war period prior to the late 1960s. And it was the radicals that provided many of the concepts in terms which are now staples of the criminological culture whatever its political and theoretical persuasion. The critique of mechanical determinism, the insistence on the social construction of statistics, the notion of the endemic rather than solely class-based nature of crime, the implication of control institutions in the creation of deviance, the ironic relationship between deviant values and crime, and the extent of the criminal victimisation of the invisible victims in racist attacks, domestic violence, sexual attacks on women and child abuse, are all largely a product of work within the radical mould.

One glance at the A-level sociology questions in crime and deviance or the standard textbooks will quickly convince one of the way in which many of these ideas have become a cultural staple, as will the, sometimes irritating, pronouncements of some of the more leftist local authorities and social services on crime and policing. All of these ideas, including new words such as "moral panic" have entered into the general social perspective of educated sections of the population as they have influenced the thinking of establishment criminology itself.

The fall-out from the new deviancy explosion has been considerable. Radical criminology has its powerbase in those areas of what one might call unsubsidised criminology. That is criminology as it is taught in the schools, the polytechnics, the universities and the colleges of education. It has not held sway over those parts of criminology which are paid for directly out of central government funds: that is the Home Office, the major University research centres and those institutions centring around the police and police studies. Its external funding, if any, has come from radical local authority services. It is common, of course, for each side of the divide to consider itself as criminology and regard the other as not really very serious. Regrettably, few sociology departments, for example, would or could teach theories of situational crime

164

prevention, few of the establishment centres would or could base their work round socialist or socialist feminist theories (Witness, Clarke and Cornish, 1983).

There has been an influence of ideas despite little melding of paradigms. It is not without a sense of irony that one reads commissioners of police defending their poor clear-up rates by insisting that the figures are bureaucratic constructions of little validity or that the rise in the rape figures are an index of police success as they are an artefact of greater reporting rather than any change in reality.

The Process of Change in British Criminology

It is important at this stage of the argument to return to the crossroads at the late sixties and see how radical criminology and its administrative counterpart developed out of positivism.

In order to more systematically understand this process of change it is necessary to first create a structure which can adequately deal with the history of the development of paradigms in the social sciences. A central insight to this is the division between the *interior* and the *exterior* histories of a discipline.[2]

The interior history is the *material* and the intellectual problems which a discipline confronts in terms of its ability to sustain practitioners in the world and the way in which the paradigm generates problems and faces anomalies. The exterior history is the *material* and *political/cultural* context in which the discipline exists. A brief (nonexhaustive) checklist of the types of instances on the development of a criminological paradigm may help to make these distinctions clearer.

The Exterior History

In a sense the material, political and social world in which the discipline exists is the major motor to changes in criminology whatever the individual criminologist thinks. For it is the exterior world which provides him or her with the problems of crime and penality, a political climate, and with fundamental conceptualisations of human nature and social order.

(a)   *Material:* The actual extent of crime, the cost and problems of crime, policing, prisons, etc. The general level of fiscal spending and the problem of crime from the point of view of Government and Public Opinion.

(b)   *Political/Cultural:* criminology, no more than any other discipline, does not exist in a vacuum. The deceit of the objective and detached scientist is belied by the obvious historical resonances of any piece of work. Political control can be immediate in terms of parameters or no-go areas in which the paradigm is constrained and no-go areas which the

---

[2] I am developing here the analysis first used by Ian Hacking (1981) in his seminal article on the history of statistics as used by Alan Phipps (1987) in his history of victimisation studies in Britain and the United States.

researcher cannot examine. But, politically and culturally, there is the more subtle influence of the way in which concepts of human nature and social order in the paradigm correspond to those prevalent in major social movement of the time.

The Interior History

(a) *Material:* The number of personnel working in the field of criminology: their distribution within the Academy (See P. Rock, this issue), the division between independent research and research funded by the State (whether within the State itself or State-funded Academic Institutions), the sources of research funding, the professional basis of the subject with different academic disciplines (in particular sociology and law), (see J. Martin, this issue) and, of course, the relationship between the Academy and practitioners working in the field. (See D. Garland, this issue.)

(b) *Political/Cultural:* The problem of explaining the extent and distribution of crime, victimisation and incarceration from the perspective of the particular paradigm, i.e. anomalies and reassurances. Taboo and preferred areas within the paradigm.

The Conditions for Paradigm Shift

I want to describe the changes which occurred within British criminology in the late 1960s/early 1970s period utilising the above distinctions between interior and exterior history. My assessment here is that a successful paradigm shift in the social sciences occurs when (i) there is a clear *empirical* problem or anomaly in the dominant paradigm (interior history); (ii) there is *material* support for the adherents of the new paradigm to enter the field (interior history); (iii) there is a material problem for those in power, i.e. a major problem of policy (exterior history) to which the new paradigm offers a solution (exterior history); (iv) there is a *political and culturally* conducive context for the emergence of the new paradigm (exterior history).[3]

Although my main aim will be to describe the process of paradigm shift in Britain, there are a series of comparative questions which I will touch on briefly which help illuminate the matter. Amongst these are: why did radical criminology take root in Britain so much more effectively than in other European countries? How does one explain the much greater success of radical criminology in Britain than the United States? How qualitatively were American ideas transposed in a British context? And, how did the transformations in establishment criminology differ from those in other western countries?

Let us look at the emergence of radical criminology and the demise of Fabian positivism in terms of this framework.

---

[3] I have developed here the work of Johnson (1971) on paradigm change in economics and Harvey (1973) in urban geography.

(a) *Exterior history*

The most immediate material problem was a rising crime rate coupled with an increasing prison population, recidivism and declining police clear-up rates.

The political context of the emergence of radical criminology, both in Britain and the United States was, of course, the emergence of the New Left in the late sixties and early seventies. Radical criminology was as much part and parcel of this train of thought as were the anti-psychiatry movement, the prison support groups and community action groups in the inner cities and sit-ins on campuses. The specific problem of some part of radical criminological theory may be explained within itself, in terms of its particular debates and controversies, but its flavour, its essence and its care core propositions were indelibly coloured by its New Left origins and this is as true today as it was in the seventies. Central to New Left thinking of the time was a critique of the extension of the state. It is important to underline the extent to which the Welfare State itself was seen as a source of oppression.[4]

(b) *Interior history*

The major problem facing positivism was what I have termed the aetiological crisis. That is, the contention that bad conditions lead to bad behaviour was undermined by the fact that as income levels rise, educational standards improved, slums were knocked down and unemployment levels dropped, crime continued to rise.

The most immediate response of positivism to the aetiological crisis was:

(a)   an increased emphasis on individual rather than social reasons for crime. Important here were notions of maternal and paternal deprivation, the greater acceptance of biological factors and the obviously *short-lived* explanation of "delinquent generations": children ill-socialised because of the war years;

(b)   bifurcation: that is an explanation of only a minority of crime and delinquency as being a product of deep-seated individual causes and the rest due to individual choice and capriciousnesses. The problem of the rapid increase was thus cut down to size and explained away as a product of causes which were not endemic to the society as a whole. (See Greenwood and Young, 1980; J. Clarke, 1980; A. Bottoms, 1977.)

Radical criminology confronted the aetiological crisis in a dramatic fashion. It deemed that there was no rise in crime. In a situation worthy of Galileo the positivists looking through the telescope at crime saw an alarming increase and invoked further and further complexities to their paradigm. The radicals blamed the telescope. They argued that the rise of crime was largely

[4] A re-read of the famous Becker-Gouldner debate, for example, reveals not merely that Becker was critical of the middle management of deviancy (the "zoo-keepers"), whilst Gouldner was critical of the master institutions of society (the "zoo"), but that both were opposed to the Welfare interventions of the State in a way which would make most present-day British radicals feel distinctly uneasy.

epiphenomenal: it was a social construction produced by increased police time, less tolerant courts and a moral panic of the public swelled up by the mass media. The criminal statistics were held to be an index more at the disposal of police forces than that of crime and, indeed, the causal link between crime and, for example, poverty was cast into grave doubt. Crime was, after all, ubiquitous. The rich engaged in crime just as much as the poor—they were simply too powerful to be apprehended. And the same was true for middle and working class juvenile delinquents and black and white crime differentials.

This break with sociological positivism was a deep flaw which was to cause radical criminology great difficulties later on. It was facilitated by the move towards individual positivism amongst the Fabians. That is, the debate with positivism was recast as a debate with reductionism. In particular, a generation of students were taught a critique of positivism which focused on atavism, biological reductionism and individual differences (e.g. I. Taylor, et al., 1973; C. Smart, 1977). If Lombroso had not existed he would have had to be invented.[5] A further result of this was, of course, that the long lineage of radical positivism in Britain was forgotten. (See Mungham, 1980, p. 21.)

On a material level there was in Britain a massive expansion of social science education in this period, both in the universities and polytechnics. Courses in criminology and the sociology of deviance sprung up in every major institution of higher education and were taught very largely by individuals in or around the new radical criminology organisation the National Deviancy Conference and to sociology students heavily imbued with the New Left ideas and practice. This development involved a tidal process of simply sweeping around the dam of establishment criminology rather than demolishing it. There was no necessity for any direct conflict between competing paradigms within the institutions. This had a positive side to it, for as Paul Wiles notes:

> The institutional rift which the emergence of the NDC created did have considerable advantages for the developing sociology of deviance in Britain. In particular, it facilitated the emergence of new theoretical and methodological concerns unfettered by the old institutional constraints, and correspondingly it provided an alternative institutional security and identity for those who wished to break with the focal concerns and ideology of traditional British criminology (1976, p. 13).

[5] As it is the Lombrosians, who were in their time extremely controversial figures, whose majority opponents were sociological positivists and who were subject to such hostile criticism that they walked out of the Second International Congress in Paris in 1889 and did not even attempt the Third Congress in 1892, have become elevated to the role of turn of the century orthodoxy. Even Quinney and Wildeman, who fully understand the controversial nature of Lombrosianism at the turn of the century seem to believe that its "influence is found in much of European criminology today" (1977, p. 56).

What I am suggesting is that the popular image of positivism as identical with Lombrosianism is a creature very largely created by the New Left, facilitated by the movement towards individual positisvism—of an almost entirely non-Lombrosian nature—by the positivists themselves. That is, the resuscitated atavistic positivism was an easy target rather than a genuine challenge.

It had also negative consequences which were the paradigms developed separately: they simply did not compete with each other.

Dominant paradigms, as John Watkins (1970) has ably pointed out, do not necessarily change because of growing empirical pressures. However, the new practitioners entering criminology in the sixties at a time of widespread disaffection with the accepted ways of understanding the word had little inducement to adopt the mainstream paradigm. In other words, you cannot teach an old dog new tricks, but new dogs may well find the old tricks quite inapplicable to the world they find themselves in. The stage was set then, in as near to optimum theoretical and empirical terrain, for the emergence of radical criminology in Britain.

In Britain the growth and impact of the new criminology has been perhaps greater than elsewhere. The extant Marxist tradition, both in the Academy and in politics in general, facilitated a rapid transition to a committed radical criminology, whilst at the same time ensuring—almost immediately—a very wide hearing compared with, for example, the United States. At the same time, British sociologists were much more open than were their European counterparts, to American deviancy theories of the sixties particularly in the subculture and interactionist traditions which were the debates out of which radical criminology developed. There is a crucial difference between Britain and the Continent. In Europe the small, but important, focuses for criminologists were in law rather than in sociology departments. These were much less open to the wholesale import of American sociology of deviance and this, in part, explains the slow, and later expansion, of radical criminology there, despite, as in Britain, a sympathetic political context. If the political orientation was to the New Left, the particular theoretical baggage which was carried into the debate derived from labelling theory and structural functionalism and both strands—the latter rarely admitted—fitted tremendously well with instrumental Marxism on the one hand and the structuralist Marxism of Althusser on the other.

What effect did the revolt of these Young Turks have on the Sultanate of establishment criminology? Its major forum was the National Deviancy Conference, which had a remarkable, almost spectacular, growth in the last few years of its existence. As Stan Cohen noted, the impact of radical criminology was much less devastating than was believed in the more heady days of the early seventies.

> There are more corners and cavities than ten years ago, but for the most part the institutional foundation of British criminology remain intact and unaltered, for the Establishment saw the new theories as simply a fashion which would eventually pass over or as a few interesting ideas which could be swallowed up without changing the existing paradigm of all (1981 p. 236).

Of course, radical criminology was not swallowed up, it made, as we have seen, remarkable headway. Its influence was felt not merely in the Academy but also in the wider political arena. For ideas emanating from radical criminology were very influential on Labour Party thinking, particularly at

169

constituency level. This was particularly true by the early eighties, when a new wave of younger Labour politicians, many of them schooled in the New Left orthodoxy of the sixties, were brought into power in the inner—city Labour strongholds. They—and in particular the police committee support units which they brought into being—became important political focuses for the ideas and concerns of radical criminology.

But what radical criminology did not do to any significant degree is challenge the criminological establishment. For the policy centres in British society were, and remain, remarkably unaffected, both in the Home Office itself and the university institutions which it helps to finance.

Both in Great Britain and the United States the size and power of the criminological establishment has actually grown over the last ten years. But its hegemony over the field has ended. Thus James Inciardi, in the introduction to a volume highly critical of radical criminology, writes:

> The discipline of criminology has endured, now, for many generations, evolving a systematic body of knowledge which focuses on the study of crime from a position which is considered, by many, as almost sacred. The mere emergence of radical criminology represents a crisis within the mainstream of the field (1980, p. 9).

Thus, even in the United States, where the political climate was probably less conductive than in any other Western country, it has become an accepted alternative paradigm, in academic circles at least (see W. Pelfrey, 1980). The main point to stress is that a weak and unsuccessful positivism was not dislodged from its position by the emergence of radical criminology. It was displaced, however, but ironically the challenge to positivism emerged quietly within its own ranks. As we shall see this was due to the rapid growth, both in Britain and the United States of what I have termed administrative criminology. Thus, the qualitative transformation of establishment criminology, the decline of positivism, occurred autonomously from the rise of radical criminology, which itself was, at first, a non-competing paradigm. But let us first follow the development of radical criminology in its recent period.

Radical Criminology: the Recent Period

Interior History

What Paul Rock omits in his survey of British criminology in this issue, is the parallel expansion of higher education in the public sector. This provided, perhaps, the last of the expansion in higher education and involved personnel in the Polytechnics and Colleges of Higher Education. Indeed, two of the most recent Centres for Criminology, Middlesex and Edge Hill, both with a radical leaning, have developed in this sector. In addition, there was the entrance of the Open University into the field to provide a course which is overwhelmingly radical in its orientation and the largest criminology course in the country. (See M. Fitzgerald et al., 1981.) These newly established sociology departments almost universally took on a radical orientation and perhaps doubled the number of radical criminologists working in the field.

Then, in a second wave, after the expansion in higher education had finished, radicals took research work in the various agencies. (e.g. Institute for the Study of Drug Dependence, N.A.C.R.O.). But most importantly, the left wing local authorities, in setting up support groups to their police committees, community safety committees, women's and race units, and police monitoring groups, provided a very substantial national base.

Most importantly was the expansion of womens studies courses, both in the University and the Polytechnic sectors, many of which had problems of the safety of women high on their research and curricula agenda. The importance of feminist work in the recent development of radical criminology cannot be overestimated. If the 1971 British Sociological Conference revolved around the early wave of radical criminology, published as *Deviance and Social Control* (Rock and McIntosh, 1974), then the 1985 Conference published as *Women, Violence and Social Control* (Hanmer and Maynard, 1987), represents the feminist influence on the second wave.

The contribution of feminist victimology has been profound. For its research:

(i)   constantly undermined the notion that fear of crime is largely irrational and without basis;

(ii)   did this by showing the biased nature of both the official statistics *and* orthodox victimisation studies;

(iii)   thus emphasised that the dark figure of crime is not merely a quantitative lacking in official statistics, but is qualitatively structured;

(iv)   thus negated the common argument that official and victimisation statistics are simply compatible with the latter merely by being more quantitatively efficient;

(v)   has been morally entrepreneurial in its exposure of not only domestic and sexual violence, but in the areas of child physical and sexual abuse. It has, in short, been the major contributor to the contemporary radical practice of exposing the invisible victim.

If the aetiological crisis was the major empirical factor galvanising criminology in the sixties, in the seventies and eighties it was the results of the various criminal victimisation studies. Throughout the seventies feminist studies of rape and domestic violence had forcefully pointed out the fashion in which the criminal victimisation of women had been ignored. This was, in essence, the beginning of radical victimology and its findings lay uneasily alongside the traditional radical tendency to play down crime as a problem. Often this cognitive dissonance was solved by a type of intellectual schizophrenia where crimes of women were readily acknowledged—but all others denied (see Lea and Young, 1984). And the victimisation studies from the mainstream also increased the dissonance. For they pointed quite clearly to the fact that working class people suffered crime more than the middle classes and that most crime was intra-class rather than between class. Furthermore, as we shall see, radical victimology itself began to flourish by the eighties with feminists expanding to survey research rather than case studies, and numerous socialist councils in Britain—for example Merseyside and Islington—conducting surveys. The widespread concern amongst working class communities with regards to crime—it being seen as the second problem after unemployment (see R. Kinsey *et al.*, 1985)—and the extraordinary levels in which inner city women were curfewed because of fear of crime had a pronounced affect on radical criminology.

Exterior History

The recent history of radical criminology in Britain has involved a rising influence of feminist and anti-racist ideas and an encasement of left wing Labour administrations in the majority of the inner city Town Halls. An initial ultra-leftism has been tempered and often transformed by a prevalent realism in the wake of the third consecutive defeat of the Labour Party on the national level and severe defeats with regards to "rate capping" in terms of local politics. The need to encompass issues which had a widespread support amongst the electorate, rather than indulge in marginal or "gesture" politics included the attempt to recapture the issue of law and order from the right. (See D. Downes, 1983; R. Kinsey *et al.*, 1986). In terms of the material exterior history there has been a continuing rise in crime in Britain, the emergence of heroin abuse as a major problem, a whole series of police scandals, and the increased and evident ineffectiveness of police in their action against crime. Thus, during the period of Conservative Government 1979 to 1986 the number of serious crimes known to the police rose by 52 per cent, over one million extra crimes a year, clear-up rates fell by over one percentile point a year, and the cost of clear-up rose to over £7,000 per crime in the Metropolitan area. (See J. Lea *et al.*, 1987.) However critical one could be about these statistics, it became increasingly difficult for radicals to deny the crisis of the crime in the urban areas. Three related imperatives have thus begun to transform radical criminology: the need to do something about crime, the need to have some audit of police practice, and the necessity of independent data. It was at this point that socialist politicians realised that it was their constituents— the working class, women and ethnic minorities who suffered most from crime—that radical criminology came of age.

Recent Radical Research

Radical research in the present period is flourishing, particularly work in the prisons, the police, drugs, juvenile delinquency, racial attacks and the victimisation of women.

It is invidious to single out recent work, but a small *selection* of books published in the last three years may be indicative of the range:
Steven Box, *Recession, Crime and Punishment*, (1987).
J. Hanmer & M. Maynard, *Women, Violence & Social Control*, (1987).
Phil Scraton, *The State of the Police* (1985).
Pat Carlen *et al. Criminal Women* (1985).

172

N. Dorn and N. South, *A Land Fit for Heroin?* (1987).
Susan Smith, *Crime, Space and Society,* (1986).

In particular there has been an emergence of a large number of victimis-ation studies specifically oriented to a radical perspective. The following selection of studies gives some indication of this growing trend and underscores the way in which the majority of them have been funded by socialist local authorities. Understandably central government largely funds establishment criminology, what is new is the local state funding of radical research.

RADICAL VICTIMIZATION SURVEYS

NAME	YEAR	FUNDING BODY	REFERENCES
Merseyside Crime Survey	1985	Merseyside County Council & Home Office	R. Kinsey, 1985 R. Kinsey *et al.* 1986
Leeds Study of Violence against Women	1981	—	Hanmer & Saunders, 1984
Women's Safety Survey	1984	GLC	R. Hall, 1985
Wandsworth Violence against Women	1983–4	GLC	J. Radford, 1987
Islington Crime Survey	1985	Islington Borough Council	T. Jones *et al.* 1986
Broadwater Farm Survey	1986	Haringey Borough Council	J. Lea, *et al.* 1986 T. Gifford, 1986
Newham Crime Survey	1986	Newham Borough Council	Newham Police Committee, 1986
Hammersmith Crime Survey	1987	Hammersmith Borough Council	K. Painter, *et al.* 1988
Manchester Women's Safety Survey	1987	Manchester City Council	Police Monitoring Unit, 1987
Camden Community Safety	1987	Camden Borough Council	Camden Community Safety Committee, 1988

The construction of alternative data bases from those of establishment criminology, often more authoritative than official data, is an important step forward for radical criminology.

To compete with the massive bureaucracies which create police and court statistics or with the central government agencies which finance victimisation studies is a difficult task. But whilst this was the case and radical criminology turned its face away from survey research, relying almost solely on case his-tories and ethnography, then the possibility of counter-voices capable of authoritatively entering into public discourse on law and order was minimal. And as this was combined with a clear disdain co-operation or communication with the mass media, then the self-marginalisation of the discipline was inevitable. The breakthrough on this score was the victimisation survey because (a) this allowed figures which were widely acknowledged as more authoritative than the police figures; (b) the logic of the focus of criminality on certain localities demanded that local surveys demanding not inconsiderable yet manageable costs had a clear advantage over national surveys which fudged and obfuscated their use of "global" figures. (See Hough and Mayhew, 1987.)

Radical Criminology: A Developing Paradigm

I want to look first at the flaws and advantages of the radical paradigm and discuss how development has occurred according to the interior and exterior histories of the subject. It is important to note at this juncture that just as establishment criminology developed into the new administrative criminology, radical criminology developed from an early left idealist to a realist phase. (See J. Young, 1986.)

I have detailed how the particular social and political context which gave birth to radical criminology impressed on the paradigm certain flaws. Important of these are:

(1) *The Unflawed Underdog.* There is a tendency to idealise oppressed groups and an inability to see anti-social behaviour and divisions within them. This has led to an underplaying of the problem of crime and the creation of taboos about such areas as inter-racial crime. This is being countered recently by the increased political focus on crimes such as domestic violence, racist attacks and child abuse.

(2) Unwillingness to Deal with Positivism

The original unwillingness to come to terms with sociological rather than biological positivism which is displayed in the above incapacity to see how outside determination causes internal divisions, is to an extent obviated, although not solved, by the passing of the aetiological crisis. That is as unemployment in Britain has risen fast over the period, it is less of a problem to relate this to higher working-class crime rates, anti-social behaviour, heroin addiction, etc.

(3) Unwillingness to Deal with Statistics

The tendency to see crime and other social problem rates as an epiphenomenon of social control is a widespread legacy of the early days of the paradigm. It is seen in, for example, in the seminal text of British radical criminology, *Policing the Crisis* (Hall *et al.*, 1978), as it is seen in social constructionism in the United States and abolitionism on the Continent. Once again, the worsening of social conditions makes such arguments much more low keyed.

(4) *Unwillingness to Deal with Reform*

The radical emphasis on the genesis of crime in the core nature of the system and its values tends to preclude reform, and the New Left heritage is, as we have seen, very critical of the interventions of the Welfare State. (See Hood, 1987.) The predicament of Britain under the "cuts" inflicted by a Thatcherite Government intent on rolling back the Welfare State has quickly reversed the attitudes of many British radicals! The importance of retaining the gains of the Welfare State and making local and national reforms becomes paramount.

All of these left idealist tendencies we have discussed elsewhere (Lea and Young, 1984; Kinsey *et al.*, 1986; Young, 1986) and, of course, it would be wrong to suggest that such a position had disappeared (witness, e.g. P. Scraton, 1987). But there has been a distinct movement which attempts to cope with these problems and respond to the demands of this present period— as was well charted by Tony Bottoms in his recent inaugural professorial lecture at the Cambridge Institute (A. Bottoms, 1987). But, contrary to Bottoms, there has also been a continuity in radical criminology from its early days through left idealism into realism (Young, 1988a). I have written enough of the flaws of the paradigm: let us look at its continuing advantages.

The Advantages of Radical Criminology

Let us spell out the advantages that radical criminology has over its establishment competitors:
1. It is not politically constrained so that it is possible to trace the line of causality of crime to situations endemic in the social structure. That is to relationships of class and patriarchy.
2. It is not politically constrained so that it is able to point to endemic problems in the administration of justice. It can, for example, engage in a fullblown critique of policing and the need for genuine public accountability.
3. It is sensitised to the fact that crime statistics are social constructs and that their reality is not something "out there" as positivism and administrative criminology would have it, but a product of behaviour and evaluation. At heart the extent of crime is a political as well as a behavioural matter. If there is one single fact that the radicals can tell a student of deviance, it is that the figures for crime, for alcoholism, for heroin addiction, for mental illness, etc. are not "hard" facts in the sense that this is true of the height and weight of physical bodies. They are moral not physical statistics.
4. It is committed to the notion that the understanding of human behaviour and hence the aetiology of crime has a subjective component and that the central dynamic of this is the experience of justice and injustice. Because of this it is against generalisations about human behaviour in terms of mechanistic laws irrespective of culture and country, whether of a positivistic or an administrative kind.
5. Radical criminology introduces politics and morality into criminology and it sites the essential causes of crime in the injustice and immorality of the system. That is, it does not believe we can understand the causes of crime,

the construction of criminal statistics or the basis of successful intervention without consideration of politics and morality. It is a sense of injustice that moves the criminal actor (however unjust his or her actions), a sense of justice that creates the moral yardstick by which crime is variously measured and which determines the effect of interventions: whether to exacerbate (if unjust) or ameliorate (if judicious). It is the inability of administrative criminology to deal with the moral and political basis of crime which is its most fundamental flaw.

The Emergence of Administrative Criminology

I have detailed elsewhere the emergence of the new administrative criminology as the major paradigm in establishment approaches to crime (1986, 1988). What is important to note is that its main thrust has been to sidestep the aetiological crisis by suggesting that the causes of crime are either relatively unimportant or politically impossible to tackle. There is no need to explain the rise in crime: it is obvious that there is a rise. Rather we must find ways of stemming its impact. The question becomes what is the most cost-effective way of making control interventions, an emphasis "on the purely technical cost-benefit ratio aspects of crime: the opportunities for crime available in the environment, and the high risks attached to criminal activity" (Downes and Rock, 1982, p. 194). It is important to note how administrative criminology, both in Britain and the United States was a result of the double failure of orthodox criminology. That is, not only was positivism seen to be not working but, a little later—in the 1970s, particularly with the publication of a series of devastating police studies in the United States—neo-classicism was palpably not working either. If there was a crisis in aetiology there was also a crisis in penalty. Conventional police work simply did not seem effective against crime (see Skolnick and Bayley, 1986), and, of course, the prisons were the havens of crisis and the harbours of recidivism. This double crisis was quite clearly perceived in the research of Ron Clarke and his co-workers at the Home Office. (See especially, Clarke and Mayhew, 1980, chapter one.) The concept of situational crime prevention coupled with rational choice theory which they have pioneered to meet this challenge is—whatever its theoretical limitations—an innovative paradigm of great importance (Cornish and Clarke, 1986). Whatever else, it has hammered home to criminologists the earthy facts of space and actual experienced choice at a particular point in time, to a criminology all too content to live in abstractions. It has also developed quite specifically in the political situation of Britain and, as Rob Reiner (1987) has pointed out, is quite distinct from the Reaganite policy of the American new administrative criminology of James Q. Wilson and the Attorney General, Edwin Meese III (1986).

The material base of administrative criminology in Britain has expanded rapidly over the period, with the Home Office Research and Planning Unit being the largest criminological research institute in Europe, whilst also funding a large number of university research projects. Indeed, as Stan Cohen has pointed out, this relationship between *power* and *criminological research* has seen:

A refinement of this connection: the Home Office Research Unit, the research branches of the Prison Department, the Metropolitan Police and allied state agencies have all expanded and become more professional and productive. This is particularly notable given the overall decline of government support for social science research. In line with what happened in the United States over this decade, the content of this type of criminology has switched (and is likely to switch even more) in the direction of "criminal justice"; that is to say, an exclusive concern with the operation of the system. Research deals mainly with matters and decision-making, manpower, evaluation and classification " (1981, p. 236).

I have no quarrel with the fact that the Government—on both a national and local level—should commission applied research on a customer-contract principle. The problem is, as Tony Bottoms has trenchantly pointed out, the national budgeting for research is so overwhelmingly in the bestow of such an orientation that there is a drastic lack of balance against basic criminological work of an explanatory character operating without political restrictions in its conceptualisation. (See A. Bottoms, 1987). As Roger Hood has indicated, the emphasis on policy relevant research as set out by central government "raises the question—what does policy relevance mean, as defined by the administrator? A short term administrative problem? Or the exploration of radical alternatives? One must at least recognise the natural defensiveness of all organisations when threatened with critical scrutiny, or even survival. Are there not problems in leaving them to set their own research agendas?" (1987, p. 537).

All the more reason, for the existence of a competing paradigm that can disagree over the facts and set a radical agenda.

From Incommensurability into Genuine Competition and Incompatibility

What is of special significance at the present period is that the two criminologies not only influence each other but they are in debate over the interpretation of the data. Most importantly that they can agree that there are common data to argue about. To return to the world of Galileo, there is a measure of agreement that there is something out there at the end of the telescope which is not just a function of the instrument itself.

There are many taboo areas which remain: the right are not able to point their telescope at police malpractice, the left is unwilling to focus on crime amongst the working class (See R. Matthews, 1988)—both right and left are extremely hesitant to examine the dimensions of inter-racial crime in other than a most apologetic fashion. But the paradigms can now begin to compete in terms of interpretation of data and most importantly in terms of predictions and anomalies. It is not a question of merely the facts being under dispute. More significantly, it is where the facts are, more or less, agreed upon but the radical paradigm provides a totally different interpretation of these "facts".

There is a further stage. And this is where anomalies in one paradigm appear which are easily explicable by another. This is the situation which occurred in the 1960s to early seventies period, when the concept of the moral panic clearly seemed (and probably, in a modified form, still does) explain the sky-rocketing rate of crime in certain offences (particularly drugs and homo-sexual soliciting) much more adequately than positivist criminology could manage. At the moment it would seem to me that realist criminology—the most recent contender from the radical stable—is able to predict and explain certain anomalies which will increasingly beset administrative criminology.

It is, perhaps, odd to talk of anomalies in a subject which seemingly thrives on encountering failure and the unexpected. But there are areas in con-temporary criminology where significant anomalies will and do occur and which I believe can more easily be explained by radical realism than by administrative criminology or positivism for that matter.[6] It is not, of course, that inadequate theories get the world completely wrong–far from it, their existence is predicated in getting quite a lot of the world partially right. In a subject overwrought with anomalies it is, therefore, difficult to imagine what can make an impact on any paradigm. My suspicion is that the problem will not occur in terms of aetiology and intervention but in terms of measurement. It is the seemingly least controversial and most secure sector of the administra-tive paradigm which is most vulnerable. And it is vulnerable precisely because of the general problem: the inability/unwillingness to acknowledge that the study of crime essentially involves moral choice and political decision.

A major flaw in establishment criminology has always been its tendency to view the criminal statistics as objective data. That is, as indices of behaviour independent of human evaluation, or as data based on a consensual scale. A realist criminology insists that criminal statistics are social constructions and the corollary of this is that, as there exist various groups in society with different, albeit highly overlapping values, there must be a plurality of statistics. (See Young, 1988b).

The search for "hard" statistics in criminology has been a long one and revolves around the palpable inadequacy of official statistics based on crimes known to the police with their unknown dark figure. In the last twenty years it has been claimed that victimisation surveys have greatly ameliorated this problem. Although the mass victimisation study was a creation of sociological positivism at its prime, the use of victimisation data has become a hallmark of administrative criminology. (See Jones, et al., 1986 pp. 1–6.) It is important to realise what a breakthrough victimisation research was seen to be. As Richard Sparks and his colleagues announced in the introduction to their pioneering British study: 'Within a mere decade... some of the oldest problems in crimin-ology have come at least within reach of a solution... Seldom in the history of social science research, can so much have been done about a single problem by

---

[6] Anomalies in other paradigms are to be found in the line of sociological positivists working in the field of homicide studies who have focused on relative deprivation, but in a totally non-subjectivist *positivist* sense (i.e. relative absolute deprivation). That is not socially perceived relative deprivation, but merely the more easily measurable disparaties in income levels. Of course, relative deprivation can often more easily rise when income disparaties narrow rather than widen. (See Runciman, 1966; Stouffer, 1949.) As can homicide. This would be an anomaly from the point of view of sociological positivism.

In the area of self-report studies the *obvious* anomaly of the identical delinquency reported by middle and working class delinquents which, from a realist viewpoint as simply a product of different definitions of crime, is used by control theorists to validate their position. See, for example, Weis, 1987.

so many in so short a time" (1977, p. 1). The whole problem of the dark figure which has beset criminology since Quetelet seemed within a hairbreadth of resolution.

But just when they thought it was safe to use criminal statistics problems began to crop up. Anomalies to a theory occur often in seemingly unimportant areas—flaws which look at first of marginal significance but whose implications are far reaching. One of these is the so-called "education effect" in victimisation data. (See Sparks, 1981.) This is the claim by educated people that they have higher rates of violence against them than those less educated. This, as Sparks put it, seems to have "no ground whatever, either in criminology theory or common sense." He adds, "Between believing such a wild implausibility and doubting the validity of the survey data, the choice should be clear: (the result) reflects clear evidence of response bias." (Ibid, p. 34.) Or does it? In fact such anomalies abound in victimisation studies, for example, the higher vandalism rates amongst the better off, the higher violence rates often found against women compared to men or even the absurdity of higher violence rates in England than in the U.S. (See Hough, 1986.) A radical realism would, of course, interpret these findings as reflecting the way in which groups (men, women; rich, poor; Britons, Americans) experience both different levels of victimisation *and* have different tolerances of crime. Both experienced behaviour and moral yardsticks vary. The fact that the figures for victimisation might relate not just to incidence but to sensitivity to crime was clearly recognised in the *Islington Crime Survey* (See Jones *et al.*, pp. 54 and 68). (Painter, 1987).

Let us now look at the impact of this on monitored crime prevention campaigns.

It is only a matter of time before longitudinal victimisation studies will generate results of great anomaly in terms of policy. These anomalies will occur when victimisation studies are used to measure improvements in particular areas as part of, say, crime prevention campaigns. For there are a whole series of crimes, for example, vandalism and "minor" violence which are extremely predicated on tolerance levels. A successful campaign may easily create a decline in tolerance to these offences, and thus a rise in the number of offences occurring, despite the fact that behaviour as measured in terms of the initial tolerance of crime has improved. For the real number of crimes is a product of behaviour and tolerance levels. Thus, it is only a matter of time before a successful crime prevention programme will create a rise in the victimisation rate in conditions where there is no dark figure to excuse it, as in the case of police statistics. What this means is that precisely the anomaly will occur which traumatised positivism in the sixties: namely a *rise* in crime despite the manifest *amelioration* of the social conditions and interventions which should have resulted in a *decrease* in crime. The effects of such findings on establishment criminology will be far-reaching: for the hope that victimisation studies would produce the "hard" data which will transform the subject into a science without the problems of human value will be destroyed. All sorts of problems will then exist in comparative work: internationally, between different parts of the city, and between different social groups. (See Hough, 1986, Young, 1988b.)

Furthermore, if there are various yardsticks measuring the criminal statistics, however overlapping they may be, then the real nature of a crime figure is invariably blurred. This does not rule out statistical methods, it just insists on a prudent period of thought before rushing the latest data to one's home computer. Furthermore, over time, such an approach will alert us to the problem that as we explore the hidden figure of child abuse, for example, we are forced also to re-examine the question of exactly what are the limits of child abuse. And as we do this our standards may become less tolerant and the hidden figure will expand. If Quetelet taught us about the existence of the dark figure of crime, radical victimisation studies—particularly those of the feminists—have indicated how it is qualitatively structured—certain crimes against certain people are more in the dark than others. Lastly, realism points out the figure is not only quantitatively high, and qualitatively structured, but that it is flexible—it expands or contracts with the values one brings to it. None of this is insurmountable but only within a paradigm capable of analysing crime, both as a product of behaviour and value. This is the theoretical lineage of radical criminology in Britain in which realism is the most recent development.

I believe that Terence Morris was right when, in the quote I used to introduce this essay, he referred to Fabianism floundering because of its failure to recognise the moral nature of human action. But it is not the Mark of Cain that haunts our crime-ridden cities, but the mark of inequality, avarice and machismo. It is impossible to solve a moral problem in the long run without a moral solution. In the last analysis administrative criminology, Fabian positivism and conservative approaches to crime all have this failing in common. Whereas the first ignores justice, the second negates it and the third turns immorality into its own form of justice. It is only radical criminology which views justice as the core of the cause, the measurement and the control of crime and by searching for the roots of crime holds the promise of its solution.

REFERENCES

BOTTOMS, A. (1977). "Reflections on the Renaissance of Dangerousness". *Howard Journal*. **16,** 70–96.

BOTTOMS, A. (1987). "Reflections on the Criminological Enterprise". *The Cambridge Law Journal*. **46,** Part 2.

CARLEN, P., *et al.* (1985). *Criminal Women*. Cambridge, Polity Press.

CLARKE, J. (1980). "Social Democratic Delinquents and Fabian Families" in National Defiancy Conference (1980).

CLARKE, R. (1980). "Situational Crime Prevention: Theory and Practice". *B. J. Criminology*. **20,** 136–147.

CLARKE, R. and CORNISH, D. (eds.) (1983). *Crime Control in Britain*. Albany, Suny Press.

CLARKE, R. and MAYHEW, P. (eds.) (1980). *Designing Out Crime*. London, HMSO.

CLOWARD, R. and OHLIN, L. (1960). *Delinquency and Opportunity*. New York, The Free Press.

COHEN, A. K. (1965). *Delinquency Boys*. New York, The Free Press.

COHEN, S. (ed.) (1971). *Images of Deviance*. Harmondsworth, Penguin.

COHEN, S. (1979). "Guilt, Justice and Tolerance" in D. Downes and P. Rock (eds.) Oxford, Martin Robertson.

COHEN, S. (1980). *Folk Devils and Moral Panics* (2nd ed.). Oxford, Martin Robertson.

COHEN, S. (1981). "Footprints in the Sand" in M. Fitzgerald, *et al*. (1981).

COHEN, S. (1983). "Social Control Talk" in D. Garland and P. Young (eds.) *The Power to Punish*. London, Heinemann.

COHEN, S. (1984). "The Deeper Structures of the Law or Beware the Rulers Bearing Justice". *Contemporary Crisis*. **8,** 83–93.

CORNISH, D. and CLARKE, R. (1986). *The Reasoning Criminal*.

DORN, N. and SOUTH, N. (eds.) (1987). *A Land Fit for Heroin?* London, Macmillan.

DOWNES, D. (1983). *Theft of an Issue*. London, Fabian Society.

DOWNES, D. and ROCK, P. (1982). *Understanding Deviance*. Oxford, Clarendon Press.

FITZGERALD, M., McLENNAN, G. and PAWSON, J. (1981). *Crime and Society*. London, Routledge and Kegan Paul.

FITZGERALD, M. and SIM, J. (1982). *British Prisons* (2nd ed.). Oxford, Blackwell.

FURLONG, V. (1985). *The Deviant Pupil*. Milton Keynes, Open University Press.

GOULDNER, A. (1973). Introduction to *The New Criminology*. I. Taylor *et al*. (1975).

GREENWOOD, V. and YOUNG, J. (1980). "Ghettoes of Freedom" in National Deviancy Conference (1980).

HACKING, I. (1981). "How should we do a History of Statistics". *Ideology and Consciousness*. 8.

HALL, R. (1985). *Ask Any Women*. Bristol. Falling Wall Press.

HALL, S., *et al.*, (1979). *Policing the Crisis*. London, Macmillan.

HANMER, J. and SAUNDERS, S. (1984). *Well-founded Fear*. London, Hutchinson.

HARRIS, A. (1977). "Sex and Theories of Deviance". *American Sociological Review*. **42,** 3–16.

HARVEY, D. (1973). *Social Justice and the City*. London, Edward Arnold.

HEAL, K. and LAYCOCK, G. (eds.) (1986). *Situational Crime Prevention*. London, HMSO.

HOOD, R. (1987). "Some Reflections on the Role of Criminology in Public Policy". *Criminal Law Review*. 527–538.

HOUGH, M. (1986). "Victims of Violence and Crime: Findings from the British Crime Survey" in E. Fattah (ed.) *From Crime Policy to Victim Policy*. London, Macmillan.

HOUGH, M. and MAYHEW, P. (1983). *The British Crime Survey*. London, HMSO.

HOUGH, M. and MAYHEW, P. (1988). "Findings of the British Crime Survey" in M. Maguire and J. Pointing (1988).

HUDSON, B. (1987). *Justice Through Punishment*. London, Macmillan.

INCIARDI, J. (1980). *Radical Criminology*. Beverley Hills, Sage.

JEFFREY, C. (1980). "Sociobiology and Criminology". in F. Sagarin (ed). *Taboos in Criminology*. Beverley Hills, Sage.

JEFFERSON, T. and GRIMSHAW, R. (1984). *Controlling the Constable*. London, Muller.

JOHNSON, H. G. (1971). "The Keynsian Revolution and Monetarist Counter-Revolution", *American Economic Review*. **16,** 1–14.

JONES, T., LEA, J. and YOUNG, J. (1987). *Saving the Inner City: The First Report of the Broadwater Farm Survey*. London, Middlesex Polytechnic, Centre for Criminology.

Jones, T., Maclean, B. and Young, J. (1986). *The Islington Crime Survey*. Aldershot, Gower.

Kinsey, R. (1984). *First Report of the Merseyside Crime Survey*. Liverpool, Merseyside County Council.

Kinsey, R., Lea, J. and Young, J. (1986). *Losing the Fight Against Crime*. Oxford, Blackwell.

Lakatos, I. and Musgrave, A. (eds.) (1970). *Criticism and the Growth of Knowledge*. Cambridge, Cambridge University Press.

Lea, J. (1988). "In Defence of Realism". *Contemporary Crises*. **II.**

Lea, J. and Young, J. (1984). *What is to be done about Law and Order*. London, Penguin.

Lea, J., Matthews, R. and Young, J. (1987). *Law and Order: Five Years On*. London, Centre for Criminology, Middlesex Polytechnic.

Maguire, M. and Pointing, J. (eds.) (1988). *Victims of Crime: A New Deal*. Milton Keynes, Open University Press.

Meese, E. III (1986). "Crime and Punishment in Modern America". P. McGuigan and J. Pascale (eds.) Washington, Free Congress Research Foundation.

Morris, T. (1976). *Deviance and Control*. London, Hutchinson.

Morris, T. (1957). *The Criminal Area*. London, Routledge and Kegan Paul.

Mungham, G. (1980). "The Career of Confusion: Radical Criminology in Britain" in J. Inciardi (1980).

National Deviancy Conference (1980). *Permissiveness and Control*. London, Macmillan.

Newman, K. (1984). *Reports of the commissioner of Police for the Metropolis* (also 1985, 1986). London, HMSO.

Painter, K. (1987). "Its Part of the Job: Violence at Work". in P. Leighton and R. Painter (eds.) *Vulnerable Workers in the UK Labour Markets*. Bradford, MCB University Press, 30–40.

Pearson, G. (1987). *The New Heroin Users*. Oxford, Blackwell.

Phipps, A. (1987). *Criminal Victimization, Crime Control and Political Action*. PhD Thesis: Centre for Criminology, Middlesex Polytechnic.

Quinney, R. and Wilderman, J. (1977). *The Problem of Crime*. New York, Harper & Row.

Radford, J. (1987). "Policing Male Violence" in J. Hanmer and M. Maynard (eds). *Women, Violence and Social Control*. London, Macmillan.

Reiner, R. (1985). *The Politics of the Police*. Brighton, Wheatsheaf.

Reiner, R. (1985). "Review of Confronting Crime". *Critical Social Policy*. 103–106.

Runciman, W. (1966). *Relative Deprivation & Social Justice*. London, Routledge and Kegan Paul.

Scraton, P. (1987). *Law, Order and the Authoritarian State*. Milton Keynes, Open University Press.

Scraton, P. (1985). *State of the Police*. London, Pluto.

Skolnick, J. and Bayley, D. (1986). *The New Blue Line*. New York, The Free Press.

Smart, C. (1977). *Women, Crime and Criminology*. London, Routledge and Kegan Paul.

Smith, D. (1983). *Police and People in London*. Vol. 1. London, PSI.

Smith, S. (1986). *Crime, Space and Society*. Cambridge, Cambridge University Press.

Sparks, R. (1981). "Surveys of Victimization in M. Tonry and N. Morris (eds.) *Crime and Justice Reviewed* (Vol. 3). Chicago, Chicago University Press. pp. 1–58.

SPARKS, R., GENN, H. and DODD, D. (1977). *Surveying Victims*. Chichester, Wiley.

STOUFFER, S. *et al.,* (1949). *The American Soldier*. Princetown, Princeton University Press.

SUMNER, C. (ed.) (1982). *Crime, Justice and Underdevelopment*. Cambridge, Cambridge University Press.

TAYLOR, I., WALTON, P., YOUNG, J. (eds.) (1975). *Critical Criminology*. London, Routledge and Kegan Paul.

WEIS, J. (1987). "Social Class & Crime". in M. Gottfredson and T. Hirschi (eds). *Positive Criminology*. Beverley Hills, Sage.

WILES, P. (1976). *The Sociology of Crime and Delinquency in Britain*. Vol. 2. Oxford, Martin Robertson.

WILLIS, P. (1977). *Learning to Labour*. Farnborough, Saxon House.

YOUNG, J. (1986). "The Failure of Criminology: The Need for Radical Realism". in R. Matthews and J. Young (eds). *Confronting Crime*. London, Sage.

YOUNG, J. (1988a). "The Tasks of a Realist Criminology". *Contemporary Crises*. **II.**

YOUNG, J. (1988b). "Risk of Crime and Fear of Crime: The Politics of Victimization Studies" in Maguire and Pointing (1988).

YOUNG, J. (1988c). *Realist Criminology*. London, Sage.